Limited Classical Reprint Library

THE BIBLICAL DOCTRINE OF JUSTIFICATION

by

Frederick Brooke Westcott

Foreword by
Dr. Cyril J. Barber

Klock & Klock Christian Publishers, Inc.
2527 Girard Avenue North
Minneapolis, Minnesota 55411

Originally published by
MacMillan and Co., Limited
London, 1913

ISBN: 0-86524-160-0

Printed by Klock & Klock in the U.S.A.
1983 Reprint

FOREWORD

Frederick Brooke Westcott (M.A., D.D., Cambridge University), son of the celebrated Brooke Foss Westcott, Bishop of Durham, followed in his fathers footsteps and became a well respected New Testament scholar.

In undertaking the task of providing his readers with a biblical exposition of the doctrine of justification, Dr. Westcott did so in the best of evangelical traditions. His treatment of the relevant passages underscoring the true nature of justification is objective, his discussion of the finer points of grammer and syntax is done with rare ability, and he expounds the New Testament teaching with consumate skill. The result is a work that handsomely repays serious investigation.

We are delighted that the publishers have seen fit to make this title available again.

Cyril J. Barber
Author, *The Minister's Library*

PREFATORY NOTE

THIS little work is put forth with very great hesitation and serious searching of heart. Circumstances required it should be printed; and since it has been printed, it may as well venture forth and see if it can find here and there an indulgent reader. None knows better than the writer how infinitely imperfect is his equipment for the task. On the other hand years of teaching, full of interest for himself, have shown him that even the young are not without a desire to have St Paul expounded, however imperfectly. Only the task must be approached without any prejudice. The Apostle must speak for himself and must not be made a mere channel for views already fixed in the mind of the commentator. Absolute honesty of interpretation must be reckoned the prime requisite.

Of erudition in these pages very little will be found. The reading of endless commentaries (not to mention tracts innumerable) has for him that writes these words exiguous attraction. His great debt to three names will be all too obvious. Bishop Lightfoot among the departed, among the living Drs Sanday and Headlam have been ever present guides. The former is cited by name. The latter are denominated 'S.,' for convenience of brevity. Their commentary is indeed a model of two great virtues, lucidity and courage. For the rest, wherever departure is made from either of these two great editions, it is made with an adequate sense of the temerity involved.

May the little book be found of use by some one !

F. B. W.

ERRATA

p. 196, *read* Glaubensgerechtigkeit.

p. 198, *for* Gen. xv. *read* Gen. xii.

p. 212 (last line), *for* Law *read* Love.

p. 231, l. 16, *for* δικαιοσύνη *read* ἁμαρτία.

p. 234, l. 6, *for* not *read* now.

p. 315, *for* inexenarrabilibus *read* inerrabilibus.

PART I

THE TEACHING OF GALATIANS

§ 1. A Word about Words

The purpose of this short Essay is to expound certain passages in the writings of St Paul, dealing with a religious question, which occupied him largely during one period of his career. The method I propose to myself will bring me face to face with the difficulties that beset any person who endeavours to set forth in one language ideas and thoughts originally stated in quite another. Differences of idiom, problems of grammar, and perhaps more especially the all but impossibility of rendering aright the niceties of vocabulary, form the chief of these difficulties.

In the case of St Paul the grammar does not present (I should say) an insurmountable barrier. He had had the great

advantage of birth in a Greek-speaking city,
and probably spoke that language from the
earliest days of his life. It was not with
him, for instance, as it was with the Fourth
Evangelist, in whose writings one comes
across, every now and then, a sentence
which will only translate by the employment of sheer violence. Vocabulary, on
the other hand, is always, and must be, a
trouble to the conscientious translator. For
words are unfortunately 'fluid,' and not
only has one to know what a Greek word
used by St Paul meant first by origin, and
then as used by him ; but also what the
English 'equivalent' (that is, would-be
equivalent : for absolute 'equivalence' is
a very rare phenomenon), employed by
our own translators, conveyed when *they*
first used it.

This opening section then will wholly
deal with words—the words that are
'master-words' in connexion with the
paragraphs to be rendered later on.

They belong to three several languages;
for students of the English New Testament

are concerned, of necessity, with English
and Latin and Greek. Hebrew (fortunately
for me) is vastly less important, for as
everybody knows the ' Old Testament ' of
the 'New Testament' writers is the Greek
and not the Hebrew.

The words I mean to discuss are δίκη
and its derivatives; '*justus*' and its
derivatives; and the various verbal and
nominal forms which derive from the
English '*right*.'

The Greek must take precedence.
In the late Dr Verrall's delightful commentary on Euripides, *Medea* (published
alas! how many years ago) he observes in
one of his notes that the original meaning
of Δίκη is the *custom* or *order* of nature.
The well-known words of the second line
of the chorus, that starts at 410,

καὶ δίκα καὶ πάντα πάλιν στρέφεται,

he renders '*Nature* and the universe are
turned upside down.'

However I am not convinced that δίκα,
in that place, means other than 'right.'

Originally, however, δίκη obviously
meant 'way.' The notion of 'right'-ness
is secondary, an accretion. This appears
from the adverbial use of the accusative in
Attic (κυνὸς δίκην 'dog's way,' or 'dog-
fashion'). But there are also indications
of the same sense in the Homeric poems.
In fact, it is not disputed. The δίκη of
'kings' means the 'way' they comport
themselves (*Od.* iv. 691)—in this case the
very opposite of anything that could be
called 'right,' mere capricious favouring of
one and disliking of another.

It is easy to imagine how 'way' or
'usage' might develope into 'right.'
Anyhow it certainly did. So we start
with the assumption that δίκη means
(roughly) 'right.' The adverb δικαίως,
in the *Odyssey*, means simply 'rightly.'
The adjective δίκαιος is more often used
of persons than it is of things. A man is
called δίκαιος when he behaves reasonably,
as a civilised person should. The δίκαιος
is not a person on a lofty ethical platform ;
he is merely one who satisfies the dictates

of common usage. The adjective, in those days, was manifestly only starting upon its upward path. We are a long way yet from the δίκαιος (say) of Plato, or again from the abstract noun that belongs to that δίκαιος, the same Master's spacious δικαιοσύνη. Of course, the Greek Old Testament inherited both these terms, when they were in the full possession of the higher, more ethical, meaning that came with the centuries.

More important however than either the noun or the adjective (at least, originally), for Pauline purposes, is the verb that is cognate with them. Δικαιοῦν in classical Greek is found with varying senses. Sometimes it means to 'set right,' as in a fragment of Pindar (151), wherein Νόμος, sovran Νόμος, is described as δικαιῶν τὸ βιαιότατον ὑπερτάτᾳ χειρί. The instance given, of this 'right' (which is 'might'), is the conduct of Herakles in 'lifting' Geryon's cattle. It is also employed (as 'justify' is in Scots) of that summary 'setting right' of an evil doer which is achieved by his abolition. More often, however, it means 'to deem right,' or else to 'demand.' But the usages of the LXX are what concern us chiefly.

Here are two or three capital instances of the verb in the Old Testament, culled thanks to the kindly aid of Dr Hatch's monumental work.

In Genesis xliv. 16 Judah says to his brother Joseph (after the discovery of the governor's cup in the sack), "wherein shall we clear ourselves?" (τί δικαιωθῶμεν ;).

In Exodus xxiii. 7 the LXX (here differing from the Hebrew, but giving an excellent sense) reads " Thou shalt not *put right* the impious for gifts" (οὐ δικαιώσεις τὸν ἀσεβῆ ἕνεκεν δώρων).

In 2 Sam. xv. 4 poor foolish Absalom says, in his disloyal way, "O that I were made judge in the land ; that every man might come unto me...and I would set him right!" (καὶ δικαιώσω αὐτόν).

There are also two passages in the Psalms which are well worth citing ; the familiar "for in Thy sight shall no man

living be *justified*" (ὅτι οὐ δικαιωθήσεται
ἐνώπιόν σου πᾶς ζῶν); and lxxiii. 13,
" Surely in vain have I set right my
heart " (ματαίως ἐδικαίωσα τὴν καρδίαν μου).
These instances, I think, will help to
bear out my contention that δικαιοῦν (in
O.T.) does not mean to '*make righteous*'
in the sense of 'right doing,' or even (as
is argued) to '*account* as right-doing,' but
simply to 'set right'—which is quite another
matter. The fact is, δίκαιος (in St Paul)
has two different senses, one technical
and one normal. Employed technically it
means 'in the right,' or simply 'right,'
corresponding to δικαιοῦν 'to set right.'
Otherwise (and the context in all cases
decides the sense) it means 'righteous,'
in the ordinary way. The same remark
applies to the abstract noun. We must
expect to find that too employed in two perfectly distinct senses. Sometimes it means
the condition of one who is 'righteous' (in
the sense 'right doing'); sometimes (and
this is the technical usage) the condition of
one who is ' right,' that is, *right with God.*

The original Latin translators, when confronted with these words, were set a difficult problem. How should they render δίκαιος, and how, as a consequence, the derivatives of that adjective ? They pitched upon 'justus,' and invented (it would seem) the compound 'justificare.' Now 'justus' will do very well for the ethical δίκαιος, but is hopelessly inadequate for the theological one. The root of the word is a root which expresses 'binding'; and 'jus,' its immediate parent, means 'natural right.' Of persons, 'justus' means 'upright'; of things either 'righteous,' that is 'well grounded' . (as in *justa causa*) ; or else 'rightful' (as in *justa uxor*). This will show that it is (as I contend) an adequate equivalent for δίκαιος in its more normal and regular sense ; that is, 'honest,' 'right dealing,' 'righteous.'

But where are we when we come to the other sense of δίκαιος ? 'Justus' obviously is no equivalent for 'right'; that is 'in the right.' This sense (which I hold to be undoubted) is really derived from δικαιοῦν,

by a kind of 'backward action.' Neither
will 'justus' do for the adjective, nor
'justificare' for the verb. 'Justus' can only
mean 'right dealing'; and 'justificare'
accordingly can only mean '*make right
dealing.*' And that can never convey the
meaning of St Paul. Nor can I think of
a way in which it could have been success-
fully rendered in Latin. 'Rectus' would
hardly do (and 'rectificare') ; and besides
the Latin translators were far more keen
to be literal than ever they were to be
lucid. So one would be inclined to conclude from studying them. In English
we are better off: for we really have
equivalents. There is 'right' (to be sure)
for δίκη; there is the verb 'to right' for
δικαιοῦν ; there is the adjective 'right' for
δίκαιος in the one sense, and 'righteous'
for it in the other. The root meaning (to
be sure) of this family of words is different
altogether from that of the corresponding
terms in Latin and in Greek. Δίκη is
the 'way'; 'jus' is 'that which binds';
while right is 'what is ruled' or 'straight.'

The 'right' man and the 'righteous' man
are the men who respectively are 'straight'
and 'straight dealing.' But is it not a
calamity that (owing to unhappy Latin
influence) δικαιοῦν should be rendered by
'justify'? At least, it seems so to me.
And moreover it appears entirely gra-
tuitous. For the resources of our English
are not, in this respect, one whit behind
the resources of Luther's German. Yet
he made his meaning plain (that is, the
Apostle's meaning) to very simple people :
and it can hardly be maintained our English
does. Later on, when we come to the
text, I hope to demonstrate it. Perhaps I
might add just this. According to Professor
Skeat the ' righteous' man is the man who
is ' wise in right' (the ' right-wise' in fact).
It is not for the ignorant to question the
results arrived at by the learned. But if the
Professor is right, and the '-eous' is not
merely terminative, then 'righteous' becomes indeed even less suitable than I
had thought it, as a rendering for δίκαιος,
where that word represents the person,

who is merely '*right-with-God.*' To call him 'wise in right' is simply hopelessly beside the mark.

§ 2. THE IDEA OF 'JUSTIFICATION' (THAT IS 'BEING SET RIGHT WITH GOD'), HOW IT AROSE

The genesis of the idea, and the consequent controversy—in which the great apostle played so decisive a part—is, for all religious people, only too simple and intelligible.

Far back, in the distant past, God made a 'covenant' with ancient Israel. He revealed Himself to them as their peculiar God, and they were to be correspondingly His own especial people.

Thus there was solved for Israel, in the days of their primitive life, the first of the two great problems Religion presents to man. That is, *How can I establish right relations for myself with God?* For the conscience of ancient Israel this riddle was easily answered. It was borne in on their

minds, by the channel of revelation, that
God had 'chosen' them. They had nothing
at all to do, but just accept the great fact,
and satisfy the conditions thereto (as they
were told) attached.

This, at first, was simple and easy.
No doubt or hesitation troubled their souls.
However, as time advanced, the other great
'first problem' began to lift its head. That
other great riddle is, *Having once secured
God's favour, how can I best retain it?*
The fact is, the Law and the Prophets,
between them, developed strongly the moral
sense in Israel. It was not enough even
for a son of Israel to have been born of
the 'Covenant' race, and to have been
himself admitted by the God-appointed
rite within the Covenant. 'Right relations' with God were his (that is, nominally
his), but how could he be sure that he had
not, by his own ill-conduct, contrived to
forfeit his privilege? How could he be
assured that he still stood with his God,
where he stood in the bygone days of
happy innocence? "In Thy sight," he

cried despairingly, "no man living shall be righted!" But plainly he could not rest in that unfruitful conclusion. Something had to be done, and done without delay. The question became acute for religious Israel, when the days of exile were over. Some stalwarts, doubtless, maintained that 'A-brahamic descent' was all-sufficient. But many were not content with that 'high and dry' position. They set to work with vigour to 'make their calling and election sure,' by indefatigable attention to the keeping of the Law. We know of one eminent man, who, drilled in the Schools of the Pharisees, set himself to this 'Danaid' task with a devotion fierce and untiring. It was Saul of Tarsus himself. Not for nothing was he born of a right warrior tribe ("*after thee, O Benjamin*"): not for nothing was he by birth a whole-hearted 'Nationalist.' Whatever Ἐβραῖος means, in connexion with the Apostle, it must at the least mean this. And indeed it is hard to believe, in view of his ready use of the Greek Old Testament Scriptures, that he

was not in other respects decisively Ἑλ-
ληνιστής. Anyhow, we have his own
testimony, that in his Jewish days he was
"*as touching the righteousness which is in
the Law*" (if that be a right translation)
"*found blameless.*" I take it, he means
thereby that, so far as a man was able to
'right' himself, by doing whatever the Law
bade ; he, Paul, had done it. I have said,
that Religion offers (the existence of God
being taken as certain; though not to be
established by any logical process) two
problems for man's solution ; How shall
I be set right with God ? and, How shall
I keep myself right ? Historically it is
the latter which is the problem of 'justification.' That is to say the latter problem
was the problem of 'justification' *for the
Jew.* It was a question for the Jew, how
he might 'qualify' for a privileged position,
ex hypothesi his already. For the Christian
on the contrary the problem of 'justification' is the problem, how to establish originally right relations. The Christian, at any
rate, this is true of the primitive believer—

the Christian was not born 'within the Covenant,' as the Son of Israel was. Therefore the problem of problems was, for him, the earlier one; for the Jew it was the later. To St Paul himself, accordingly, the question presented itself *at the first* (in pre-Christian days) in the 'Jewish' form. For he was born 'privileged,' even beyond the common run of his countrymen. He possessed advantages innumerable. 'Philippians' tells us how (in his regenerate days) he regarded these advantages. By a vigorous oxymoron he counted them '*less than nothing.*' Like the character in Hans Andersen, who asks contemptuously, 'Do you call that a *hill*? *We* should call it a *hole*,' St Paul declares he reckoned his ' κέρδη ' as mere ' ζημίαν.' No more would he go about (as he did in these old days) to keep himself 'right with God,' by doing and doing and doing. He would not even assume that he started 'right with God,' and only had to keep so, by loyalty to the Covenant. His point of view was transformed. All was merged in one great

question, How shall I *become* right with
God—right once for all ?   And the answer
came, 'Through Christ.'   Here was the
new way, the God-appointed way.   Henceforth he never wavered in heart and soul
conviction that 'justification' for him was
an accomplished fact.   He had 'become
right' with God, 'in Christ Jesus,' as a
result of 'faith.'   It was the wholly new
beginning of a wholly new existence.

But though he had himself escaped from
the riddle which beset his countrymen, he
had by no means heard the last of it.
Other folks were not prepared to accept his
solution; yes, even nominal believers.   The
thing cropped up again (inside the Christian
Church) in spite of all his preaching—and
just where he would have least expected it.
When after a lapse of years (which is one
of those mysteries of the Book of the 'Acts'
we should most dearly love to solve) he
had been brought to Antioch by Barnabas,
and subsequently despatched, with that
very notable saint, on the mission of relief
to Jerusalem ; he started (as every one

knows) the work to which Christ had called
him, as the Prince of Mission Preachers.

The Churches first evangelised con-
tained (as Zahn declares) 'a few full-born
Jews, a number of proselytes of different
grades, and a much larger number of
Gentiles,' and 'received through Paul the
stamp of "law-free" Gentile Churches.'
These early churches, I assume, are the
'Churches of Galatia.'

It is possible, of course, that at some
later date (before 'Galatians' was written)
the Apostle may have touched the fringe
of Bishop Lightfoot's 'Galatia,' with its
Celtic population. But Professor Ramsay
would appear to have established his main
position. The geographical argument appears to me wholly conclusive. The
interpretation of Acts xvi. 6 would (no
doubt) be open to question, *by itself*. But,
that Ramsay is wholly right in his grip of
St Paul's 'objective,' and in his strong
contention that 'Celtic Galatia' lay entirely
off the track of his evangelistic ambitions,
I cannot for a moment doubt. Perhaps

it may be of interest to some among
Cambridge students, if I say that the
Bishop's lifelong friend told me, shortly
before he died, that he was himself a convert to the 'South Galatian' theory.

It was amongst these earliest of the
numerous Pauline Churches that St Paul
first found himself confronted with the
question originally raised by Judaisers at
Antioch.   At Antioch, of course, he must
have borne his part in opposing the new
heresy.   But Antioch, after all, was not
primarily his 'business.'   The Galatian
churches were.   And though one might
have thought that the letter from Jerusalem
would have finally settled the question, it
obviously did not; though (presumably) it
went further, in regard to making con-
cessions to Jewish prejudices, than St Paul
himself would have gone.

It was after St Paul had passed (so
singularly shepherded by the "*Spirit of
Jesus*") on his adventurous way to Europe,
that the trouble in Galatia came to a head.
How the apostle came to know of the

inroads, that were made into his earliest converts' convictions by the 'Judaic' emissaries, we cannot determine for certain. He may have learned at Corinth, in the course of his eighteen months' residence (as in Acts xviii. 11). If he did, this letter was written from the capital of Achaia, and becomes the earliest of all extant Pauline Letters. On the other hand, the trouble may not have revealed itself to him in all its seriousness, till he found himself once more in his 'base' at Antioch (xviii. 22). If so, the letter was written from there before he started forth on his third great Missionary tour. That still leaves the Galatian letter the earliest of its group, though it then is but third of all in date, no longer first. Perhaps the only objection to this latter theory (though it is rather a serious one) is the fact that one would not gather, from the text of the letter itself, that the writer had it in mind to follow close on the heels of the bearer of his Epistle—as he obviously did from the record of 'Acts.'

About actual date I say nothing. The
computation of Pauline chronology is a
fascinating problem; but it belongs to those
who are experts. All I am concerned about
is the order of events, and not the actual
years, in which they severally befell. There
is fairly substantial agreement with regard
to the latter : and (even were there not) it
would not much affect the purpose of this
Essay, which is to set forth what St Paul
taught upon a topic, which was at once
for him, at one stage of his career, of
singular importance, and touches all religion,
in all time, very deeply and decisively.
Let us then get to the text and ponder its
mysteries!

§ 3. THE FIRST PARAGRAPH FROM GALATIANS

St Paul, in his opening words, affirms
his Apostolate, in unmistakeable terms, and
also the Divine authenticity of his message.
This leads on to an exposition as to how

he came by it. It is no 'human' message:
it came (he expressly says) by definite
revelation. He repeats the familiar tale
of his pre-conversion days ; how he was
a persecutor ; an out and out 'legalist' ;
an upholder of 'tradition' altogether beyond
the common. Others (the suggestion is)
may be 'zealots' for the Law, but not to
the extent that he has been.

Then follows, after the wonderful verse
and a half (*vv.* 15, 16) in which the mystery
of his 'call' is described, the well-known
summary of his relations with the chief
Apostles. He did not go up to Jerusalem
(he tells us) to those who were Apostles
"before him " ; on the contrary, he was in
" Arabia " (a geographical term indubitably
employed in a very broad sense) and returned from there to Damascus. It was
μετὰ τριὰ ἔτη that he went up to visit
Cephas and spent a fortnight with him.
James the brother of the Lord was the
only other leader of the Mother Church
he saw on that occasion.

These statements the Apostle makes in

the most solemn form conceivable. Then
came the Cilician sojourn (of Acts ix. 30
presumably). The pronouncement the
Apostle makes (with regard to his relations,
up till then, with "the Churches of Judaea")
is beset with puzzling questions, but does
not concern us now. Next the readers are
told of the second visit to Jerusalem (διὰ
δεκατεσσάρων ἐτῶν) with Barnabas and
Titus. By this time St Paul is very plainly
at work, preaching to Gentiles (ὃ κηρύσσω
ἐν τοῖς ἔθνεσιν, ii. 2). This would seem,
at first sight, to suggest an identification
of this visit with that in Acts xv. But
probably those are right who rather see
in it the 'Relief Visit' of Acts xi. 30. If
that be so, the Apostle had very early
made up his own mind on the question of
circumcision for Gentile converts : for,
surely, it is certain that Titus was *not*
circumcised.

However all attempts to harmonise
'Galatians' with the 'Acts' involve us in
some difficulty. If the visit "after 14
years" is to be taken as the Relief Visit,

then what are we to say about the 'elders' of Acts xi. 30 ? That verse seems to imply that 'the Twelve' were already gone from Jerusalem. On the other hand Gal. ii. 6—11 very decidedly suggests that the very "pillars of the Church," "James and Cephas and John," were actually there, and struck a bargain with him, freely acknowledging his mission (and Barnabas') to the Gentiles, but begging him to remember the poor at Jerusalem—the which, indeed, as he says, he had already been forward to do.

All the various problems involved in Galatians i. and ii. form a fascinating theme for full discussion. Yet, when all is said and done, there seems little likelihood of any consensus of scholars upon disputed points. The ball is tossed to and fro ; now one theory is in favour, and now another. For doctrinal purposes the upshot matters little. All we are concerned to know is, that the Apostle roundly declares that his mission was independent and not controlled from Jerusalem ; that the heads of the

Mother Church freely recognised it was so
—in short, that the loud-voiced contention
of Judaising emissaries, as to the inferiority
of his status (compared with οἱ δοκοῦντες),
had no existence in fact, nor yet in the
minds of those who were foremost in the
Church. It is at this point, quite incidentally, that we come upon the first of
the passages of which I propose to speak.

Gal. ii. 11—14. " But when
Cephas came to Antioch I withstood
him to the face, because he was
without defence. Before there came
'certain from James,' he had been
joining in food with Gentiles ; but
after they came he was disposed to
withdraw and separate himself, from
fear of the Circumcision Party. And
his insincere conduct was joined by
the other Jewish *Christians.* Inso-
much that even Barnabas was carried
away in the stream of their in-
sincerity."

" But when I saw they were not
walking by the standard of Gospel

truth, I said to Cephas, in the presence of them all : If you, a Jew to start with, live as the Gentiles do, and not as Jews do ; on what principle are you for forcing the Gentiles to live as Jews ?"

At this point let me halt for a word or two of comment.　Of this visit of Cephas to Antioch, which must have taken place anyhow after the close of what we are told in Acts xii. 25—that is, after the return of Saul and Barnabas from the mission of relief, we know nothing from other sources. But we can easily understand that St Peter must have taken to heart the lesson so singularly taught him in connexion with Cornelius.　Up till then he had recognised it as an "unlawful thing for a Jew" to have intimate relations with, or even to enter the house of, an 'alien' (κολλᾶσθαι ἢ προσέρχεσθαι ἀλλοφύλῳ, Acts x. 28).　At any time after that (and we note that he is invited to "*stay on* with them certain days" at Caesarea, which presumably he did : see Acts x. 48) the Apostle may have

made it a practice to join at table with
Gentile believers. It was made a reproach
against him, on his return to Jerusalem,
by οἱ ἐκ περιτομῆς (designated in Acts as
here), that he had actually done so once, on
the occasion of that visit. And we should
gather that his defence was successful for
a time, and silenced his Judaic critics.
This had befallen some considerable time
before Saul was fetched from Tarsus to
join the work at Antioch; and he had been
a full year at that before the 'Relief'
mission. It is to be hoped, and believed,
that the custom of St Peter—for 'Cephas'
in the text can be no other : the existence
of the variant Πέτρος is decisive evidence
for early church belief—set forth in the
συνήσθιεν (Gal. ii. 12), was a habit of
some standing. Nor, indeed, is it even
certain that he actually gave it up when
the Judaisers came. The Greek, of course,
is not decisive for that interpretation. All
it sets before us is a tendency, a back-
wardness, an unwillingness to do as he
had done (at any rate *in Antioch*) under

Judaising pressure. St Paul stigmatises this weakness as sheer ὑπόκρισις, and it is difficult indeed to blame him for calling it so. The defection of Barnabas, the one man broad-minded enough and courageous enough to hold out the hand of fellowship to the ex-Pharisee and persecutor (as we are told in Acts ix. 27) may well have tried his comrade very severely. There could be no stronger proof of the influence exercised by the emissaries " from James." The language of ii. 14 is interesting. Ὀρθοποδοῦσιν (a most expressive term) may have been a word of Antioch, or even of Tarsus : it has about it, one can't help thinking, a kind of ' sporting ' ring. Πῶς, I imagine, represents the τί μαθών of classical Greek. In idiomatic English it would be ' Why on earth ?' or the like.

It seems to be fairly certain that St Paul, on this eventful occasion, would only have flashed forth one sharp, indignant question. No one supposes he went on with all that is contained in *vv.* 15—21. But, if he did not say all of it, seeing

how it all hangs together, it is very hard
to tell where the break should be supposed.
It is better, I have no doubt, to punctuate
as is done in 'W. H.' Very possibly St
Paul felt then exactly what he now sets
down in 'black and white.' But it would
have savoured of the absurd to have so
delivered himself at Antioch. There is
only one consideration that might give us
pause : that is the opening ἡμεῖς. But
St Paul, and all Jewish Christians who felt
with him, were called upon to defend themselves, as often as this attack was made by
the ' circumcision people.' It is for himself and them St Paul is speaking here.
There is nothing surprising in the sudden-
ness of the turn. It is highly characteristic
of the writer.

Otherwise we might regard the passage
as a sort of soliloquy, in which the Apostle
mentally apostrophises his great brother.

Gal. i. 15. "We are Jews born,
and not 'sinners' from among the
Gentiles; yet being sure that a man
is not 'set right' (*with God*) from

doing things Law bids, (*but*) only
through faith in Christ Jesus ; we too
became believers in Christ Jesus, that
we might be set right with God on the
ground of faith in Christ, and not of
legal doings. For no living creature
shall be set right *with God* as a
consequence of achieving law."

This somewhat rude translation will
speak, I think, for itself. 'Sinners' is, of
course, used as contemptuous Jews would
use it, of folks not born ' in the Covenant,'
or even insufficiently educated. Εἰδότες
expresses a truth intuitively discerned,
about which one does not reason, for the
thing is self-evident. It is not easy to
represent the distinction between the ἐξ
and the διὰ of *v.* 16—if indeed (for practical
purposes) there be any distinction at all.
The latter part of the verse, in which ἐξ is
used thrice running, would plainly suggest
there is none. The εἰς with Χριστόν in
v. 16 (ἐπιστεύσαμεν εἰς Χριστόν) means no
more than "in." There is no 'pregnant'
conception of 'incorporation,' or the like.

The aorist is certainly 'ingressive.' The
citation of the Psalm is an instance of that
free handling of O.T. Scripture which
startles the modern reader when studying
the New Testament.   And it comes in
' Romans ' too in precisely the same form,
with the addition (from the LXX) of
ἐνώπιόν σου.   For the Psalmist the pronouncement *is* of universal application.
Whether we read πᾶς ζῶν or πᾶσα σάρξ
makes no sort of difference.   Still the first
time the modern reader comes across
the Pauline insertion he cannot but feel
troubled.   He is vexed to have to say to
himself : 'if the statement is universally
true, it must be true in the case imagined
by St Paul ; the most careful " legalist "
must fail of δικαιοσύνη.'   We should feel
happier if we might expand a little and
say : " neither by 'legal works,' *nor any
other way*, shall any living man be righted
in God's eyes."

Apart from the famous citation the
two verses present no difficulty.   Now we
come to harder matter.

Gal. ii. 17, 18. " But if in our eagerness to be set right in Christ, we, even we, found ourselves in the category of 'sinners,' is Christ an agent of sin ? Out, impious thought ! If I build up again what *once* I demolished, it is I that am transgressor."

The argument in *v.* 17 is of the nature of a ' reductio ad absurdum.' To become ' believers in Christ' the Apostles and their fellows had to sink, in the eyes of their countrymen, to the level of Gentile ' outcasts.' They too became ' sinners.' But it was Christ that set them there. Ergo, the sinfulness of that ' sinner ' state was none. It was just a necessary consequence of seeking life in Him. With regard to ἐν Χριστῷ, the question must arise, is this the familiar Pauline phrase to express the ' vital union,' which obtains between Christ and believers ; or, should we rather regard the ἐν as being of an 'instrumental' character? 'Εν Χριστῷ might be virtually equivalent to διὰ Χριστοῦ. If we have

here the full 'pregnant' phrase, it would
be better to adopt the rendering "by
union with Christ." The one rendering is
grammatically simpler; but the other is
probably right. Verse 15 shows that the
boot is on the other leg. It is addressed
to all such Jewish believers as showed
a disposition to 'weaken' in the face
of Judaic bigotry; in fact manifested a
tendency to 'run both with hare and
hounds.' St Paul elsewhere declares that
whatever is not 'of conviction' is 'sin.'
To accept the Christian position, to take
Christ for 'all in all,' and then to hark back
to the Law, as if that had 'saving' virtue—
that was plainly tantamount to self-con-
viction. The παραβάτην ἐμαυτὸν συν-
ιστάνω recalls the κατεγνωσμένος of *v.* 11.
The Apostle, after his manner, employs
the first person here, but in the very next
verse he is at the pains of explaining that
this is by no means *his* case—the case of
him, Paul.

Verse 19 is very hard of rendering:
one can only guess, at the best.

c. ii. 19—21. " Law led me to die
to Law, that I might live to God.
Christ's crucifixion is mine. There
lives no longer I ; it is Christ lives in
me. And so far as I now live the
life of common man, I live in faith—
faith in the Son of God, that loved
me and gave Himself up for me. I
do not nullify the grace of God. If
by Law acceptance comes *with God*,
then was Christ's death for naught !"

Here is indeed a passage sufficiently
perplexing. The thought seems plain in
regard to its general drift. But there is
a very baffling conciseness of expression,
as well as an element of the ' mystical' in
the teaching, that does not contribute to
make it easier of exposition.

The opening phrase of *v.* 19 is an excellent instance of highly perplexing conciseness. The thought appears to be : I was
once a follower of Law, and followed with
might and main : but it led to nothing,
nothing. The more I tried, the more
hopeless seemed the task. Law finally

demonstrated its hopeless inefficacy. So
'Law' became for St Paul the death
of 'Law.' Only he does not put it so.
Instead of saying 'Law died for me,' he
says 'I died for Law.' But (I take it) the
reason for his thus converting the proposi-
tion is the clause that follows next, ἵνα Θεῷ
ζήσω. Law, indeed, died for him : he had
no more interest in it or use for it. He
found a real 'life' elsewhere—in the
spiritual sphere. His 'death *to* Law' led
him on to 'life *for* God.' The datives are
very difficult, and the latter more so than
the former. The former is a species
familiar enough in classical Greek. I
used to call it myself the 'dative of personal limitation.' The name implies that
the predication contained in the verb is
limited to a certain (and a personal) application. 'Law' is here personified. The
Νόμῳ, then, means 'as far as Law was
concerned I ceased to be ' (which is only a
way of saying ; Law became nothing for
me). The Θεῷ is a different matter. The
dative, apparently the same, is (on further

consideration) obviously other. St Paul
entered a new life, not merely relatively to
God, but altogether. Νόμῳ ἀπέθανον and
Θεῷ ζήσω are not in perfect balance. But
that is a common phenomenon in Pauline
sentences. The reader may recall a closely
similar variation of datives in one sentence,
that occurs in Romans vi. 10, "In that He
died, He died to sin once for all : in that
He liveth, He liveth for God." The
relations there expressed by the datives
are similarly different. St Paul, in fact,
uses ζῆν τινί, not infrequently, in the sense
'to live in the interest of.' This is not,
so far as I know, a classical usage. The
phrase Χριστῷ συνεσταύρωμαι is full of
interest. Owing to the non-existence in
English of an adequate equivalent for the
perfect tense in Greek (for our perfect is
widely different) it can only be rendered
by some cumbrous periphrasis. One can
either say, I am 'crucified with Christ,' or
else (as above) 'Christ's crucifixion is mine
too.' The perfect represents the fact as
permanent and ever fruitful. The same

idea is found in Romans (vi. 6) stated in
the other possible tense, the aorist.   That
represents the thing as an event in historic
time, a thing that once befell.   Here the
'death,' implied in crucifixion, is set forth
as perennially lasting.   There must be a
death before the new life can begin.   So,
spiritually also, 'death' is the 'gate to life.'
It follows that, as a consequence, Paul (in
a way) is no longer alive.   The old 'Paul'
is gone for ever.   There is a new 'Paul'
now : only this new 'Paul' is not really
'Paul' at all ; it is Christ alive in Paul.
Accordingly he continues ζῶ δὲ οὐκέτι
ἐγώ, which I rendered above, 'There lives
no longer I.'   Greek idiom requires that
the verb should be in the first person.   It
is like the "θαρσεῖτε, ἐγώ εἰμι" of the
Gospel story.   This however (the ζῇ ἐν
ἐμοὶ Χριστός) represents only the mystical
truth.   There is a natural life coincident
with it : there is a palpable 'Paul,' who
behaves as other men in outward things,
who eats and sleeps, and so forth.   Yet even
his life is different from the life of other

men, not merely in a mystical sense, but
in intelligible ways. It is lived in a different
atmosphere. That atmosphere is 'faith'
—"faith in the Son of God, that loved me
and gave Himself for me." This personal
appropriation of the love of Christ by St
Paul may be said to have its rationale in
the fact that Christ is Divine. At first
one is tempted to say Christ could only
die for the world. And indeed that might
have been so were He other than He is.

Believers in every age have sided with
the Apostle in his strong 'personal' conviction : and (seemingly) they have been
right. What self-surrender is this of which
the Apostle speaks τοῦ...παραδόντος ἑαυ-
τόν ? Surely it must cover the death.
How far it would be justifiable to see in
the ὑπὲρ ἐμοῦ the idea of 'vicarious
suffering,' it is not easy to say. Speaking
in strict grammar, one could not insist on
its presence. But life (ordinary human life)
is very full of it : in fact, love would be at
a loss, if this channel were closed to it.
The χάριν of *v.* 21 would appear to be

'concrete.' It is the 'loving favour' shown in an especial way, in the giving of the Son.

To translate δικαιοσύνη by 'righteousness' (in *v.* 21) appears to me absurd. The word is meant to express the condition of the technically δίκαιος—of the man 'who is right with God.' It is by no means easy to 'English.' One can 'right' a man, or 'set him right'; but 'rightness' would mean nothing. The Latin says 'justitia.' It would have been somewhat happier, had it said 'justificatio.'

One often hears people make mention of 'legal fiction' in connexion with the idea of 'justification.' This appears to me to proceed entirely from a failure to recognise the purely technical sense of δίκαιος and of δικαιοσύνη. It plainly lies with the Deity to dictate the terms and conditions on which He will admit a man within His Covenant. At least it appears to me so.

§ 4. THE SECOND PARAGRAPH FROM GALATIANS

(being the whole of chapter iii.)

The second passage from 'Galatians' follows immediately after the first. It opens with an appeal to actual experience. The Galatian Church enjoyed the gift of the Holy Spirit. The question is, how did they get it? To this there could be but one answer. They had only to question themselves, in sincerity and honesty, and they would gratefully acknowledge it had not come by 'law.' And the Spirit is, of course, the seal of God's acceptance. But here is what the Apostle says:

(iii. 1.) "O foolish Galatians, who has bewitched you? Why, before your very eyes Jesus Christ was plainly writ, as crucified."

In this verse the opening metaphor is drawn from the 'evil eye.' They must have been 'overlooked' (as peasants say in the West). Nothing else would account for it. Lightfoot avers that προεγράφη contains no idea of 'painting': it simply means 'posted up,' 'placarded.' The ἐν ὑμῖν is rejected by modern editors. Notwithstanding it is possible. It may be intended to reiterate the vividness with which the crucifixion was presented. The πρό of προεγράφη means, I think, merely 'plainly,' as in προλέγειν.

(iii. 2—6.) "This only would I learn of you. Did the gift of the Spirit come from doing what Law bade, or from *believing* what you were told? Are you as foolish as all that? Having started in the Spirit, are you now seeking fulfilment in the flesh? Have all your experiences gone for nothing—if indeed they have gone for nothing? He that ministers to you the Spirit, I ask again, and makes mighty powers to work amongst you, (*does He* it) because you do what Law commands, or because you hear and believe? As *Abraham believed God and it was reckoned to him for righteousness.*"

Gen. xv. 6

The paraphrase here given sets forth what I think to be the Apostolic meaning.

The gift of the Holy Spirit (to begin with) is, in the Apostle's thought, and in the minds of his readers, a fact entirely beyond dispute. They actually possessed this high endowment, with all its visible and palpable accompaniments. The only question is the question the Apostle puts : how did it come ?

In the latter part of *v.* 2 we have two balancing clauses, which are not exactly parallel. The former of them is plain enough as to its meaning, the latter much more intangible. That ἐξ ἔργων νόμου means " by doing the various things Law bids," I should say, none would dispute. Ἐξ ἀκοῆς πίστεως is plainly a harder phrase. But, seeing that πίστεως is obviously the more important member of what is in effect a compound noun (after the Teutonic model), we cannot be wrong in rendering, either " from believing hearing," or " from believing what you were told." The latter I myself prefer. It is the repetition of the

phrase below (*v.* 5), in immediate connexion
with the mention of Abraham's 'belief,'
that makes this rendering likely. Verse 3
contains one of those curious passive uses,
which are regarded as 'quasi-middle.'
"Having started in the 'spirit,' are you
seeking completion (ἐπιτελεῖσθε) in the
'flesh'?" Here I should say that the
so-called 'middle' force is really due to the
'tentative' character, which often attaches
to the 'present stem' tenses in Greek.
An old scholar might have rendered it
"are you for being completed?" The
two datives πνεύματι and σαρκί are very
baffling for the translator. For all intents
and purposes they are equivalent to adverbs; but we have no English adverbs
that could serve as equivalents. Verse 4
is ambiguous. It may refer to persecution;
"have you suffered all you have suffered"
(which would recall such passages as Acts
xiv. 1, 2, and—even more particularly—
Acts xiv. 22; where St Paul and Barnabas
expressly warn the converts of Lystra,
Iconium and Antioch, that we must "enter

into God's Kingdom διὰ πολλῶν θλίψεων");
or it may be of broader reference, recalling
all that methodists would denominate 'experience.' This I conceive to be the
likelier. The adverb which closes the
verse plainly means 'without effect,' that
is, 'without being the better, the more
faithful, for it all.' It is odd that the
Vulgate should say 'si tamen,' instead of
'si quidem.' Verse 5 merely reproduces
the old question in a new form. The οὖν
is, of course, 'resumptive.' The ἐπί of
ἐπιχορηγεῖν is probably not 'intensive,' but
merely employed because later Greek
preferred the compound to the simple
verb χορηγεῖν. Ἐνεργῶν δυνάμεις ἐν ὑμῖν
is doubly ambiguous. Δυνάμεις may be
'miraculous powers,' or actual 'miracles':
ἐν ὑμῖν may be 'among you,' or actually
'in you.' It is difficult to be sure, in either
case. For the rest, the question's answer
is so inevitable, that it is not stated at all.
We have to supply it. For writer and for
reader, it 'goes without saying.' 'For our
believing' is, of course, the answer; *as*

Abraham believed God and it was counted to him for righteousness.

The quotation from Gen. xv. 6 (the 'LXX' of that passage) is not developed here, as it is in Romans iv. The student cannot decide, how far the writer read into the words of the ancient Greek the technical sense he himself generally attributes to the term for 'righteousness.' The Hebrew (I should apprehend) means only "God accounted it as a thing well and rightly done"; 'righteousness' being little more than 'a righteous act.' Anyhow, in Abraham's case, *belief* it was pleased God, and won acceptance with Him. The particular 'belief' in question was the belief in the promised 'seed' (*tell the stars, if thou shalt be able to number them: and He said unto him, So shall thy seed be*).

The passage continues :

iii. 7—9. " You can see then, that the men of faith—they are the sons of Abraham. And the Scripture, seeing beforehand that it is by faith God means to 'justify' the Gentiles, had

promised before to Abraham, *In thee
shall all the nations be blessed.* Accordingly it is the men of faith who
are blessed with faithful Abraham."

The opening verb in *v.* 7 is an appeal
to the reader's good sense. Unquestioning
belief constitutes, beyond a doubt, that
trait in the Patriarch, which commended
him to God, beyond all other men. It
is a fair deduction from this, that a like
attitude in ourselves will produce a like
result. At least that is how the writer
appears to put it (γινώσκετε ἄρα). The
'Scripture' of *v.* 8 is an earlier passage in
Genesis, in fact the primal promise made
to Abraham at his call (Gen. xii. 3).

The δικαιοῖ either expresses the wont
of the Almighty—the way He habitually
deals—or else must be regarded (with
Lightfoot) as 'prophetic.' This is how
I have taken it. About the 'pluperfect'
rendering of προευηγγελίσατο, I don't feel
certain. Possibly however it is safer. The
personification of 'the Scripture' is singular
and unique. It was God, to be sure, who

made the promise to Abraham, and not
'the Scripture' at all.   That only records
it for us.   If we were expressing it in
words of our own, we should put it something like this.   We should say : "And,
seeing it was God's intent to justify the
heathen through faith, the Scripture tells
us how God had made promise before to
Abraham, saying...."

In the conclusion of *v.* 8 St Paul (as
his manner is) takes the ancient Greek
translation of O.T. in the sense it naturally
bears (as read in Greek) for one not con-
versant with the Hebrew text.   It is true
that he does not quote LXX exactly,
but it is only the change of a word (ἔθνη
for φυλαί).

It is hardly necessary (and indeed is
inadvisable) to postulate the 'fusion' of
Gen. xii. 3 with Gen. xviii. 18, to account
for the change of noun.   The context in
fact demands an earlier citation than one
in chap. xv.   Therefore the Apostle is
plainly citing Gen. xii. from memory.
Stress is laid on the sense of the *Greek*,

because it would appear that the *Hebrew*
means something other. The words in
Gen. xlviii. 20 (*In thee shall Israel bless,
saying, God make thee as Ephraim and
Manasseh*) seem to make it fairly clear
that " In thee shall the nations bless themselves" must be taken as merely meaning
'the nations shall pray that they may be
as happy as you.' However (as I have
said) the Apostle took the LXX as he
found it, and expounded it as it stood.
How it ever came to pass that the LXX
should be the 'O.T.' of Gamaliel's pupil is
one of the strangest problems that faces
the 'N.T.' student. But so it certainly is.
Can it be that he laid aside the Hebrew
for the Greek, from the day when he
knew himself the Apostle of the Gentiles?
The importance of the change from the
one version to the other it is hard to
overestimate. Indeed have we, Christian
students, sufficiently realised yet what it
means *for us*, that the Christian 'O.T.' is
the Version of Alexandria, and not the
Hebrew at all—just because it is the

version of all the N.T. writers, broadly
speaking; unmistakeably of St Paul? In
any case it is plain that the Greek of Gen.
xii. 3 (as we have it and St Paul had it)
must inevitably mean, " *Through thee* shall
all the nations be blessed." It is the
Scripture, interpreted so, that solely meets
the facts of the Christian revelation. I
should say that in this place (as in several
others) the later wisdom of Israel was
actually 'guided' in the interpretation it
set on primitive Scripture. In so far the
LXX becomes, not only the 'Christian'
version, but actually the 'better' version,
as containing the latest light vouchsafed
to Israel. We are here faced with a
dilemma which I do not intend to state.
The thoughtful 'N.T.' reader will discern
it for himself.

Another point should be mentioned
before we pass on further. It is this. The
genius of our language (and this is clearly
seen from the study of A.V.) dislikes per-
sistently employing one family of words to
set forth one family of ideas. For instance,

πιστεύειν and πίστις occur several times, each of them, in the course of this section. But we, in rendering, are forced to 'ring the changes' between 'belief' and 'faith.' You may say 'the men of belief' or 'the men of faith'—whichever you will. One thing only you may not do. You may not render πίστις, wherever it may occur, consistently by either. Sometimes it must be 'faith,' sometimes 'belief.' It must be neither all the time. Being very sure of this, I have varied the rendering in my own paraphrase. Of course one might say "And so the men of belief share the blessing of believing Abraham." But it would only be pedantic, and mistaken pedantry too.

At this point in the argument a new idea is introduced. '*Blessing*' suggests its antithesis, and the Apostle passes on to argue that so far from being a source of 'blessing,' the Law is a source of 'curse' and condemnation.

    iii. 10—12. "Why, all that are of the school of legal doings are under a curse. For it stands written,

Accursed is everyone that abideth not in all the things that are written in the Book of the Law for to do them."

"And that by Law no man is righted in the eyes of God is plain : because *The just shall live by faith.* Whereas the Law is not matter of faith, but, *He that achieveth the commands shall live by them.*"

Lev. xviii. 5

The opening clause of *v.* 10 is rendered by Lightfoot, 'those who are of works of law.' It is not a perspicuous phrase. The meaning clearly is, 'the whole tribe, or fellowship, of "doers."' The 'circumcision party' are described in Acts xi. 2 by a similar periphrasis. The quotation in the same verse is a somewhat free citation, LXX in character, of Deut. xxvii. 26, the final sentence of 'cursing' from Mount Ebal. The πᾶς and πᾶσι of the Greek are not represented in Hebrew, though our Authorised Version inserts an 'all' before the "*words of this law.*" The quotation in *v.* 11 is a very notable one. It comes (as everyone knows)

from Habakkuk ii. 4, where again in our
English Version the citation by St Paul
has influenced the rendering. In Hebrew,
strictly speaking, there is no word for
'faith' (in any N.T. sense). The πίστις
of LXX stands for 'loyalty' or 'stedfastness,' rather than 'faith': but St Paul
avails himself here of the double meaning.
What the prophet is declaring amounts to
this: in an era of disaster the 'faithful,' or
'loyal,' among Israel shall not perish. In
fact it is the doctrine of the 'remnant'
stated in another form. The same citation
is found in Romans i., employed as it is
here. In Hebrews x. 38, it is found in
full LXX form, and further is interpreted
in accordance with the original sense, as
'loyalty' or 'stedfastness' and not as the
theological virtue. Πίστις (it should be
added) occurs often in LXX, but always
in the sense of 'faithfulness.' Bishop
Lightfoot observes, in this connexion, that
the Apostle gives the prophetic words 'a
spiritual meaning and a general application.' He applies them to 'moral' ruin,

not 'material'; and avers that 'stedfast loyalty' shall not fail of its reward. However, the modern reader can hardly fail to be conscious of something of discomfort, in view of the sense attached by St Paul to Habakkuk's words. 'Faith' (in the Pauline sense) and 'faithfulness to God' (which is what the Prophet had in mind), in the long run, *are* the same thing. But the Western mind would shrink from identifying them for purposes of argument. 'Law' and 'Faith' are far apart; but 'Law' and 'Loyalty' are not so disconnected. For loyalty is revealed in prompt and ready obedience. Howbeit in this passage the Pauline antithesis is not developed, and the Habakkuk citation is not of vital moment for the argument. 'Law' lands its votaries finally in 'cursing' rather than 'blessing,' because only perfect 'obedience' can satisfy its claims; and 'perfect obedience' is (or, at any rate, then was) impossible for man. Accordingly *vv.* 11 and 12 might well be set in a bracket, as parenthetical.

iii. 13, 14. "CHRIST it was redeemed us from the curse that Law
involves, by becoming for us a ' curse'
(for it is written, *Accursed is everyone* Deut. xxi
that hangeth on a tree); that the [23]
blessing of Abraham might in Christ
Jesus extend to the Gentiles ; to the
end we might be given the promise of
the Spirit, through faith."

It will be seen we have ' worked back '
to the question which was asked in *v.* 2
above.   The ' Promise of the Spirit ' is
identified with Abraham's 'blessing' (the
'blessing' promised in Gen. xii.).   Probably in the phrase "the promise of the
Spirit," the ' promise' is meant to be, *not*
the promise made by Christ on earth,
but the promise made to Abraham.   The
' Spirit,' in short, is the 'promise'; is its
splendid realisation delayed till the time
of Christ.   The verb ' redeem ' ($\dot{\epsilon}\xi\alpha\gamma o\rho\acute{\alpha}$-
$\zeta\epsilon\iota\nu$) here employed occurs only once in
LXX, in the curious phrase of Daniel
ii. 8, $\kappa\alpha\iota\rho\grave{o}\nu\ldots\dot{\epsilon}\xi\alpha\gamma o\rho\acute{\alpha}\zeta\epsilon\iota\nu$.   'To become
a curse' is, in English, by no means so

intelligible as it is in the language of Israel.
A person exceptionally ill-starred might
call himself a 'curse,' as Anna (the mother
of the Blessed Virgin Mary) does in an
Apocryphal Gospel cited by Lightfoot.
For 'sin' and for 'sin offering' there is
but one word in Hebrew.   In relation to
the statement here used of Christ, one
recalls the 'scapegoat' (and its heathen
analogies, the φαρμακοί at Athens, or the
victims in ancient Egypt whereof Herodo-
tus speaks).   In 2 Cor. v. 21 it is said
of Christ, "Him that knew not sin on
our behalf, He made *sin*."   That is even
stranger than this "becoming a curse."
In the citation from Deuteronomy the
Apostle alters the phrase in the LXX text
'κεκατηραμένος ὑπὸ Θεοῦ' (which he could
not have anyhow used, as hardly with
reverence to be applied to Christ—even in
view of Psalm xxii.) into the simple ἐπι-
κατάρατος, which brings it into line with
the quotation of *v.* 10.   For myself, I
cannot see how we can extrude from the
passage before us the thought of 'vicarious

suffering.' Christ 'redeems' us by 'becoming a curse'—that is by taking on
Himself the penalty involved in the failure
to achieve the claims of God's Holiness.

It is always difficult, when following
Pauline argument, to be certain as to what
is essential in the course of the reasoning
and what unessential. At first sight one is
tempted to say, in considering this passage,
that the introduction of the thought of the
'curse,' which Law entails, interrupts the
sequence of thought. 'How did you get
the Spirit? it came to you by faith, as
Abraham's blessing came to him. Your
blessing *had* to come in the self-same
manner; for so is the way of God in
dealing with men.' This might seem to
us to be the essential argument. But it
is not. *It leaves out Christ.* It is not by
'faith,' pure and simple, that men are
'saved' at all, according to the Apostle;
but '*by* faith *in* Jesus Christ.' For centuries before He came men had been
striving to 'right themselves' by scrupulous
obedience. But this was a hopeless task.

They rested evermore beneath the shadow
of Ebal and its doom. Over everyone
there hovered, be he never so careful in
'doing,' the shadow of dismal failure—
the 'curse' that is linked with Law.
Christ it was who dispelled the shadow.
He did something: He bore something:
He 'became' something. The 'curse' (we
cannot fathom how) He somehow transferred to Himself. He was the 'scapegoat' of mankind. I do not see myself (I
say again) how we can avoid the conclusion
that His *death*, in the Apostle's thought,
made life possible for our race. Till then
(one is led to infer) 'faith' itself was
ineffectual. But, with that life once lived,
that death once died, faith received her
proper object, and the blessing—the long-
promised blessing—could descend on man.
On the readers it had descended, the seal
of their acceptance. And—*it had come by
'faith.'*

iii. 15—18. "My brothers, take
a human analogy! A man's will,
though it be but a man's, when once

ratified, none sets aside or alters by
addition."

" To Abraham were the promises
spoken *and to his seed.* It says not
and to his seeds, as if there had been
many, but as in the case of *one, And
to thy seed*, which is Christ."

" But what I am saying is this.
A covenant ratified of old by God, the
Law, that came four hundred and
thirty years after, does not cancel, so
as to do away with the Promise."

" For if the inheritance comes by
Law, it does not come by promise.
But to Abraham God's free giving is
by promise."

In this passage the Apostle is haunted
by the ever present Judaic contention that
it is the Law that matters. Mark how it
begins with 'man,' and ends with God
(κεχάρισται ὁ Θεός). No doubt there is
involved in this the force of an ' a fortiori.'
If man's διαθήκη stands, what shall we say
of God's ? The curiously placed ὅμως is
exactly illustrated by 1 Cor. xiv. 7. With

regard to διαθήκη, two things must be observed. The first is that with St Paul the διαθήκη in question is the pre-Mosaic 'Covenant'; the other, that he avails himself of the double sense of διαθήκη—the regular (but not universal) 'classical' sense of 'will,' and the regular LXX sense of 'covenant.' In spite of all contention to the contrary, we cannot blink the fact that all through O.T. Scripture 'covenant' *is* διαθήκη in Greek—a word very likely used of deliberate intent, because God's 'covenant' is not a set agreement between two contracting parties, but a gracious purpose of God, offered to man upon conditions. That is, it is a 'disposition' but not a 'testament.' In Heb. ix. 15—17 we have the famous 'amphiboly,' wherein it would seem the writer uses διαθήκη in both senses. That same 'amphiboly' is here. Ἀνθρώπου διαθήκη must be a 'will' —so much is shown by the technical term ἐπιδιατάσσεται ; for ἐπιδιαθήκη means an 'amended will' or 'codicil': but the διαθήκη of God is obviously other. The idea

of 'testamentary disposition' is wholly impossible in such a connexion.

A human will is 'ratified' when duly
sealed : and further (it would seem to be
implied) when the man who made it is
dead. The Covenant of God is ratified by
His own gracious declaration, and 'sealed,'
on the human side (for there *is* a human
side), by the God-appointed symbol. The
εἰς Χριστόν (of *v.* 17), which I have omitted
with the editors, might be interpreted as
due to what *v.* 16 says. It would have to
be translated either as 'pointing to Christ,'
or 'till Christ should come.' The latter
sense is supported by *v.* 19 below (ἄχρις
οὗ ἔλθῃ τὸ σπέρμα). Awkward as εἰς
Χριστόν is, it is worth while to observe
that only by keeping it can we account
for the curious *v.* 16. That verse contains
a citation from Genesis xiii. 5 ("all the
land which thou seest, to thee will I give
it *and to thy seed* for ever "). Remark that
this citation is unmistakeably LXX.

The Greek σπέρμα has a plural ; the
Hebrew word has none. The argument

of St Paul (which does not appear to us precisely convincing) depends on the possibility of substituting σπέρμασιν. Moreover, note this further, that, though the actual citation is as stated ; the importance of the identification is intimately associated with the memory of that other word, "and in thy *seed* shall all the families of the earth be blessed." That passage must have been, at the moment of writing, in the back of the Apostle's mind. In *v.* 18 we should note the exceeding advantage Greek has in the flexibility, which allows the omission of a verb. We, in English, have to choose between ' was ' and 'is.' It is far better to have neither. The latter part of οὐκέτι is due to Greek idiom : we need not, indeed we must not, say ' no longer.' The κεχάρισται of *v.* 18 recalls the famous χάρισμα in Romans. Unhappily English possesses no verb that completely corresponds.

In *vv.* 19, 20 we come to close grip with the question, ' Then how about the Law ?'

Here is the Apostle's answer. He demonstrates that the Law had a reason ; that it was only temporary ; and that it was palpably inferior, as being 'mediated'— and all this in the compass of a single verse.

iii. 19, 20. "To what end then served the Law? It was an addition made for transgressions' sake, till such time as the seed should come, for whom the Promise is ; appointed in the presence of angels by the hand of an intermediary. Now God is One ; and the very idea of one excludes an intermediary."

Τί οὖν ὁ νόμος; is not to be regarded as parallel to 1 Cor. iii. 5 ("what then *is* Apollos ?") The τί is probably accusative ("What then *did* the Law ?") The words that follow set forth the 'Law,' as a sort of 'afterthought' (προσετέθη)—no part of the original purpose. Τῶν παραβάσεων χάριν is explained by statements in Romans. Law's purpose (according to St Paul) is not to 'check' sin, but to 'define' it—in effect, as he says, to 'create' it. (See Romans iii. 20, iv. 15, v. 20, vii. 7.) Ἐπήγγελται appears to be 'impersonal passive.' The tense points to the record of Scripture, which stands as long as earth stands.

The mention of 'angels' in connexion with the giving of the Law is probably post-canonical. There is a possible reference in Deut. xxxiii. 2, but *not in the LXX text*. In Acts vii. 53 the 'angels' are spoken of as enhancing Law's dignity: here (as more decisively in Heb. ii. 2) the angels depreciate Law, as moving God farther off: they are suggestive of 'intermediaries.' Ἐν χειρὶ μεσίτου is difficult of rendering: it means really "*worked by* a mediator." But that one could hardly say. In the LXX, we may add, this special formula is actually consecrated to this connexion (see Numb. iv. 37).

About *v.* 20 commentators have been amazingly at variance. Lightfoot declares its interpretations mount to 250 or 300 in number. The conciseness of the Greek and the lack of definite outline which appertains to the genitive, constitute between them the difficulty.

The free paraphrase given above expresses what I believe to be its meaning. There appears to be an antithesis between the 'mediate' character of the Mosaic 'covenant' and the wholly 'immediate' nature (as coming direct from GOD) of the Abrahamic 'Promise.' At least, so I should hold.

The Apostle has now explained how the Law came into being. For the sake of greater precision, and to avoid all misunderstanding, he asks yet another question :

iii. 21. " Does then the Law conflict with the promises of God ? God forbid it should do so ! If a Law had been given, that could bring real life, then truly 'acceptance with God' would have been by Law. But" —(*so far is this from being so*)—" the Scripture has made all the prisoners of Sin, that the promise might be given to believers, thanks to faith in Jesus Christ."

The 'promises' of God, mentioned in *v.* 21, are all summed up in one Promise (as we see below). Maybe the plural is here used because the one Promise is made more times than once. Ζωοποιῆσαι suggests a virtual state of death. Ἡ δικαιοσύνη may mean 'the righteousness we have in view,' or merely 'righteousness.' The singular figure συνέκλεισεν comes once again in Romans, in a somewhat similar phrase (xi. 32). Τὰ πάντα is noticeable. St Paul uses the neuter plural to make what he wishes to say as comprehensive as possible. He is thinking of people, of course, in spite of the gender. 'The Scripture,' one inclines to think, must be a Scripture already cited. If so, it clearly must be that quoted in *v.* 10. Apart from that necessity, other Scriptures would have suited, such as Psalm cxiv. 3, or Psalm cxliv. 3 (which latter has been quoted in ii. 16). The 'promise' is the Spirit, God's gift to believers, consequent on faith in Jesus Christ.

iii. 23—27. " Before faith came, we were kept safe under Law, fast prisoners till the faith should come, that was going to be revealed. Accordingly the Law was our 'tutor,' till Christ came, that we might be set right with God in consequence of faith. Since faith has come, we are no longer under a tutor. Aye, you are all Sons of God, *through* faith, *in* Jesus Christ. For all of you that have been baptised in Christ have put on Christ."

The ἐφρουρούμεθα of *v.* 23 suggests zealous watch and ward : the perfect συγκεκλεισμένοι is preferable, I should say, to the present participle, in spite of MS. authority. The εἰς is plainly ' temporal,' as in several other places. The order of the words, at the end of 22, is thoroughly ' classical.' In *v.* 24 the γέγονεν is one of the ' irrational ' perfects we sometimes find in the case of that particular verb. We must translate it as though it were an aorist, not a perfect. The figure of the παιδαγωγός developes, and further softens,

the metaphor of ἐφρουρούμεθα. The Law
may have had a tight grip, and held its
prisoners fast, but its purpose was a loving
one. The mention of the παιδαγωγός
(seeing what the functions were of such a
confidential slave) makes εἰς Χριστοῦ rather
tempting. Yet εἰς Χριστόν is right. With
the latter we must assume a temporal
sense. God's 'Sons' (a term of privilege)
are beyond all slavish restraint.

In *vv.* 26 and 27 two questions suggest
themselves with regard to the prepositions.
Is it " sons of God...in Christ Jesus"? or
is the genesis of that 'sonship' described
in its twofold aspect, as brought about by
faith, but resting on union with Christ? I
incline to the latter belief. Again, in *v.* 27,
does it mean "all ye that were baptised in
Christ," or " baptised into Christ" (which
indeed is no true English, but a clumsy
way of representing what is called a
'pregnant' sense)? I believe 'to baptise
in Christ' means to 'baptise in the name
of Christ'—in which case εἰς is used.
Anyhow, the 'sonship of God' is due to

union with Christ, here described by the bold figure "have put on Christ."

iii. 28, 29. "There is *there* no Jew nor Gentile; no bond nor free; no 'male and female.' Ye all are one man in Christ Jesus. And if ye are Christ's, then are ye Abraham's seed, and heirs according to promise."

Lightfoot's comments on *v.* 28 are highly illuminating. The ἔνι, he observes, 'negatives not the fact but the possibility'; and again, 'all distinctions are swept away, even the primal one of sex' (*male and female created He them*). For the masculine singular εἷς, see Ephesians ii. 15.

In *v.* 29 we see that it is the 'vital union,' obtaining between Christ and believers, that constitutes them the 'seed' of the patriarch Abraham. Strictly speaking, Christ is the seed, as in *v.* 16 above. But they that are Χριστοῦ (which *may* mean 'members of Christ') are necessarily 'seed' too, and as such inherit the promise.

§ 5. THE THIRD PARAGRAPH FROM GALATIANS

(Chapter iv. 1—11.)

In chap. iii. we were told that the Law—in that case plainly the Law of Moses—was a παιδαγωγός, a temporary παιδαγωγός, till 'faith' should come, that is definite Christian faith, and release from such discipline. This state of tutelage has now been merged in 'sonship.' It is past and gone for ever. But we have not exhausted the topic. It reappears in chap. iv. For the Apostle is anxious exceedingly to make it clear to his readers, that this bygone state of tutelage was tantamount to 'bondage.' The freedom of the Christian is ever a prominent feature of his teaching.

In the next section we are puzzled by two difficult questions. The first is, to what extent the terms the Apostle employs are strictly technical—a comparatively small matter : the other, what class of converts

he has in view, whether Jews primarily, or
Gentiles. From the record in Acts we
should gather that the Churches of Galatia
were predominantly Gentile.

In the earlier part of Acts xiii., it is
true, we have record of a discourse made
to Jews and Jewish sympathisers, in the
course of which (by the way), in *vv.* 38
and 39, we have a doctrinal statement,
which is closely parallel to the teaching of
this letter :

" Be it known unto you therefore,
Sirs and brethren, that through Him
remission of sins is proclaimed to
you, and that in Him everyone that
believes is cleared " ($\delta\iota\kappa\alpha\iota o\hat{\upsilon}\tau\alpha\iota$ apparently means 'is acquitted') "from all
those things, wherefrom ye could not
be cleared by Moses' Law."

The form of this last statement is worthy
of remark, '$o\dot{\upsilon}\kappa$ $\dot{\eta}\delta\upsilon\nu\dot{\eta}\theta\eta\tau\epsilon$ $\delta\iota\kappa\alpha\iota\omega\theta\hat{\eta}\nu\alpha\iota$.'
It dwells upon the inefficacy of Law in
regard to setting man right with God, as
a condition of things now over, a condition
that has given place to a something new and

better.   Possibly the sense of δικαιοῦσθαι is not so plainly 'technical,' as it is in Galatians, but the general drift of the teaching is obviously identical.

Passing on to *v.* 49 we should gather that in Antioch Gentile Christians far outnumbered the Israelitish converts.   In Iconium, on the other hand, the proportion of the two classes was much more equal (Acts xiv. 2).   Yet the general effect, produced upon the reader by xiii. and xiv. together, is of a Church far more largely Gentile.   Let us assume that it is so.

In Gal. iv. it is hard to determine, at any given point, whether the Apostle is speaking to Jews, or speaking to Gentiles. He seems to pass almost imperceptibly from the one sort to the other.   This will appear as we deal with the text.

iv. 1.   "Now mark! as long as the heir is not grown up, he differs no whit from a slave, although he be absolute owner; but is controlled by tutors and guardians, till the time his father has appointed."

The language here, I should hold, must not be regarded as drawn, with any sort of accuracy, from strictly legal sources. It is neither Roman law, nor is it Greek. Νήπιος (after the Pauline manner) is broadly opposed to ἀνήρ (as 'minor' to one of full age). Προθεσμία is a good Greek term for a fixed or settled day, a day appointed for payment, or the like. But there is no reason to suppose that, in a general way, whether in Galatia or elsewhere, coming of age depended on a father's will. But it does (as all will admit) in the case of the Heavenly Father.

The 'appointed day' accordingly must be regarded as a necessary modification of detail imported into the image by the writer. The two words used for 'guardian' cannot be accurately distinguished: the whole phrase is merely equivalent to 'guardians of one sort or another.' The more definite 'guardian' in this chapter takes the place of the 'paedagogue' (for whom we have a female analogue in a 'nursery governess') set before us in chap. iii.

iv. 3—5. "So we too, in our
childish days, were under the 'worldly
rudiments' in a state of slavery.   But
when the full time was come, God sent
forth His own Son, born of a woman,
born under Law, that He might redeem
them that were under Law, that we
might receive the intended adoption."

Is the wording of these verses intentionally vague ?   Is '*we*' Jews, or Gentiles,
or both ?   Is the phrase the 'worldly rudiments' so designed as to cover effectually
both the Jewish discipline of Law (the
Mosaic Law), as well as such Gentile
'propaideia' as is set forth in Rom. i. 19,
20 ?   Or, does the thought of the Gentiles
not enter in, till the person of the verb is
altered in *v.* 8 (for the second time) ?   These
are all questions far more easy to ask than
to get answered.

There seems to be little doubt that
στοιχεῖα (as in Heb. v. 12) means 'A B C,'
or 'rudiments.'   And plainly the phrase is
disparaging, as we gather from the two
Col. ii. 8,   places where it occurs in the Colossian
20.

Epistle. It marks, as Lightfoot says, an intellectual stage, and an intellectual stage that is obviously 'unspiritual.' St Paul (as a matter of fact) does not definitely identify this rudimentary (and 'worldly') discipline with the Law. But it is difficult not to believe *that* was uppermost in his mind. In Colossians the phrase would seem to have decisively wider reference. Yet even in that passage 'sabbaths' and 'new moons' are mentioned, so that it is hard to disentangle an asceticism, which might be heathen, from distinctly Jewish ordinances. Δεδουλωμένοι comes in at the end of the clause, with independent weight, as who should say, 'bondsmen, bound hand and foot.' About "the fulness of time" (where the '*the*' of R.V.—I should say—is nothing but a mistake : you can't say, in Greek anyhow, τὸ πλήρωμα χρόνου) a good deal might be said, but it is not necessary. In regard to ἐξαπέστειλεν, I don't think we need be concerned to find a special force for each of the prepositions in the double compound. " Born of a woman," one would

say, must mark the humiliation involved in
the Incarnation. This particular phase of
the verb (γενόμενος or ἐγένετο) is specially
associated with that prodigious event. The
anarthrous νόμον that follows is puzzling
enough. Is it anarthrous because 'woman'
before it has no article? This is wholly
conceivable. Or, because (as Lightfoot
thinks) 'law' is meant to cover more than
merely the Law of Moses? I should say
that 1 Cor. ix. 20—though there again
Lightfoot detects the same extension—tells
somewhat against this alternative.

In view of what has gone before, it is
hard to attach any other force to ἵνα τοὺς
ὑπὸ νόμον ἐξαγοράσῃ than simply this ; that
it is meant to set before us the 'redemption'
of believing Israel from the bondage of
the Law of Moses—in fact, just such a
redemption as St Paul had himself ex-
perienced.

On the whole it seems wisest to say
that till *v.* 5 is ended, St Paul has *Jews*
in view. In *v.* 6 the ἐστέ covers Jews and
Gentiles. Υἱοθεσία reminds us that the

'sonship,' wherewith we are 'sons,' is not as the Sonship of Christ. The word is itself late Greek. The preposition in ἀπολάβωμεν doubtless points to an age-long purpose in the mind of the All Father. Or, to put it otherwise, the ἀπό regards the promise made centuries before. Anyhow, it is just and right to lay stress on the normal sense of this particular compound.

iv. 6, 7. "And because ye are *sons*, God hath sent the spirit of His own Son into our hearts crying, Abba, Father. So that thou art no longer a slave, but a son, and if a son, also an heir through God."

In these two verses we have an unusually striking example of the tendency of St Paul to pass from person to person. We start with "Ye are"; there follows one line after "into our hearts," and the very next verse begins "and so thou art no longer." Ἡμῶν and ὑμῶν, of course, are frequently confused. Yet the editors are of opinion that ἡμῶν is right. Ἐξαπέστειλεν must be translated not 'sent,'

but 'has sent.'   The aorist is an indefinite
past tense, not a definite.   The verb here
merely states what has happened, whether
it be long ago or lately.   The 'sending' of
this 'spirit' is just an event in the past.
We note the double compound once again
(as in *v.* 4).   'Has sent from afar' may be
right (compare Acts xxii. 21).   "The spirit
of His own Son" must not, I think, be
regarded as a definite reference to the gift
of Pentecost.   It describes rather that
essential attitude of 'son' to 'father,' which
has its supreme manifestation in the relation
of the Eternal Son towards the Eternal
Father.   This relation towards the Father
is precisely what we note in the Gospel
story as specially inculcated by Our Lord.
No doubt, the actual mission of the Spirit
it was, that implanted it in man.   But it
is not the same thing.   It is just a vivid
consciousness that God *is* Father—*Our
Father*.   And yet one can hardly say 'consciousness'; for that indeed goes too far.
From Romans viii. 26 we should rather
gather that there is in the true believer

a Something which pleads earnestly (and
intelligibly to God), yet unbeknown to him.
And if a critic should say, Nay, but that is
the Holy Spirit, as commonly understood :
one must answer, In 'Romans' possibly ;
but the words 'His own' would seem to
exclude identification here.   Κράζον recalls
to our minds Romans viii. 15, where we
are told that 'in' (or, through) 'the spirit
of adoption' (that is, 'the spirit of adopted
sons') we '*cry*' (as here).   Moreover
we cannot forget the κραυγὴ ἰσχυρά of
Hebrews v. 7.   The formula Ἀββᾶ ὁ
Πατήρ (attributed in St Mark to Our Lord
Himself) reminds us that Christ was 'bilingual' ; and so was the early Church of
Jerusalem.   In view of the sacred memory
attaching to the phrase, it is curious that it
should ever have dropped from use ; for
once apparently it was in use.   In *v.* 7 the
change to the singular illustrates a Pauline
tendency, exhibited elsewhere, to lay stress
on the 'individual' aspect of the new life
in Christ.   He is speaking to all conscious
believers, 'You...and you...and you.'   The

Church, as a whole, has the life, but only
because its members are truly 'alive.' The
reading at the end of the verse is curiously
wavering. Editors read what I have translated. The lection "heir of God, through
Christ" is too simple to be taken, as against
the strange "heir through God."

The Apostle himself claims, at the
opening of the letter, to have received his
commission "through Jesus Christ and
God the Father that raised Him from the
dead." That however is hardly the same.
Διά, in Pauline usage, essentially belongs
to the Incarnate Son. Yet one could
hardly without misgiving assume it is the
Son, that is meant in the words "through
God."

Up till this point St Paul has been
speaking to Jew-Christians, or all Christians;
but now he turns his thoughts to that
Gentile element, which was probably pre-
dominant in the Churches of Galatia.

The ἀλλά, with which the new section
starts, is not very luminous. "Howbeit"
says our English: but it would puzzle one

to find where any sense of logical opposition enters in. Γάρ or οὖν would appear
to be far more natural particles to introduce
the new sentence. In translation it were
better to take no account of the ἀλλά.

iv. 8—11. "In old days, not
knowing God, you were slaves to
what are really" (this seems to be the
meaning of φύσει) "no gods at all.
Now, having come to the knowledge
of God, or rather to His knowledge
of you—why do ye turn once more to
the weak and beggarly rudiments,
whereto ye want to be slaves all over
again? Ye are closely observing days
and months and seasons and years.
I am afraid of you, that all my pains
over you are gone for nothing."

Plainly Gentiles are here addressed.
Yet the old phrase, slightly varied, appears
once more, the phrase about the "rudiments." It would seem St Paul regarded
all close attention to minute details as
having in it something of the 'heathenish,'
or 'worldly'; what he styles the 'rudimentary.' Religion is, for him (as in the

famous teaching of St John iv. 23), a matter of 'spirit' and 'truth.' All that is not 'spiritual,' all that is not 'true,' partakes of the nature of slavery. Into such a slavery he feared they were drifting back. But is it not, for us, an astonishing thing that he should (to all appearance) place in one category the nullities of heathenism and the unprofitable 'rudimentary' ordinances that formed, for the ordinary Jew, the heart of his religion? Strictly speaking, these Gentile Christian Galatians were not returning to 'heathenism,' in any sense; they were only substituting for vital Christianity a system of forms and rules and trivial ordinances. Yet he speaks, we must observe, as if this conduct of theirs were virtually a 'reversion' (and nothing else) even for them.

For the "really no gods" of *v.* 8, one compares the λεγόμενοι θεοί of 1 Cor. viii. 5. The amended statement ("but rather known of God") recalls 1 Cor. viii. 2 and xiii. 12. It is characteristic of St Paul to keep before men's minds the weighty truth, that religion starts with God and not with us.

The adjectives 'weak' and 'beggarly' describe the essential unprofitableness of all religion that stands in 'forms,' under two vigorous figures. It is 'weak' because it has no effect ; it is 'poor' (or 'beggarly') because there is 'nothing in it.' No one is one penny the better for it. Remember how the Apostle loves to speak of 'spiritual' things under metaphors derived from wealth or riches. 'Beggarly' (in our English) is not altogether happy. It sounds as if it were mere abuse and vituperation. Of course, it is not. In *v.* 10 we should not say 'observe,' but 'narrowly observe.' That is the verb's proper meaning. For the catalogue of things the 'Galatians' were wrongly 'observing' (that is, 'observing' as if they were matters of first-rate importance ; for clearly the Apostle himself did not wholly disregard forms, as witness what he says about the need of orderly worship) one must compare that other list in Colossians ii. 16. There we have, in addition to 'meat' and 'drink,' 'feast days,' 'new moons' and 'sabbaths.'

'Months' in this place (one is tempted to think) should rather be 'moons.' The 'seasons' is somewhat odd, because one would have thought that 'days' would cover it. But the 'years' is odder still. Of course, there were 'Sabbatic' and 'Jubilee' years in the Code; but one would have hardly thought that any would have wished to impose such institutions upon the Gentile converts in far Galatia.

The "pains" (κεκοπίακα) of *v.* 11 remind us that the Apostle regularly speaks of his mission labours as very heavy and onerous. Nor is any likely to question the justice of his claim, who follows with care his story.

§ 6. THE FOURTH PARAGRAPH FROM GALATIANS

(Chapter iv. 21—31.)

The next nine verses I propose to omit. Verse 12 is indeed obscure, but need not detain us now. He begs them to be, as he is ; and passing on (though disclaiming

any ground for distinct complaint) mentions with sorrow and regret the change
that has come over them.   In *v.* 13 the sense
would be plainer if a small change might be
admitted, and we were allowed to read δι'
ἀσθενείας (circumstantial, "in ill health")
in place of δι' ἀσθένειαν.   The latter can
be explained, though not without difficulty.
The former would demand no sort of
explanation.   Further, we gather from
these verses that he had paid them hitherto
two visits.   It was on the former occasion
his health was somehow amiss.   Then they
were all sympathy.   They welcomed him
as a messenger of God, nay even (as he
declares, using a bold figure) as if he had
been the Master Himself.   Then they
spoke of themselves as the happiest of
men, to have the Apostle among them.
Nothing would have been too good for
him.   They would have torn out their
very eyes and given them him.

Now all is sadly altered.   His influence
has been undermined.   He suggests he
has been too sincere, while others have

been employing the arts of the flatterer.
This seeming friendliness will not end in
good for them.   In the upshot it will only
lead to their exclusion from Christ (for
such would seem to be the meaning of
v. 17).   Verse 18, once again, is far from
transparent.   A good deal must be supplied.
But the gist of it seems to be that friendliness is all very well and honourable
attention.   In fact St Paul himself prized
their kindly attentions to him.   But he
does not want 'fair weather' friends—
people who are kindly to his face but not
behind his back.   The section ends with a
pathetic cry :

> iv. 19, 20.   "O my little children !
> over whom I once more endure the
> pangs of birth, till Christ shall be
> formed in you!   I wish I could be
> with you now, and change my tone :
> for I am sore puzzled about you."

Why the wish of *v.* 20 is put as a thing
impracticable, it is a little hard to see, more
especially if it was so, that he actually did
visit them very shortly after he wrote.

But now we have reached the point where we must return to the text:

iv. 21—27. "Tell me, ye that would be under Law, do ye not heed the Law? It is written, you know, that Abraham had two sons, one by the serving maid and one by the freewoman. The child of the serving maid is" (that is, in the page of Holy Writ) "a child of nature: the child of the freewoman comes by promise. There is in it all a hidden meaning. The two mothers are the two covenants; the one of them from Mount Sinai, engendering to bondage—which is Agar" (here the ἥτις might be equal to *quippe quae*, but I should conceive it is not, but is used as a definite relative, like ἅτινα just above): "and Agar represents Mount Sinai in Arabia, and ranks with the present Jerusalem; for she is in bondage and so are her children: whereas the Jerusalem above is free—which is *our* Mother. For it is written,

Isaiah liv.
1 (LXX).

*Rejoice, thou barren, that bearest not !
break forth into speech and cry, thou
that travailest not ! for more are the
children of the lone woman than of her
that has a mate."*

Here the Galatians are regarded as
filled with a desire to return to the old
regime, the bondage of ordinances. The
Pentateuch (had they 'ears to hear') should
have taught them better. They should
have seen the meaning of the tale of
Ishmael and Isaac. This the Apostle proceeds to unfold. The one of them was
'slave born,' the other 'free born'; the one
born in the ordinary way, the other contrary to nature, to all intent, miraculously.
How αὗται (in *v.* 24) should be interpreted
I don't feel certain ; but the demonstrative
is attracted to the gender of διαθῆκαι. It
might be safer to say, " Here we have the
two Covenants." In any case the one
Covenant had its birth at Sinai. Its
children are 'slave children.' That Covenant is Agar. The reading of *v.* 25 is
curiously varied. Some copies omit *Agar*,

some omit *Sinai*, while others again read
both, with γάρ or δέ. On the whole the
reading of W.H. (and the Revisers) seems
to have the preference. 'Hagar' or
'Chagar' stands for 'rock,' and Chrysostom
speaks of the mountain as ὁμώνυμον τῇ
δουλῇ. In that case the ἐστίν is as the
ἦν of 1 Cor. x. 4 ("that rock *was* Christ").
This reading has the advantage of re-
ducing the phrase ἐν τῇ Ἀραβίᾳ to a mere
statement of geography. It is difficult to
see in what sense Arabia could be regarded
as a land essentially of 'bondage.' The
idea of bondage, I should say, is associated
with the Law, not with Arabia at all. The
meaning of the συστοιχεῖ is clearly given
by Lightfoot. There are two categories,
the 'earthly' and the 'heavenly,' or the
'temporal' and the 'eternal': to the one
belong Hagar, Ishmael, the earthly Jerusalem, the Law, the Old Covenant; to the
other, Sarah, Isaac, the heavenly Jerusalem,
the Gospel, the New Covenant. In each
'rank' part is type and part is antitype.
If we assign a 'Mountain' to each: Sinai
is the Mount of the one; Sion (as in

Hebrews xii.) the Mount of the other.
The subject of δουλεύει (in *v.* 25) is primarily
Agar-Sinai, only secondarily the earthly
Jerusalem.   In *v.* 26 (as so often in St
Paul) the sentence takes a fresh start and
all symmetry is sacrificed.   We should have
expected it to go on, " But the other from
Mount Sion, engendering to freedom, is
Sarah.   She is free and ranks with the
heavenly Jerusalem...."   But the mention
of the earthly city at once suggests the
heavenly, and the Apostle is in haste to get
to the thought of freedom.   Accordingly
he does not stay to develope his figure
fully.

The MSS. are divided between " our
Mother" and " your Mother."   The former
seems the likelier.   The quotation from
Isaiah, which occupies *v.* 27, is adapted by
the writer to his purpose.   This will at
once appear from a study of the passage
quoted.   There Israel is the bride, Jehovah
Himself the husband.

But we have not yet exhausted the
lessons to be learned from the story of
Isaac and Ishmael.

iv. 28—31. " We, brethren " (says (Cf. Rom. ix.6,7,8,9. the Apostle), " as Isaac was, are promise-children. But as then the naturally born persecuted the spiritually born, so is it now. Howbeit what says the Scripture ? *Cast out the bondmaid and her son! For the son of the bondmaid shall never inherit with the son of the free."*

" Accordingly, my brethren, we are not the children of a bondmaid ; we are the children of the free."

Upon these words let me make a handful of comments. ' Promise-children ' is, in effect, a compound noun. As for the ' persecution ' mentioned, that can hardly be found in Genesis (see Gen. xxi. 9). Yet the LXX goes further than our Hebrew text : for whereas that says merely '*mocking*,' the Greek version reads παίζοντα μετὰ Ἰσαὰκ τοῦ υἱοῦ αὐτῆς. Moreover in after days the enmity of the 'Hagarenes' against Israel became a commonplace (see Psalm lxxxiii. 5, 6). ·And as for the meaning St Paul saw underlying the story, had not

he, the child of promise, the son of faith,
known what it was to feel the ruthless hatred
of the 'natural sons' of the patriarch—his
descendants 'after the flesh'? The words
of 'the Scripture' that follow, though
setting forth the unseen Will, are (in the
story) the words of Sarah. They express
(St Paul would have us recognise) the
eternal Purpose of God. The real Israel
is the Israel of faith; the real 'circumcision' the 'circumcision of spirit' (as we
learn afterwards from Romans). For the
present we rest content with this conclusion: "we" (that is, all believers) "are the
antitype of Isaac—we are the children of
the 'free woman.'"

The moral is unfolded in the section
that follows next.

§ 7. THE FIFTH PARAGRAPH FROM GALATIANS

(Chapter v. 1—12.)

It is at this point we have revealed to
us the exact nature of the dreadful change

which had come over the Galatians. What
it was we could have gathered from Acts,
but here it is in black and white. Jew
believers and Gentiles alike, they had
yielded to the suggestion that Christ would
not serve alone, but that it must be *Christ
and Moses*. The contest was between the
liberty of Christ and the heavy bondage of
the Lawgiver.

Accordingly the Apostle continues :

v. 1. "For freedom Christ hath made
us believers free. Stand firm and be
not caught again in the yoke of slavery!"

The shorter reading here is the reading
of the Editors. The rendering of the
dative (now, I believe, usually followed)
was the rendering preferred by the
American Revisers of 1881. The definite
article seems to make it all but inevitable.
Without it we might have rendered "Christ
has made us wholly free," on the analogy
of such a phrase as ἐπιθυμίᾳ ἐπεθύμησα.
As it is, the simple dative here seems to
carry the same meaning as the ἐπ' ἐλευθερίᾳ of *v*. 13. The curious word στήκειν

is all but only Pauline in the pages of
N.T. : it is found three times in the
Septuagint. Plainly it is a useful form,
though rather startling at first. We might
have had βήκειν too, or even γνώκειν !
' Yokes' are so unfamiliar to us that I
venture to say 'be not caught'; although
a ' yoke ' is hardly a thing in which one is
' caught,' and the tense does not really
imply a momentary experience. In English
one cannot say ' be not held again.' And
"entangled " (as in R.V.) is a desperate
mixing of metaphors. The earlier translations in our language (except Wycliffe
and the Rheims) were even more unhappy,
"wrap not yourselves again." The weighty
warning of the verse should be left to
stand by itself. It can neither be closely
attached to what goes before nor to that
which follows after.

v. 2—5.   " Lo ! I Paul say to you,
that if you are ' circumcisers,' Christ
will profit you not one whit. Once
again I solemnly protest to every man
that is ready to submit to circumcision,

that he is absolutely bound to carry
out the Law in its entirety. Your
relation with Christ has come to
nothing, you that seek to right yourselves with God by Law. You have
fallen from grace. We (true believers)
look for and hope for acceptance with
Him, spiritually, by faith."

" I, Paul," here seems to imply, not ' I,
Paul, that am accused of preaching circumcision' (which indeed is possible), but
rather, ' I, the Paul you know,' ' your own
evangelist.' This is made likely (I think)
by the λέγω ὑμῖν which follows. Ἐὰν
περιτέμνησθε does not mean so much as
"if ye be circumcised"; but rather "if ye
be for circumcising," expressing a tendency
of the will. For me, I should say the
verb must be thought of in connexion
with the Pauline phrase οἱ περιτεμνόμενοι ('the circumcisers,' or 'circumcision
people'). That is why I have paraphrased
it so. If they yield to this weakness, he
says, so far from being 'saved' through
Christ, they will gain no good whatever.

Μαρτύρομαι, three times out of five in the
N.T., is used in this non-classical way.
The meaning is plain enough. ' I solemnly
protest to you,' or ' assure you.' The same
construction is found in LXX, though only
in one place (Judith vii. 28). 'Οφειλέτης
appears to mark a high degree of obligation:
it is only Pauline in this figurative use,
though the verb is common enough in a
similar sense. "To do" the Law means
to carry it out, achieve it; here the phrase
is very strong, "to carry it out in every
particular." The very curious formula
καταργεῖσθαι ἀπό is found in Romans also
(vii. 2). 'Από may imply 'separation' or
' direction ' (' on the side of '). The former
is more likely; in that case the usage is
'pregnant.' Two ideas are combined in one;
"you are frustrated and dissevered from
Christ." That is, your union with Christ
is dissolved. The tense (as in St John xv.
6) appears to be ' instantaneous.' The very
notion of seeking circumcision, as an aid
towards justification, has this disastrous
effect at once. Christ becomes nothing to

you and you to Him. The relative here
keeps its common 'generic' force. 'Grace'
means the condition of Divine favour
secured by union with Christ. In *v.* 5 the
compact adverbial dative πνεύματι is very
difficult of rendering. Law, and all external ordinances, would be similarly
characterised by a brief and comprehensive
σαρκί. So much meaning lies in πνεύματι
that in English we really need to make it a
separate clause. Otherwise the stress that
lies upon the word cannot be adequately
reproduced. "We Christians look for
acceptance by faith—a spiritual thing."
Ἐλπίδα δικαιοσύνης literally means "an
acceptance that we hope for." Δικαιοσύνη
is here used in the very unusual sense of
'*final redemption.*' The same idea is
found in Phil. iii. 20, and a similar expression (perhaps) in 2 Tim. iv. 8.

v. 6. "Where Christ Jesus is, you
know, neither circumcision matters at
all, nor uncircumcision : no (the only
thing that counts is) faith operating
through love."

'Εν Χριστῷ 'Ιησοῦ, one apprehends, is equivalent to such a phrase as 'for real Christians.' It is altogether possible that it is ' Pauline' for τοῖς ἐν Χριστῷ 'Ιησοῦ. The remainder of the clause is put with characteristic vigour. The addition of the 'οὔτε ἀκροβυστία' (or rather, the "neither... nor...") brings home to our minds the absolute ' indifference' of any such rite as circumcision. As is well known, in 1 Cor. iii. 7 we have a parallel elliptical construction; and in 1 Cor. vii. 19 the same statement is conveyed to the reader in all but identical terms. The verbal phrase to be supplied in the latter member of our sentence would be something like πάντα ἰσχύει.

In three places the nullity of circumcision is insisted on, and each time something else is contrasted with that nullity. Here it is " faith operating through love," as the only thing that does matter; in chap. vi. 15 it is καινὴ κτίσις (which is only another way of expressing the same phenomenon). In 1 Cor. vii. 19, on the

other hand, we have "circumcision is
nothing, and uncircumcision is nothing,
ἀλλὰ τήρησις ἐντολῶν θεοῦ." It is difficult
indeed to bring that into line with either
of the 'Galatian' instances. One might,
to be sure, illustrate it by quoting what
Christ says to the rich young man in St
Matthew xix. 17. But, I suspect, St Paul
is making excuse for the pious Israelite, to
whom Christ is not known. 'Circumcision' had a merit, till Christ came, and
a very obvious merit. It was a 'fulfilling
of righteousness' by obedience to a positive
enactment. And that, maybe, is what
ἀλλὰ τήρησις ἐντολῶν θεοῦ implies: "only
the keeping of a Divine ordinance."
Ἐνεργουμένη may be passive, but I believe
it is deponent. 'Love' does not make
'faith' work; but 'faith' does express
itself in 'love.' And, as everybody is
aware, St Paul did not contemplate for one
moment a 'barren' faith. The life of
Christ in a man must 'work' and 'bear
fruit'—or die.

v. 7. "Oh! you were running

bravely! Who is it has hindered you from heeding the Truth? It is not a Godly influence to which you are yielding. Stop in time, oh, stop in time! I am confident of you, with a Christian confidence, that you will be minded as I say. And he that disturbs you, shall answer for it to God—be he who he may!"

The imperfect ἐτρέχετε is full of picturesque vigour. All was going well till this intrusive influence came. They were making a brave show in the Christian race. Ἐνέκοψε certainly means 'hinder' (as in 1 Thess. ii. 18; Rom. xv. 22), but what the underlying figure is, it were difficult to say—it can hardly be 'breaking up a road.' Ἀνακόπτειν (read by some here) is used in Thucydides for 'beating back' an assailant. The τίς would seem to imply that the Apostle actually did not know who was ringleader of 'the disturbers' (v. 12); apparently however he suspected that it was some one of consequence. Ὁ καλῶν ὑμᾶς (as always) is God the Father.

Πεισμονή would seem to have some connexion with the foregoing πείθεσθαι. But
what ? As the word (in N.T. Scripture)
is found only here, the meaning is of
necessity uncertain. The proverb of *v.* 9
is found also in 1 Cor. v. 6. It is a warning
to beware of the 'thin end of the wedge.'
Leaven, in Holy Writ, nearly always
typifies some evil influence. It was
thought by the ancients to be a process
of corruption ; but, I take it, modern
science would hardly regard it so. Our
Lord applies the figure in a purely neutral
sense to the teaching of the Pharisees.
He called their instruction 'leaven,' not so
much, as I should hold, because it was
'bad,' but because it was 'generative.'
Only in His own Parables does 'leaven'
appear as a symbol of beneficent working ;
and even then the point of comparison is
not the 'goodness' of the influence, but
the unseen and rapid effect of it.

The dark and ominous phrase used with
regard to 'ὁ ταράσσων' in *v.* 10 I have
interpreted in accordance with the Pauline

use of κρίμα. I don't think that there can be any doubt that the 'judgment' contemplated is the judgment of God. With regard to ὅστις ἂν ᾖ one would naturally suggest that the ringleader might easily shelter himself behind the weighty name of James, the brother of the Lord. But, be he who he may be, plainly those who disturb the Church of God will have to answer for it to God.

In the two verses that follow next reference is made to a malicious statement current in the Churches of Galatia, about the Apostle himself. They said that he himself had demonstrated in act the importance he attached to circumcision. It would appear that the insinuation was based on the fact recorded in Acts xvi. 3. There we read of a 'Galatian' who was actually circumcised by St Paul himself, and that not on his first visit, but his second—to wit, his convert Timothy. Of him we read: "(Paul) took and circumcised him, because of the Jews that were in those parts." The fact the Apostle does

not deny; he does deny the inference.
Timothy was circumcised out of a desire
to conciliate—the event showed a mistaken
desire. As St Paul says in *v.* 11, the truth
of the insinuation was disproved by the
bitter enmity of the Circumcision Party.

> v. 11, 12. "As for me, my
> brothers, if at this time of day I am
> 'preaching circumcision,' why am I
> still assailed?"

> "It would seem the offence of the
> Cross is wholly cancelled."

> "Oh! I could wish they did not
> stop short at circumcision—these folk
> that would upset you!"

The two ἔτι's of *v.* 11 are both idiomatic: the first is as in i. 10, the other as in
Rom. iii. 7. The ἄρα of *v.* 11 introduces
a false inference. It is of the nature of
a *reductio ad absurdum*. The Apostle's
steps were dogged with an absolutely
ruthless rancour. And the objection to
him was that he preached consistently the
'crucified Messiah.' This (as he tells us
in 1 Cor. i. 23) was an idea of horror

to the Jews and matter for ridicule to the
Gentiles. As long as the Apostle preached
it, so long was it inconceivable that Jews
would tolerate him. But, if this disturbing
influence came from a Jewish Christian
quarter (which indeed we must suppose),
it is a little hard to see wherein their
' Christianity' consisted. One would have
thought that if they could not accept a
' Messiah' who was crucified, they would
either have to deny the Messiahship of
Jesus or to disbelieve in His crucifixion.
And it is very difficult to see how they
could do either. As for St Paul, not only
did he believe Jesus to be Christ, although
He was crucified, but he also based on this
astounding fact the hope of all mankind.
He preached 'Christ crucified' as the
source of δικαιοσύνη—the one hope of
man's acceptance with the All Holy.

v. 12 is the sudden outburst of a pent-
up indignation. It is like the " God shall
smite thee, thou whited wall!" of Acts
xxiii. 3. What it means is only too plain.
" Utinam et abscindantur," says the steadily

literal Vulgate.   Whether that is intended to convey the meaning of the Greek (as set forth in the paraphrase) or whether it represents " I would they should be cut off," I do not know.   Either rendering would be possible.   The reference plainly is to those horrible self-mutilations which were practised, especially in honour of Cybele, by Asiatic votaries.   The people of Galatia were familiar with such practices. The Greek (of course) means ' I wish they would,' not ' I wish they had.'

§ 8.   The Last Section from Galatians

(Chapter vi. 11—end.)

The writer now passes for a time from questions of doctrine to questions of practical life.   Freedom is of the essence of the Christian life, but Christian ' freedom '—in accordance with the fundamental paradox of Christ—involves (yes, even is)

'slavery,' the slavery of love. This love
the Galatians were very far from having
realised. They were fighting among themselves. Such contention, the Apostle ad-
mits, is highly natural, but it is wholly
unspiritual. One can't have it both ways.
The 'flesh' is one thing, the 'spirit' another.
To follow 'natural' desire is to be unspiritual. And it is only 'spirit life' which
is really free. *v.* 18 would seem to be
parenthetical. It does not state the essence
of 'spirit life,' but only a consequence
of it.

"And if ye are led by spirit" (says the
Apostle) "then is there no 'law' for you."
Where the Spirit is, Love is; and where
Love is, law vanishes. The last part of
chap. v. is taken up with the list of typical
'products' (ἔργα) of the 'flesh,' and the
corresponding list of the things which proceed without effort from the presence of
the Spirit in a man. These various virtues
and graces are denominated καρπός. The
latter member of *v.* 23 presents, in another
form, the absolute 'freedom' of the spirit

life. " In face of these" (κατὰ τῶν τοιούτων)
" Law" (in any of its forms) " does not
exist."

But the operation of the Spirit and its
influence on men is not wholly automatic.
In *vv.* 24 and 25 we are brought up against
the solid fact of the need of human effort.
" If we owe our life to spirit, let our acts
too correspond." Something like this, I
suppose, is the meaning of *v.* 25.

The sixth chapter, in its earlier portion,
deals with mutual help in the Church, the
need of the life of service, and, more particularly, with the claims of generous
giving.

The latter half of the chapter I should
like to paraphrase.

vi. 11—12. " See, with what huge
characters I write, with my own hand!"

And (apparently) he writes the next
sentence *in capitals*—writes it himself,
not employing, as usually, a friend as
amanuensis :

" ALL THAT WANT TO MAKE A FAIR
SHOW OUTWARDLY, SEEK TO FORCE YOU

TO CIRCUMCISION. ONLY BECAUSE THEY
WANT TO AVOID THE PERSECUTION EN-
TAILED BY THE CROSS OF CHRIST."

That is to say, St Paul affirms, with all
the emphasis he can command (typified by
enormous letters), that the 'circumcision
party' were solely influenced by lack of
moral courage. They shrank from the
reproach of their countrymen. That was
all. They found that if they submitted to
circumcision, or rather persuaded others to
submit to circumcision (for they were, *ex
hypothesi*, already circumcised themselves),
they could disarm all Israelite enmity.
They might believe exactly what they
liked and teach exactly what they liked,
provided they accepted that rite, which
placed them under the Old Covenant.
Their zeal for circumcision was just to
'save their face.' They did not realise—
they shut their eyes to the fact—that it
was flat treason to the New Covenant. On
the other hand, they did not trouble themselves, nor would anyone outside trouble
them, to keep the whole of the Law. It

was enough, for Jewish zealots, that they
should accept the one rite that counted.

vi. 13. " Why, not even the circumcisers themselves trouble about
keeping the Law.   No, they want you
circumcised that they may win glory
for themselves over *your* external submission."

" Not so I ! God forbid that I seek
glory, save in the Cross of Our Lord
Jesus Christ ! whereby the world is
'crucified' for me, and I for the
world."

Οἱ περιτεμνόμενοι is St Paul's con-
venient term (coined on true Attic
principles) for the circumcision party.   We
are not to conclude that, so far, these weak-
kneed brethren had prevailed in Galatia.
They had not as yet ' Judaised ' the bulk
of the Galatian Church.   Only they were
trying hard, and the danger was imminent.
' Glory ' was what they wanted—the credit
of standing well with men.   ' Glory ' the
Apostle also wants, but *his* glory stands in
his ' shame '—the reproach of the Cross of

Christ he has embraced with heart and soul. All else is dead for him (for 'crucifixion' connotes death) and he for all else. The two terms 'world' and 'flesh' have, of course, a good deal in common. Circumcision, in the light of the revelation of Christ, was 'fleshly,' was also 'worldly.' The Apostle would have none of it. To be sure, he had been circumcised: but to that he now attached no importance whatsoever. So he continues:

> vi. 15. "In Christ Jesus circumcision is nothing, and uncircumcision is nothing. A man is a new being."

As I have said already, I hold it probable that ἐν Χριστῷ Ἰησοῦ represents τοῖς ἐν Χριστῷ Ἰησοῦ. The translation of ἀλλὰ καινὴ κτίσις is not an easy matter. The choice seems to be between "but a new creation *is everything*" (as in 1 Cor. iii. 7) and the version I have given. The general effect is much the same, whichever we believe to be the Apostle's meaning. Καινὴ κτίσις (one would gather from

Lightfoot's statement) is more likely to have reference to an individual believer.

vi. 16. "And all that are going to walk by this standard, peace be on them and mercy—aye, on the Israel of God!"

The phrase στοιχεῖν κανόνι appears to be unexampled. What is the κανών in question? Probably 'Christ and Christ only.' The person St Paul regards as a genuine Christian, as one of the 'Israel of God,' is the man who has taken Christ for 'all in all.' That is the man St Paul can regard as a genuine brother.

The last καί (in *v.* 16) is a καί of identity.

The general sense of *v.* 17 would appear to be that on this point the Apostle himself is unassailable : it is no use troubling him. He is 'Christ's man' altogether, as anyone can detect who sees him face to face. What the figure underlying the στίγματα may be, it is hard to tell. I suspect tattooing rather than branding. It may be the thought of an ordinary slave, or of an *hierodule*, or

of a soldier that he has before him.   In his
case the marks of allegiance were somehow
visibly stamped.   Why they are called, by
a usage far from common in St Paul, "the
marks of *Jesus*" is a difficult problem.

The brief expression of blessing in
v. 18 is notable for three things ; for the
pathetic appeal in ἀδελφοί, with which it
ends ; for the reminder in the word χάρις
of the way δικαιοσύνη comes ; and for the
significant hint (μετὰ τοῦ πνεύματος ὑμῶν)
that Christianity is, in essence, an inward,
not an outward thing.

§ 9.   SOME CONCLUDING REMARKS ON THE TEACHING OF THE EPISTLE

So ends the Epistle, which began with
so tremendous an assertion of Apostolic
authority (backed up by the added weight
of "all the brethren, which are with me ")
and an expression of deep wonderment at
the rapid falling away of believers in Galatia

from their one time loyalty, both to their own original teacher and to the one and only Gospel, which he brought. That Gospel centred, as the first few verses witness, in the Person of the Lord Jesus Christ, who "gave Himself for our sins," —the manner of the 'giving' is undefined —"that He might deliver 'believers' from the present evil age." Its compass has been restated in the course of the brief letter. It may be well to sum up here the main points of that restatement.

For Jews it amounts to this. Assuming that all men wish to 'right themselves,' or 'be righted,' in the eyes of God; they cannot possibly achieve this by obedience to the Law. The Apostle quotes Scripture in support. Yet it may be safely said that no further argument is needed than ordinary human conscience. Those who have tried hardest know best the futility of trying. Experiment clearly demonstrates that the thing is impracticable.

In chap. ii. we are merely told that St Paul and others, his fellows, pinned their faith on Jesus Christ, being assured that only that way, by faith in Jesus Christ, could the condition they desired be actually attained. This involved for them, as Jews, distressful consequences. They were regarded as 'renegades.' They had become 'sinners,' like the Gentiles. As the Apostle parenthetically remarks, they might truly regard themselves as backsliders, or transgressors, if they returned to the old position they had given up so deliberately. As for St Paul—he has no such intention. His life is a wholly new life: it is dominated by Christ. Even his natural relations to the life about him are coloured by the prodigious change.

We are not very clearly told the manner of its coming: but it came *through faith in Christ*—Christ, the Son of God, who had loved Paul and "given Himself up" for Paul. The faith has for its object not merely Christ, it is plain, but the Christ who died. Somehow—we are not told how—this 'faith' brings new life to a man, begetting in him the assurance of his acceptance with God. As for the way of 'law,' it is just a delusion. He who follows after law frustrates and nullifies the grace of God. It is an inconceivable thought that Christ should have died for nothing.

This Gospel of acceptance with God through Christ alone had been preached before to the Galatians. But they had other evidence, to convince them of its truth, beside Apostolic affirmation. They had the evidence of the Spirit—that amazing gift of God, that came to them through faith. It had been with them, as it was with Abraham; it was faith that had led to blessing. The mention of Abraham suggests many new ideas. The true doctrine about Abraham is stated at some length; for a good deal of Jewish error was associated with the Patriarch. First of all, it is plain that his real descendants are his 'spiritual' descendants, who will share his 'blessing' thanks to the same means by which he won it, to wit, faith. As for law, no 'blessing' comes that way, but only a 'curse'; and from that curse Christ redeemed us by the sacrifice of Himself. It is so that a 'blessing' may come upon the Gentiles (it had come on the Galatians), a blessing identified with the gift of the Holy Spirit. It cannot be seriously contended that the Law had superseded this primal Abrahamic 'Covenant.' How could it? 'Wills' and 'Covenants' are not so lightly superseded. Once made, they stand. The Abrahamic 'Covenant' has precedence of the Law. It rests on the primal promise. The Law cannot cancel the promise, any more than it can bring effective life. Yet it served a useful end. It defined sin; it quickened conscience; it kept Israel in safety, till the hour of Redemption should come. But its elementary character must not be overlooked. It belonged to 'nursery' days. When the Son came, 'Sonship' also came; and with Sonship the great appeal of the Spirit in us to the Father.

As for the Gentiles, they of old have served 'gods,' that were none. Now that they 'know' God, what folly to return to

primitive discipline! Let them recall
with what joy they welcomed the new
message at the first hearing, and beware
of treacherous friends. The story of
Isaac and Ishmael testifies to the 'freedom' that belongs to the spirit-child—the
freedom that is theirs. To hark back to
circumcision (even for the uncircumcised
believer the submission to circumcision is
a real retrogression) is really to give up
Christ. To affirm that their Apostle
himself laid stress on circumcision, is to
fly in the face of facts. Freedom belongs
to those alone who follow the Spirit's
guidance. The talk of the 'circumcision
party' is all delusion, and delusion prompted
by self-seeking. It is Christ, and His
Cross, that matter; nothing else. The
Apostle prays for blessing on those who
cling to Him alone. Of his own whole-
hearted loyalty none can doubt.

As one peruses the Epistle, it is borne
in on the mind that, whatever it may be,
it is not a formal treatise. It has all the
free discursiveness of a thoroughly natural

letter. Great ideas pervade it throughout ;
but they appear to defy analysis. And
one feels (one cannot help feeling) that
St Paul would have been mightily surprised if he could have learned of the
dogmatic superstructure to be afterwards
upreared on the great ideas thrown out in
the course of his eager writing.

These ideas, on a broad survey, would
appear to be chiefly two.

Granted all would stand well with God,
they can only attain their wish by what is
called 'faith in Christ.' This is not very
clearly defined, probably primarily because
it defies all definition. From this 'faith,'
further, flows a notable consequence, the
gift of the Holy Spirit.

These two fundamental realities exclude once and for all any question of
'circumcision,' as an essential to God's
acceptance. Christianity, so far from being
an expanded Judaism, is a wholly different
thing. Rightly regarded, Judaism is no
more than an episode. As compared with
Christianity, it is as bondage is to liberty.

Religion began long before the Law. And it has found its consummation wholly apart from Law, or anything which partakes of a legal character. The whole-hearted acceptance by man of God's gift in Jesus Christ is the kernel of the matter. When one grasps this great simplicity of teaching, one can easily understand the appeal the brief but splendid letter made to our Protestant reformers. Surely never was the heart of religion set forth more plainly and unmistakeably by any living man. It is the realisation of a Love, which works in a definite way.

PART II

THE TEACHING OF ROMANS

§ 1. A BRIEF FOREWORD TO 'ROMANS'

The Epistle to the Galatians I have taken, as it stands, without any close enquiry as to its circumstance and origin, still less as to its authenticity. So likewise I propose to deal with 'Romans,' that longer and fuller letter, which followed shortly after the Asiatic one, and developed its teaching not a little. 'Romans' (I assume) was written from Corinth, where the Apostle was lodging with Gaius, and very shortly before he started on that journey which so dramatically ended in bonds and imprisonment. That is to say it came at the end of the period of fruitful ministry, mainly centred around Ephesus, before the opening of which the shorter 'Galatians' was penned. St Paul had

never been to Rome; though he fully
hoped to get there, before many months
were past. He had no personal knowledge of the 'Church' in the great capital.
His readers to-day, in like manner, are
strangely in the dark with regard to the
Church's origin. How the Gospel got to
Rome, we can only guess. In all probability, the seed of 'the word' was sown
by immigrants from Jerusalem, or by
visitors to that city, belonging to the
very large community of Jews who had
settled in the metropolis. The Church was,
therefore, originally a Church of Jewish
believers. But we notice, with some astonishment, that when the great Apostle
did get to Rome the Jewish leaders there
(Acts xxviii. 17) apparently knew nothing
about it. The little knot of Hebrew
Christians, that is to say, was wholly
lost in the multitude of their countrymen
long resident at Rome.

It is well known how hard it is to be
sure, at any given moment or in any given
passage, whether the Apostle is addressing

himself to Jews or Gentiles. That diffi-
culty is present in ' Romans,' as elsewhere.
Whether there was a larger proportion of
Israelites, or non-Israelites, in the little
Church at Rome, it is very hard to settle ;
and indeed it is useless to try.

Zahn inclines to the belief that Jews
preponderated. He also acutely observes
that, though the Church was mainly
' Jewish,' and founded, years before, by
Palestinian Jews, yet there was to be
detected in it no element of apostacy, or
reversion to Judaism. St Paul did not
write to them, because they were exposed
to reactionary influences. He wrote rather
to pave the way for his anticipated visit, by
introducing to their notice both himself and
the doctrine he taught.

Whether Zahn is right in saying that
Rome was, for St Paul, rather a place with
which he must establish friendly relations
(as a base for future Western mission
activities) than an actual centre of work,
I cannot tell. ' Acts ' (one would have
been inclined to say) suggests the great

city was a goal and an end in itself. He had set his ambitions on it years before, and although his schemes expanded with the profuse magnificence of an Alexander or a Napoleon in the sphere of mundane conquest, yet it seems not wholly unreasonable to suppose he still set his heart on Rome, as Rome, when he wrote.

With the question of the genuineness of certain sections of the letter, I am fortunately not concerned. All the sections I have to treat of come before those passages about which there are doubts and questionings.

§ 2.   INTRODUCTORY VERSES. (i. 1—17)

The great Epistle opens with a sentence of what one might call 'Ephesian' complexity. This I do not propose to render. I would merely like to observe that the mention of the 'Prophets' and of 'Holy Scriptures' in *v.* 2 ; together with the reference to Christ's 'Davidic' descent, in

the verse that follows; make the modern
reader think of a Jewish-Christian community, in the main, as the body addressed.
Further I would like to suggest that the
antecedent of the 'ἐν οἷς,' at the opening
of *v*. 6, is to be looked for in the phrase εἰς
ὑπακοὴν πίστεως, and not in the πᾶσι τοῖς
ἔθνεσιν. Here was the meeting point of all
Christians whatsoever, Jews and Gentiles:
they had all 'heard and believed.' And,
if it should be noticed, that St Paul here
claims a mission to Jew as well as to
Gentile—as, for my part, I believe he
does; for I don't believe the ἐλάβομεν
covers more than just himself; whereas in
other places, notably in xi. 13 of this
Epistle, he lays stress on his 'Gentile'
apostolate—the natural answer is, that
wherever he went and preached, he always
addressed himself to his fellow countrymen
first. The fact is, his Gentile mission did
not exclude the faithful following of Christ's
precept 'Israel first' wherever occasion
arose, in an unevangelised district. Even
at Rome itself the Apostle at once

established relations with the Jewish leaders, and earnestly spoke to them of Israel's hope. For why? They were out of touch with all Christian influences—altogether beyond the reach of the members of the small and obscure community, which (all unknown to them) had arisen in the ranks of their Roman co-religionists. In *v.* 7 πᾶσι τοῖς οὖσιν may be taken to refer to a body, which has in it more elements than one. If Jews predominate, there are Gentile 'brethren' too.

The next paragraph (*vv.* 8—16) tells us a good many things of considerable interest. The first verse, with its thanksgiving for the world-wide proclamation of their faith, would seem to have in it something of loving exaggeration. But at least it does contain a striking testimony to 'Roman' orthodoxy. Whether the Church were large or small, it was certainly sound and loyal. The next two verses set forth the attitude of the writer to this distant, unvisited Church. He prays for them 'unceasingly,' and especially for this, that

"at last" (ἤδη ποτέ), by the Will of God,
a way may be found for him to come to
them.   Rome had been for many a year
the goal of his ambitions.   But he does
not say so here.   It is not Rome that he
is thinking of; it is the Church at Rome.
It is to them his heart goes out.   Doubtless he would have loved to have been
allowed to have brought the Gospel to the
capital; as he had taken it already to
Ephesus and to Corinth.   In this he had
been forestalled, probably by years and
years.   Yet even so it was not wholly
beyond his power to help the growing
Church: for it had never been privileged
to welcome an 'Apostle.'   Still he mentions
the possibility with characteristic caution.
"*I long* (he cries) *to see you*"—observe, he
does not claim that this 'longing' is a
matter of years: the ἤδη ποτέ refers to the
old long-cherished ambition to visit Rome:
the desire to visit *them* is altogether a later
born longing—"to the end I may impart
to you some spiritual endowment, for your
confirming."   So far the words imply that

he will be the giver and they the recipi-
ents. A natural Christian humility, coupled
with a reasonable desire to conciliate a
body, which (maybe) had never heard of
him and certainly did not know him as he
was known in Galatia and Macedonia, in
Greece and in 'Asia,' leads him to qualify
this very decisive statement. The 'giving'
is not to be all on one side. He, in the
plenitude of Apostolic endowment, can
help them, as none other, not being an
Apostle. But they can help him too, in
a very human way, by the sympathy and
encouragement that spring from a common
faith. Moreover he cannot conceal (whatever may be the requirements of Christian
courtesy and even of Christian prudence)
his very eager desire to help forward the
Church at Rome, not only in the direction
of strengthening its members, but also by
the gathering in of large numbers of new
converts. For that is his foremost duty
and therein lies his special capacity.

i. 13—17. "I want you to know,
my brothers, that often I have purposed

to come to you (though up till now without success) that I might get some fruit amongst you too" (that is, I presume, in Rome) "as I have amongst other nations"—we are not called upon to emphasise the definite article before 'other nations.'

At this point the whole eagerness of his missionary heart flashes forth:

"To Greeks and to non-Greeks—to educated and uneducated, I have a duty."

"So, as far as lies with me, I am eager to preach the Gospel to you too, that are in Rome."

"Oh! I am not ashamed of the Gospel. It is a power of God, issuing in 'salvation,' for everyone that believes; for Jew first, but for Gentile too."

"In it there is revealed a God-appointed 'righteousness,' springing from faith and leading to faith—as it stands written, *The righteous shall live by faith.*"

It is characteristic of the Pauline method that in this short passage we should have the word 'Greek' employed in two different senses. In *v.* 16, as in 'Acts' not infrequently, it probably means 'non-Jew'—a singular tribute to the range of Greek speech and Greek habit, from Rome to the Euphrates. The βαρβάροις of *v.* 14 makes it equally certain that it is the 'Greek,' in a narrower sense, who is there in view, the 'Greek' of Hellenic culture, if not of Hellenic birth. The σοφοῖς τε καὶ ἀνοήτοις (for the two phrases appear identical) seems to imply that he is thinking, not so much of Hellenic blood, as of Hellenic modes of thought and Hellenic civilisation. On the other hand, it is arguable that the words are used (in *v.* 14) in their strict and classical sense. Then the whole double phrase would mean, " I have a duty to discharge for men of every race, whether learned or unlearned." It is the same spirit which in a later age possessed the soul of John Wesley. All races, all sorts and conditions of men, have a claim on the Apostle's great heart. He has room for the people of Rome as well as for all the rest. In his eagerness to say it, he wholly disregards the niceties of grammar. Τὸ κατ᾽ ἐμὲ πρόθυμον undeniably presents a very awkward brachylogy. It would appear to mean, " I, to the best of my powers, am ready."

In *v.* 16 we must note a curious indication of the pain which was caused St Paul by the incessant and ruthless attacks of those who called him 'renegade.' " I am not ashamed" he cries. Why should he speak of 'shame'? Plainly, because he was ever being held up to Jewish opprobrium. However loyal his heart might be to his Lord and Master, he could not escape the anguish which came from those ceaseless attacks. There was only one cure for it, to make up his brave heart to 'glory' in his 'shame.' This he does in Galatians; and this he does also here. In the latter part of the verse, though the construction of the words is not after the classical model, δύναμις Θεοῦ εἰς σωτηρίαν

should be regarded as one compound expression.   It means a power heaven sent,
heaven ordained, issuing in σωτηρία.
Whether σωτηρία should be taken in a
strictly theological sense, or in the broader
sense of 'wealth,' 'well-being' (as frequently in the κοινή), it is difficult to say.
There is a certain attractiveness in the
meaning 'eternal weal,' in this particular
connexion.   On the other hand v. 17
rather points to the stricter sense, and
possibly even more so v. 18.

The πρῶτον is eminently puzzling. The
Jew has a right of priority, but otherwise
no pre-eminence, in regard to the Gospel
message.   Therefore it would appear that
the meaning must be temporal. But it
cannot be maintained that it is phrased in
a natural way, if it means what I have set
down above in paraphrase.

"A righteousness of God" must (I think)
be technical.   Plainly, from the words that
follow, this 'righteousness' is a thing God
appoints and man enjoys. We have nothing
here to do with the 'righteousness,' which

is God's. For this 'righteousness' rests on 'faith.' We must then assume that it means a way of attaining God's favour, of 'standing well' with Him. The prepositional phrases coupled with it, much as εἰς σωτηρίαν above, are very loosely attached. 'Such as rests on faith, leads to faith' would seem to be their meaning. The former statement one would expect: for 'faith' and δικαιοσύνη are normally coupled together, as cause and effect. But what are we to say about the " εἰς πίστιν " ? The words appear to be linked with the foregoing ἐκ πίστεως, which is essential to the argument, by way of heightening and emphasis. Faith is first and faith is last, and faith is everywhere, as a means to " δικαιοσύνη."

The quotation from Habakkuk is found also in Galatians iii. 11. It is employed there as an argument to establish the impossibility of attaining to God's favour by the aid of 'Law.' What I would wish to say about it has been said in that connexion.

§ 3. THE WORLD'S SINFULNESS

In the former of the two Epistles, in which 'justification' was regarded from a somewhat narrower standpoint, there was no development of any doctrine of Sin. In the section that follows here we find such a doctrine. The Gospel reveals to men the method of redemption, the means whereby they shall be 'righted' with God. Corresponding to this revelation there is another. We read of it in the next verse. This second "*is revealed*" is not precisely the same (in regard to grammatical value) as the other in the verse above. The Gospel is a new thing : the revelation it embodies is likewise new. That other revelation of the "Wrath of God" is no new thing. It has been going on through the ages, though all have not had skill to read its teachings. The enlightened Christian can. Even the enlightened heathen is not without some power to "discern the signs of the times."

i. 18. "For there is revealed *a wrath of God from heaven,* on all impiety and wickedness of men...."

The prepositional qualification ἐπὶ πᾶσαν ἀσέβειαν undoubtedly belongs to the ὀργὴ Θεοῦ, and not to the ἀποκαλύπτεται. It follows, in my opinion, that ἀπ' οὐρανοῦ does too. Heaven is the source of the ὀργή, and not of the revelation. That ὀργή is directed against human wickedness in fullest comprehensiveness. The clause, which completes the sentence, is of singular obscurity. It sets forth the condemnation of mankind as a whole. I would paraphrase

v. 18 (continued). "...that check the truth of God by wicked ways."

Of the two senses of κατέχειν ('hold fast' and 'hold down'), the latter alone is possible. "God's truth" cannot be 'held' by men that are wicked at all. They have it indeed potentially: but that is not κατέχειν, in the former of its two senses. Ἐν ἀδικίᾳ is probably instrumental: yet it might be equivalent to 'being in wickedness.' In any case the sense is the same. "God's truth"—His Revelation of Himself in His wonderful works—by rights should make headway. But it does not do so—men will not allow it.

i. 19, 20. "For what can be known of God is plain, and they can read it. For He has made it plain to them. For the things the eye cannot see of Him, His everlasting Power and Godhead, are plainly seen and discerned by the works of His hands, since the creation of the world. So that they are without excuse."

Here γνωστόν might be 'known': but it probably is 'knowable.' "The knowable of God" is, so much of God as may be known, or apprehended, by men. Ἐν αὐτοῖς (as S. observes) is as the ἐν ἐμοί of Gal. i. 16. The use appears to be of Hebrew origin: ἐν αὐτοῖς means little more than the simple dative. In *v.* 20 "ἀπὸ κτίσεως κόσμου" is plainly a phrase of time. Where it belongs it is hard to say. It is conceivable the meaning may be, "what the eye has not been able to see since the world began." Yet it is every bit as likely that the temporal clause attaches to the words that follow. Ever since there has been a world, the eye of the thoughtful mind has been in a position to read the teachings conveyed in that Book the which 'who runs may read.' However νοούμενα καθορᾶται expresses rather a potentiality than an actual fact. For the bulk of men it is true, they might have known, but they did not. The evidence was plain; but they failed to read it. The writer goes further here than he did when he spoke at Athens (Acts xvii. 22—31). The passages should be compared. Verses 30 and 31 there suggest that the 'revelation' of 'the Wrath' may not be as I have said, a revelation of the centuries; but a revelation of the 'now' (compare Acts xvii. 30). If so, the two ἀποκαλύπτεται's are precisely parallel. The world will be judged anon: the 'Wrath' will fall: but whoso has attained to 'righteousness' by faith will escape the impending doom. For, while a 'wrath' is unveiled, there is also further unveiled a way of escape from it.

We cannot pursue, in detail, all St Paul has to say about the way of human sin. But the gist of the matter is this. Unworthy conceptions of God, whose nature should have been known—and here, though much of modern thought will not find itself in sympathy everywhere with Pauline exposition, most thinking men would agree with him—unworthy conceptions of God brought in their train a series of dire consequences. The first of these is idolatry. And, as 'the reward of a precept is a precept,' so is the reward of error further error. Wrong thought leads on inevitably (so is the Will of God) to wrongful action. So idolatry became the fruitful mother of vice. And history is witness to the truth of what is said by the Apostolic writer. The more we know of idolatrous worship, the more we realise how hopelessly it was entangled with myriad immoralities. Prostitution and

sodomy were two of its necessary consequences. Because men refused to know
God (*v.* 28) their whole ideas of life became
utterly corrupt. They were 'delivered,'
in the Apostle's language, to a 'reprobate
mind.' The inevitable sequel is that catalogue of sins which occupies four whole
verses. And all the time men knew that
they were utterly wrong. But they were
obstinate in error. Not only did they do
wrong, but they also acquiesced, even
cheerfully acquiesced, in the wrongdoing
of others.

In the whole of this dismal indictment,
there are two phrases which chiefly grip
the mind of the modern student and set
him wondering. The first is the γνόντες
τὸν Θεόν of *v.* 21 : the other the striking
statement contained in the earlier part of
the verse which closes the chapter. What
shall we say of them ?

The γνόντες τὸν Θεόν appears of the
nature of a paradox. It seems indeed to
state what might have been, what should
have been, as if it actually were. Yet, for

the mind of the ancient world, the existence
of a god (or gods) was axiomatic. They
'knew'; yet they did not 'know.' Had
they read Nature's book aright, St Paul
implies, they must have known. That
they failed to read it so, brought inevitable
punishment. Yet, all the same, we are
puzzled by the directness of this γνόντες.

The other 'hard saying' I must paraphrase :

> "People who, recognising God's
> decree, that they who act in such
> ways are deserving of death, not only
> do the things, but go heart and soul
> also with them that do them."

The word " δικαίωμα " here means 'that
which one thinks right.' In viii. 4 will be
found a partially similar usage. Between
the ποιεῖν and the πράσσειν I doubt if it be
desirable to draw any strict distinction (as
is done by many commentators). It is
the closing words of the sentence which
make such distinction unlikely. But, what
of the ἐπιγνόντες ? where, when and how
did they 'recognise' it ? Perhaps we ought

to conclude that St Paul is appealing here
to the universal conscience. This 'conscience' is, for him, the revelation of the
δικαίωμα of God.   For them maybe it was
not : but none the less it existed. Wrongdoing they knew as wrongdoing. They
could not pretend they did not.   And
wrongdoing called for punishment ; called
for the retribution of death.   Notwithstanding, there will never be a full realisation of
sin, till the Being of God is grasped to an
adequate degree.

§ 4.   Gentile and Jew, how they stand

Up till now the writer has been drawing
a picture of the sinfulness that prevails in
the Gentile world.   But the Jew is not to
escape his ruthless analysis.   His turn is
coming.   When precisely he appears upon
the scene it is a little hard to say.   The
matter is handled indeed with very great
skill and delicacy.   Only we feel sure of
this, that the Jew is present in thought

some time before he appears in unmistakeable black and white. It is not till *v.* 17
of the second chapter that he is directly
addressed. But from the moment when
'judgment' is mentioned (human judgment
of human conduct), and that is in *v.* 1, we
feel certain that the writer is thinking of
his countrymen. For Israel was a very
stern critic of heathen morality, and
many heathen practices were positively
abhorrent to the law-instructed Israelite.
We may feel fairly certain that, when
the Apostle apostrophises ἄνθρωπε πᾶς ὁ
κρίνων (ii. 1), his thought is in transition
from Gentile to Jewish sinfulness. The
Gentile's normal attitude towards human
frailty is complacent toleration (συνευ-
δοκεῖν); it is the Jew who 'judges.' In i. 20
it was laid down that the Gentile world, in
general, is inexcusable. Now we are told
that all who 'judge' are also inexcusable.
For 'judge' and 'judged' are alike—all
partakers in the same ill-doing. In *v.* 2 it
is laid down that God's judgment is in all
cases 'in accordance with the facts'—κατ᾽

ἀλήθειαν certainly means "corresponding
to reality." The same teaching is repeated lower down, in *v.* 6, where it says
that "God shall render to each man in
accordance with his doings." In the verses
that come between it is assumed that all
are wrongdoers ; that all presume alike
upon God's patience and forbearance. Or,
maybe, we should not say 'all.' For in
the verses that follow, rather to the reader's
surprise, it is suggested that there are, who
will win "eternal life," because they set
themselves to the splendid quest after
"glory and honour and immortality"
(ἀφθαρσίαν), καθ' ὑπομονὴν ἔργου ἀγαθοῦ,
"by resolute persistence in good doing."
Now this statement would be less surprising, did it apply to Gentiles only. But it is
plainly stated, it does not : it covers both
Jew and Gentile (*vv.* 7—10). In this regard
all stand upon one footing, "for with God
there is no respect for outward circumstance" (*v.* 11).

But it would appear that for the Jew
ὑπομονὴ ἔργου ἀγαθοῦ, though conceivable

in thought, is incapable of realisation in actual practice. So declare the verses that follow, especially *v.* 13.

 ii. 12—16. "For all that have sinned without Law, without Law shall also perish. And all that have sinned within Law, by Law shall have their judgment. For not the hearers of Law are 'right' in the eyes of God. No! it is the doers of Law that shall be set right with Him."

 "For whenever Gentile folks, that have not Law, do naturally what Law bids; these, though they have no Law, are a Law for themselves. They display the effect of Law engraved upon their hearts. Their conscience bears them witness. Their thoughts, in inner conclave, accuse them or (maybe) defend them...(*for so surely it shall be*) in the day when God shall judge the world, as I state it in my preaching, by the agency of Christ Jesus."

In perusing this striking passage, the

reader cannot but feel that the hope of attaining God's favour, by 'resolute well doing,' is a very shadowy one. For Jews it fades away, all but entirely; for Gentiles it becomes exceedingly faint. 'Self-condemnation' (*v.* 15) is plainly the normal lot, even of the virtuous Gentile. His own 'self-knowledge' judges him; for 'conscience,' it is well known, in Pauline writings is a narrower faculty than in ordinary modern speech. It judges a man while he lives; and further, when he is passed to his great account, it will judge him—his 'thoughts' will judge him (for the λογισμοί are elements in the συνείδησις)—when he stands before Christ's Tribunal. This teaching of impending 'judgment' (compare, once again, the speech at Athens), St Paul says, is a regular feature in the 'good tidings' as he tells them.

In *v.* 12 ἀνόμως is curiously used. It must stand for 'outside Law,' a phrase meant to cover all Gentiles. The antithesis makes this inevitable. Ἐν νόμῳ (in

spite of the absence of any definite article
—and that need not at all surprise us, for
it is wholly in keeping with well-attested
classical usage) equally certainly covers
Jews. The statement in *v.* 13 ("but it is
the doers of the Law that shall be righted")
is, for all intents and purposes, a citation
of Holy writ. It is plainly equivalent to
that saying of Leviticus (xviii. 5), which is
referred to in x. 5, as also in Galatians.
What is said in *vv.* 14 and 15 has often
proved a stumbling block to Christian theologians. S. says that in the Talmud is ' no
such liberal teaching.' Ἑαυτοῖς εἰσι νόμος
is curiously hard to render, so as to convey
the proper meaning. Perhaps we might
venture upon, "these, having not a Law,
are their own Law"; that is, they do without one. The figure in *v.* 15 is, as Pauline
figures often are, confused and baffling.
The conception of a Law 'in the heart,' or
' written on the heart,' is, of course, familiar
' O. T.' But here it is not the 'Law' which
is graven upon the heart. It is the ἔργον
of the Law, a very different matter. Now

the 'ἔργον of the Law' would possibly mean, that which the Law bids be done; though it is not beyond the power of grammatical pedantry to vow that should rather be ἔργα. I have ventured to say 'effect,' taking ἔργον in the sense of 'product.' My own idea would be that the Apostolic writer is saying two things at once. It might be said of these people that 'they display the Law written on their hearts'; or, again, it might be said of them, that 'they display *the effect of Law* in their daily conduct.' What St Paul does actually say is, I believe, a combination of these two, or of two similar statements. In any case the 'figuration' (one has to coin the word) changes in *v.* 15 with wonderfu͘ rapidity. We have barely grasped the idea of the Law which is 'on the heart,' before we find ourselves transported to the Court in permanent session within the virtuous man. And even here the figure is not very easy to grasp. For it too shifts and varies with kaleidoscopic swiftness. First the man sits in judgment himself, with 'self-knowledge' for friendly witness. Anon the picture is more defined. Conscience becomes the judge; some 'thoughts' appear as accusers, and some as defenders. And then, before we can visualise the picture set before us, the whole judgment is transferred to the great Hereafter. Christ it is who sits supreme; the man is standing before Him; and his own 'conscience' is pleading for him—or alas! more often condemning him. And thereby a light is thrown on processes of judgment, which is full of instructive significance for any one who reads. This transference of the moral audit, from the man's own heart to heaven, is so exceedingly abrupt that the translator is almost forced to fill in the details of the sentence. I have done this (with the words in italics) in the course of my paraphrase.

And now the Jew is confronted decisively and definitely. He is 'shown up' to himself. Yet even here 'circumcision,' which the normal Jewish teacher regarded as an absolute *sine qua non*, is kept well

in the background. And, of course, it was
on this that the hard-fought controversy,
which embittered the Apostle's life, pre-
eminently turned. However the voice of
this strife had not been heard in Rome.
Accordingly the writer happily found himself in a position to develope what he had
to say in the order which best pleased
him.

ii. 17—20. "And if you, sir, call
yourself 'Jew,' and rest upon the Law,
and glory in God, and can read the
(heavenly) will, and pursue the loftiest,
thanks to Law's most plain instruc-
tions; and are confident about yourself, that you are a leader of the blind,
a light of people in darkness, an in-
structor of the foolish, a teacher of
the childish, because in the Law you
have a power of shaping knowledge
and (attaining to) God's Truth...."

Here we have the Jewish position—as
the Jew thought of himself, contrasted with
the unenlightened Gentile—very clearly
set before us. Two facts, above all, stand

out. God, the supreme Creator of Heaven and Earth, is in a peculiar sense the God of Israel. He is 'our God and the God of our fathers.' Moreover the Israelite has a priceless heritage in the possession of the Law of Moses. This gives him an unique standing. All other men, by contrast, are 'blind,' are 'in the dark,' are 'fools' (a Stoical term, from the School of Tarsus), are 'infants.' By the study of the Law (and in it he has been very soundly drilled) he can attain to real 'knowledge'; he can realise God's 'Truth.'

And here, by the way, we should notice the exact force of "$\mu\acute{o}\rho\phi\omega\sigma\iota\nu$." It is not the $\mu\rho\phi\acute{\eta}$ of knowledge the Law provides. It is not a solid fact, but a potentiality. Those very unhappy backsliders, of whom we read in 2 Timothy, possessed a $\mu\acute{o}\rho$-$\phi\omega\sigma\iota\varsigma$ of Godliness, but of Godliness they had none. They failed to actualise it. (2 Tim. iii. 5) Here the Israelite apostrophised claims that he has the 'key of knowledge,' and does not let it rust unused.

But the stern Apostle affirms that his

practice is not as his preaching. He teaches other people, but he fails to teach himself. It is as it always has been. The Name of Israel's God is dishonoured among (Isai. lii. 5 LXX.) the nations, through the fault of His own people

One phrase in this indictment is perplexing to the reader. It is the latter part of *v.* 22, "You, who abominate idols, are you a despoiler of temples?" In what sense, the reader asks himself, could a Jew be a 'robber of temples'? Anything that had even remotely to do with an idol temple was considered 'abomination.' To have anything to do with such (and we know, from early Christian experience, what difficulties were involved, in the avoidance of idol-contact) might be classed as ἱεροσυλεῖν. At least, so we may suppose. One finds it hard to believe that a normal, respectable Jew would pilfer from heathen shrines. But then, it might be urged, neither would he steal.

And now, for the first time, comes mention of circumcision.

ii. 25—27. " Circumcision is of
service, provided you keep the Law.
But if you transgress the Law your
circumcision becomes *ipso facto* uncircumcision. If then an uncircumised
person shall zealously observe the
requirements of Law, will not his
uncircumcision be reckoned as circumcision ? and accordingly Uncircumcision, born so, because it achieves
the Law, judge you, who transgress
the Law with the letter and circumcision ? "

In these verses there is no difficulty,
though there are interesting points of
grammar. For instance, one asks oneself,
is there any significance in the variation
of phrasing, as between νόμον πράσσῃς
and παραβάτης νόμου ᾖς? The combination (in *v.* 26) of ἡ ἀκροβυστία with ἡ
ἀκροβυστία αὐτοῦ is also remarkable. One
would have expected the abstract, so used,
to have stood for a plural noun, instead of
for one person. Ἐκ φύσεως (in *v.* 27) appears
to be temporal, and mean " from birth."

The διά, in the closing words, is of the
'circumstantial' variety. In translation it
needs some expansion, for it represents
all this; 'though you possess the commandments in black and white, and have been
circumcised.' In *v.* 26 I have omitted to
say that the second definite article in τὰ
δικαιώματα τοῦ νόμου need not reappear in
English. It may be either "of the Law,"
or simply "of Law." In Greek the article
could not have been omitted.

In the last two verses of the chapter
we have an idea brought forward, which reappears in chap. ix. The sentence is highly
elliptical, and it is by no means certain
how it ought to be expanded in English
reproduction. I should deal with it as
follows :

ii. 28, 29. "For it is not the outward Jew"—'ostensible' and 'palpable' seem, both of them, impossible
—"that is a Jew; nor the outward,
material circumcision, that is circumcision. No! it is the inward Jew,
that is a Jew; and the heart has a

circumcision—a circumcision spiritual, not literal. His praise comes not of men ; it comes of God."

In Jeremiah (ix. 26) and in Deuteronomy (x. 16) this conception of the 'inward' circumcision may be found. It is worth noting how St Paul almost invariably avoids a perfectly balanced antithesis. As far as the second Ἰουδαῖος, the sentence, though elliptical, maintains a proper balance. Then the order is disturbed. Why πνεύματι has an ἐν, and γράμματι not, it would be difficult to say. Possibly the writer shrank from an unsupported πνεύματι, but did not feel the need of repeating the preposition. What is the antecedent of οὗ ? One would have expected the feminine gender. It is just conceivable that the masculine (for it probably is *masculine*) was called for by the fact that the very name 'Jew' (Ἰουδαῖος) has a connexion with the word for "praise." However, that may be a mere coincidence.

At this point comes a digression. The Jew is so convinced of his privileged position, so utterly sure of himself as the favoured son of God, that St Paul feels called upon to meet an inevitable (though unformulated) objection.

> iii. 1, 2. "Where then is the Jew's superiority? or, where is the advantage which belongs to the Circumcision? There is much, in every way. To begin with, they were entrusted with the oracles of God...."

Tὸ περισσόν is equivalent, I think, to an abstract noun, literally "the 'over and above'-ness." The 'Circumcision,' in the second question, means the whole of the Jewish people. It might be taken, of course, as signifying, 'Where is the use of being circumcised?' But the other seems to me preferable. For, although the question is put twice, it is really only one question. The supposed objector cries, What is the good of being a Jew, if what you say is correct? The answer comes, There is much good! The superiority is palpable; it is also manifold. The writer makes as though he would enumerate

various points in which Israel is highly
favoured. But he only mentions one.
Others he might have mentioned will be
found in chap. ix. Then, he suddenly
breaks off, in a very perplexing manner.
His tendency to fly off, as it were, at a
tangent is well known to all commentators.
But generally it is more easy to see what
diverted his thoughts than it is in the
passage before us. Anyhow *vv.* 3—9 are
a digression in a digression—and a digression so far-fetched, that one is almost
tempted to wonder whether the section
can be misplaced. Yet that is made
unlikely by the undoubted fact of the
break. The expected enumeration never
comes.

For the rest, what can we say, unless
that the thought of 'trust,' contained in
ἐπιστεύθησαν, instantaneously calls up the
thought of the people's untrustworthiness?
To have been 'entrusted' with the Law,
and with the Prophets, was indeed a substantial privilege, though it was only one of
several. And how did Israel respond?

Was he loyal? was he trustworthy? Did
his 'faithfulness' in any sense answer
to the 'faithfulness' of his God? Alas!
the record of history is all to the contrary.
The story of Israel is a story of trust
unjustified, of love Divine betrayed. But
it is not merely this the Apostle says. If
it were we should follow the thought with
less of hesitation. He passes, with light-
ning rapidity, from one consideration to
another. He answers thoughts of his own
and unexpressed objections of an imagined
opponent in controversy. The effect is
bewildering to the modern reader. However, let us take it as it stands.

iii. 3, 4. "Why! Suppose that
some were faithless; will their un-
faithfulness annul the faith of God?"
(The "faith of God," obviously, can only
mean one thing, His being true to Himself
and true to His promises.)

"Of course, of course, it cannot!
Nay, let God be proved true, though
every man be a liar: as it stands in
Holy Writ, *That Thou mayst be proved*

right in Thy pleadings, and prevail ^{Ps. li. 4} *when on Thy trial.*"

In this citation from the Psalm (in which the writer follows the LXX variations from the Hebrew—for Professor Cheyne renders *that thou mightest be justified when thou speakest, be clear when thou judgest*) St Paul regards the Most High as Himself before a tribunal, and amply vindicated. The Hebrew presents us with a very different picture. There *man's* sin is so palpable, so undisguised, so freely admitted ; that the sentence passed by God, the Great Judge of all, however heavy it be, can only be accepted as altogether justified. The Septuagint translators may have meant to employ a deponent. But if they so intended, St Paul disregards their intention ; thus attaching to their words a wider range of meaning, and, for the moment, dissevering them from the context, in which we find them. As here quoted they have the sense : what God says is always right ; whenever His acts are questioned they are found beyond all question.

Next it would seem, we must suppose, this unchallenged eternal 'Rightness' is disputed on the subtle ground that if our 'wrongness' establishes God's 'rightness' it cannot be just and equitable that He should punish us. But this contention receives short shrift and sharp. It is simply inconceivable that the Judge of all the Earth should not do right. Yet it crops up once again, in prompt restatement (*v.* 7) in a form amazingly involved; only to be repudiated in the grim and stern pronouncement "Whose condemnation is just."

Cf. Gen. xviii. 25.

Before the passage is left, let me give a paraphrase of it.

iii. 5—8. " But if our wickedness establishes God's righteousness, what are we to say? Can it be—I speak as a man—that God, who inflicts on us His wrath, is dealing unjustly? Never! If that were so, how is He to judge the world? If the truthfulness of God redounded through my lie, why, that being so, am I judged as a sinner? Moreover, why should we not cry; as they malign us, aye, some aver we say; Let us do evil that good may come of it? The condemnation of such talk is just."

The last sentence here in the text is formed very irregularly. A τί must be supplied, but also a λέγωμεν. The latter has been absorbed in the λέγειν dependent on φασί. Furthermore the very thing, which we ask if we are to say, stands as a dependent clause in construction with the φασί. Such irregularities are found in classical writers, but hardly in a form so intricate and complex as this we have before us.

There is nothing more I can say about the section. I have done the best I can to give a definite meaning to a sentence such as fills the most courageous interpreter with a sinking of the heart.

§ 5.   Jew and Gentile alike guilty

The digression into which we plunged
at the end of *v*. 2, and the train of specula-
tion that it brought, are now a thing of the
past. We return to the main argument,
leading on to the conclusion that all the
world alike is hopelessly involved in sin.
In the case of the Gentiles, the fact is
beyond dispute. Israel too, in spite of his
privileged position, is really in no better
case. So we now proceed to show. Verse
9 (as it happens) contains a curious problem
of vocabulary. What is the meaning of
προεχόμεθα ? Looking at the sentence in
general one notes that excellent sense
would be made if προεχόμεθα should mean
either 'are we better off than they,' or 'are
they better off than we'; either 'have they
the advantage of us,' or, 'have we the
advantage of them.' Whichever the question may be, the answer is 'not at all.'
I think that stands out clearly. But how
shall we decide? All classical students

know that certain compounds of ἔχω are
used in the active voice with a neuter
sense. This is the case with κατέχειν,
ἀνέχειν and προέχειν. Our own 'hold'
supplies in English an obvious illustration.
Προέχειν in the active means to 'jut out'
(of headlands), and then generally to 'be in
advance,' to 'be superior.' Can the middle
have a similar meaning? There is no
evidence whatever to show it. Προέχεσθαι
(passive) exists in Plutarch (only I cannot
trace the reference) with the meaning 'be
exalted.' The Greek O.T. affords us no
aid. The word, in any case, occurs only
once and then it would appear that προσ-
έχειν, rather than προέχειν, is the reading to
be followed (Job xxvii. 6). The fact is,
we must wait till some fortunate exhumed
sherd, or strip of papyrus, from the ran-
sacked dustheaps of Egypt comes to throw
new light upon it. Harking back to *vv.* 1
and 2, I feel certain that the sense required
is, "are we in better case?" That is, to
be sure, precisely what the ordinary Jew believed with fervency of devotion ; precisely

what St Paul was minded to contest.
Therefore (even in the absence of all
evidence for such a meaning) I make bold
to believe it is right. It is, no doubt, a
term of common speech, involving some
metaphor not easy to discern. There are
plenty of such usages to be found in every
language. It is on the racecourse, or the
drillground, or the rialto, one has to look
for their primal origin.

> iii. 9. "How then? Are we in
> better case than they? Not one whit!
> We have already charged both Jews
> and Gentiles, all of them, with being
> under sin; as Holy Scripture says..."

In i. 21, we were told that the heathen
are 'without excuse'; and that was followed up by the long and familiar catalogue
of definite iniquities. At the opening of
chap. ii. the same epithet (ἀναπολόγητος)
was apparently applied to the Israelite in
his proud consciousness of moral superiority. To this, as I conceive, is reference
in προῃτιασάμεθα. It is 'charge' rather
than 'demonstration'; though the Gentile,

in all probability, would have let judgment go 'by default.' His attitude towards sin, as we have already seen, is an attitude of cheerful acquiescence. 'They all do it' would be his plea. Why should he wish to be either better than his neighbours, or better than his gods? The Jew would be less prepared to 'give himself away,' by admitting his sinfulness. The 'conflate' quotation that follows, I assume, is addressed to him. Indeed, in *v.* 19, the writer distinctly says so. The string of 'texts' (in the vulgar sense of the word) runs something as follows:

iii. 10—12. *"There is not a single one righteous; there is not who has understanding; there is not who searches after God. All have swerved from the* Ps. xiv. *way; all alike have become corrupted;* 1—3. *there is not who follows goodness, no, not even one."*

So far the writer has drawn upon the opening of Psalm xiv., the complaint of a servant of God in an age of infidelity. The words quoted give us a picture of 'the

fool' and of his fellows; that is, of the
reckless unbeliever. The next four 'texts'
are taken from various places, Psalm v.,
Psalm cxl., Psalm x., Isaiah lix. Save
the passage from Isaiah, which is a national
indictment, the rest all come from pictures
of the professedly unrighteous, of the
enemies of God and of His servants.

Says the first (Psalm v. 10 (LXX)),

> iii. 13. *A grave wide open is their
> gullet; with their tongues they have
> wrought deceitfully.*

(Here ἐδολιοῦσαν is 'imperfect' in form
—a very awkward tense; we need ἐδολίω-
σαν.)

The second says (Psalm cxl. 3 (LXX)),

> *The poison of asps is under their
> lips:*

the third (a very free citation of Psalm x. 7),

> *whose mouth is full of cursing and
> bitterness:*

the fourth is from Isaiah lix. 7, 8 (in a form
both abridged and free),

> *Swift are their feet to pour out
> blood...destruction and misery is in*

> *their ways, and the Way of Peace have*
> *they not known :*

last of all come part of the opening words
of Psalm xxxvi.

> *...there is no fear of God before his*
> *eyes.*

These last five sayings have made
their way from 'Romans' into the common
Christian version of Psalm xiv.—they are
found in our 'LXX' manuscripts—and
so into the Prayer Book version of our
Church.

Roughly speaking, the whole citation,
which is after Rabbinic models, describes
the 'wickedness' of the 'wicked.' St Paul
however makes bold to apply it universally.

> iii. 19. "Now we know that all
> the Law says, it says to those in the
> Law; so that every mouth may be
> stopped and (*thus*) all the world be
> proved liable to God's vengeance."

The 'Law' means, of course, all the
Scriptures : in this case, the Psalms and
Isaiah. Their message is to God's people,
to those who own His allegiance and

accept His holy commandments. Accordingly their indictment brings condemnation
on Israel. The result is—for the ἵνα cannot be taken as strictly 'telic'; save in so
far as all that is, corresponds with a hidden
'purpose'—the result is, that all opposition
is silenced, and none can dispute God's
justice. "Every mouth," both of Jew and
Gentile, is "stopped"; "all the world,"
whether heathen or other, is liable to such
penalty as the Almighty shall choose to
inflict.

This conclusion is finally clinched by
the citation we have already met in Galatians ii. 16. The form of it and the use of
it are just the same as there. Only here
we have an addition, a very pithy statement of the purpose served by Law in the
Divine economy.

iii. 20. "Because by works of
Law *'no living creature shall be
righted in'* His *'Presence.'* By Law,
you know, there comes the recognition
of sin."

The actual quotation (from Psalm cxliii.

2) is enclosed in single commas. The idea of the function of Law as stimulating conscience by definition of wrongdoing is repeated, in another form, in chap. vii. below.

§ 6.   THE NEW 'RIGHTNESS,' OR 'RIGHTEOUSNESS'

And now, having set before the reader, in black and white, the deplorable condition of all the world in respect to sinfulness, St Paul proceeds to unfold the doctrine of the new 'Righteousness.' The message first touches the Israelite, as is plainly indicated in the very opening phrases. It is a section of fundamental importance and calls for very careful handling.

iii. 21, 22. "But now, quite apart from Law, a 'righteousness of God' has been (and is) displayed ; a 'righteousness' whereto the Law and the Prophets testify—a 'righteousness of God' (operating) through faith in Jesus

Christ, (and) extending to all believers;
for there is no distinction."

The very last verse declared that "*no
living creature shall be set right.*" So it
was till the New Age came. It was in
such a sense, I should hold, the Apostle
interpreted the words of Psalm xiv. There
he did not take δίκαιος to mean 'right-
doing'; but 'right' in a narrower sense,
that is 'right with God.' *That* no one
was, nor could be τότε—in the days before
the great φανέρωσις. Χωρὶς νόμου briefly
hints at the stage of futile effort, which
Saul the Pharisee had known so well.
Many still were engaged upon it: there were
Jews in Rome so engaged. The two words
simply insist that 'all that' is a delusion
and must be set aside. "A righteousness
of God" I take to mean a way whereby a
man may attain to 'right'-ness with God,
by God's own plan and appointment. It
has nothing to do with conduct: it deals
with *status* only: but *status*, where God is
concerned, is for man the very first of all
considerations. God's own 'righteousness.'

in the ethical sense, has nothing to do with the matter. The Θεοῦ does not mark Him as the possessor of the 'righteousness.' It only marks it as being associated with Him—we apprehend, of course, as its fountainhead and source. "God's righteousness" is contrasted with a "righteousness" of man, that is, any system whereby a man may hope to attain to the definitely unattainable. But, though this way to acceptance is new in point of time, it is not unprepared for. The 'Law' has testified of it, no doubt, both in its words of promise and also (perhaps more plainly) in the symbolism of appointed Ritual. As for the 'Prophets,' one thinks at once of the great utterances of Isaiah. In *v.* 22 we meet prepositions somewhat heavily weighted, even overweighted, with meaning. The διά has to bear a good deal; but so also has the εἰς. There seems to have been a time when copyists were uncertain whether ἐπί or εἰς should be read. If one might have a choice in the matter, one would be disposed to vote for ἐπί, as definitely better adapted to express the idea of extension. In English we cannot well, without sacrifice of clearness, refrain from some expanding. The meaning of the phrase πίστεως Ἰησοῦ Χριστοῦ has been disputed like everything else. That the 'faith' is not our Lord's faith (notwithstanding Heb. xii. 2), is made certain by Gal. ii. 16, where we read how "we"... "being sure that man is not 'justified' by works of Law, only by faith in Christ Jesus, even we became believers in Christ Jesus" —which is surely proof positive as to what the writer means here. The closing words of *v.* 22 (οὐ γάρ ἐστι διαστολή), belong to what goes before. Διαστολή itself, as it happens, is found once again in the Epistle (it occurs three times altogether, the remaining place being 1 Cor. xiv. 7) in such a connexion as shows that the absence of difference spoken of is in relation to 'believers' and not to 'sinners.' The sense is "on all believers, without distinction." At least that is the conclusion suggested by x. 11, 12. However, in the end, it

comes to the same thing. Jew and Gentile
—all are 'justified' only by the way of
'faith.' For why? The sequel shows.

    iii. 23, 24. "For all have sinned
and (consciously) fall short of the
Divine Glory; and are freely justified
by His own 'grace,' through the
'redemption' that was wrought in
Jesus Christ...."

The πάντες ἥμαρτον here is an excellent
instance of the danger of identifying the
Greek aorist with our preterite. All the
phrase means is just this, that every man
on earth, and woman too, at one time or
another, has done amiss. Presumably it
was this kind of usage that induced old
world grammarians to designate the tense
'the undefined tense.' Now, our English
preterite is, in a general way, precisely
the opposite. 'I struck' means that I so
did upon some given occasion. When we
wish to be 'indefinite' we naturally say 'I
have struck,' not 'I struck.' 'Again and
again I *have* seen' is what our idiom requires.
Therefore "all have sinned" is right. Only

we must be careful to remember, it does not refer to any 'corporate' sin, any sin in which we all had part and lot—as the older theology says men all share in the sin of Adam. It merely states a truth we are none of us prepared to deny, that, at one time or another, we have done what we blush to recall; what we feel to be incompatible with any 'acceptance' by God. This 'sin' is always past, even if perpetrated just this moment: the 'consciousness' it entails is inevitably present. Because we did wrong to-day, last week, last year, whenever it may be, we feel in our hearts uncomfortable at the contemplation of God and His Supreme Holiness. And there is more in it than that. Not only do we 'feel' unfit; we actually are unfit. As for the voice of ὑστεροῦνται, it is worth while to observe that 'sense' verbs in early Greek are very apt to be 'middle.' There is in them an element of 'reflexive' force. A careful consideration of the places where ὑστερεῖν and ὑστερεῖσθαι are found in the New Testament.

seems to give good reason for thinking
that the former means 'to be behind,' and
the latter 'to feel want,' or to 'feel oneself
behind.' Yet it is not wholly certain. St
Luke xv. 14 and 1 Cor. xii. 24 might be
taken as examples of the meaning of 'conscious' want or 'conscious' failing. It
seems reasonable to suppose that the Divine
'Glory' is an expression for God's realised
Holiness. He has said " *Ye shall be holy,
for I am holy,*" but unhappy man in his
heart is only too well aware he is nothing
of the sort. Before the amazing splendour
of that transcendent Holiness he stands
completely abashed. The "glory of God"
however might mean that moral dignity
which the great Creator meant His creature
man to have. But the other interpretation
appears to be the likelier. Verse 24 is full
of important technical terms. Χάρις means
(in strict accordance with regular Pauline
usage) the 'undeserved favour' of God.
'Απολύτρωσις I will speak of anon. Δικαιούμενοι is used in the formal 'theological' sense, not "made righteous," that

is, but "righted." Luther's German gives it exactly: "*und werden ohne Verdienst gerecht.*"

There is, we must freely admit, a singular grammatical difficulty to be faced in this same verse. It is this; that the main predication is conveyed in a participle, δικαιούμενοι. Yet plainly there are before us only two alternatives. Either all words after πιστεύοντας till τῆς δόξης τοῦ θεοῦ must be taken as a parenthesis, and δικαιού-μενοι be regarded as one of those 'irrational' participial appositions we sometimes find in St Paul: or else we must boldly say that δικαιούμενοι is virtually equivalent to καὶ δικαιοῦνται. Our familiar "being justified freely" is only possible because it is apprehended not as a *present* participle, but as a *past* one. As translation it will not do. At any rate so I should hold.

However, let us be honest. I have said that I incline to regard the word δικαιούμενοι as equivalent to καὶ δικαι-οῦνται. Then, unless we are prepared to admit some laxity of expression, it undoubtedly means too much. " All " have sinned, but " all " are not " justified." It is the πιστεύοντες only, be they Jew, or be they Gentile, that reach that happy condition. If accordingly we incline to take it as I have taken it, we must supply a qualifying phrase (at least, in thought) " and are justified—*if they are justified—* by no merit of their own but by His free Grace."

The question is; is this, or is it not, beyond the bonds of that licence in manipulation of grammar St Paul so freely assumes? And now for ἀπολύτρωσις. The usage of the Septuagint undoubtedly eliminates from this term the idea of 'ransom.' The word means 'redemption,' that is, in the sense of mere 'deliverance.' All idea of ' price' has vanished. Has it also vanished in St Paul? Elsewhere the thought of ' price' is emphasised by our writer, though not in connexion with 'ransom,' or any such metaphor. In the famous saying of Christ we have our definite λύτρον. It might be argued therefore that here too the second element in the famous compound noun is not asleep or dead. Take it altogether, however, I think that it is safer to regard the noun as used in its common 'O. T.' sense. After all, the λύτρον of Christ was all His own. It does not seem to have had any sort of root in the past. The λύτρα of O. T. are literal λύτρα. Let us then dissociate ἀπολύτρωσις from all λύτρον in this context.

Lastly, before we pass on, we must observe that this ἀπολύτρωσις is characterised as being ἐν Χριστῷ Ἰησοῦ. The ἐν awakes some questioning. Is it like this one in 'Galatians' (ii. 4) τὴν ἐλευθερίαν ἣν ἔχομεν ἐν Χριστῷ Ἰησοῦ? or this other, in the same Epistle (ii. 17), ζητοῦντες δικαιω-θῆναι ἐν Χριστῷ? And, even if it be, what is the force of it? The truth is, of all prepositions none is more elusive than ἐν. Here, I take it, we have to choose between two conceptions. The 'redemption' either comes "through Christ Jesus" (for I conceive that there are places where ἐν is not far in sense from διά with the

genitive): or else, it must be viewed as
centred in His Person. This latter is easier
to say than to grasp or to explain. Maybe
the Johannic "In Him was Light" would
help us. The ἐν in vi. 11 is, I should say,
more decisively quasi-instrumental—unless,
by a considerable stretch of the 'pregnant'
principle, we make bold to see in that the
doctrine of the 'vital union.' I remember,
when I first read 'Romans' as a schoolboy
years ago, all ἐν's had somehow to be forced
into relation with the idea of locality. But
such desperate expedients need not trouble
us to-day. The effect of this qualification,
attached to our Redemption, is plain for all
practical purposes: it comes 'through' the
Lord Christ—primarily through His Incarnation and Death.

Let us venture forward two more
verses:

> iii. 25, 26. "Whom God.........to
> be atoning, by means of faith, through
> His own blood; with a view to demon-
> stration of God's own 'righteousness'
> —because former sins had been passed

over, in the time when He was patient
—I say, for the demonstration of His
'righteousness' at this present, to the
end He may be 'righteous' *yet also*
'righting' him, that is of those that
believe in Jesus."

The verb I have left a blank, because it
is so hard to make up one's mind about it.
Προτίθεσθαι comes but three times in all
the N.T. Twice it certainly means 'propose' (that is, set before oneself, as an
object to pursue). In the 'LXX' the
middle is found three times in this tense;
and in each of the three it has a reflexive
force. It belongs to the phrase of the
Psalms 'to set God before one's eyes.'
Can it mean here "Whom God purposed
to Himself to be"? Or, are we to find in
it a usage somewhat removed from all
Biblical usage whatever, and take it as
merely meaning "set forward," "displayed"?
That could be supported by classical instances—even if we dissociate it from that
more special usage, whereby it often means
'lay out for burial.'

On the whole, I should prefer to render "Whom God purposed to be atoning...."

With regard to ἱλαστήριον, I feel certain S. is right. So far as form is concerned, the word could easily be an adjectival form. And 'adjectival,' in fact, it is, in Josephus and elsewhere (*testibus L.S.*, who give two references). In LXX, to be sure, it always means "mercy seat" as it does also in Hebrews ix.—the only other place, where it is found in the N.T. Yet it cannot possibly mean "mercy seat" here. And should you say, such a usage of an adjective is not Greek, then I answer, you will find an instance in Aeschylus, who employs in *Theb.* 562 κακῶν τῶνδε βουλευτήριον for 'the man that counselled these naughty deeds.'

The two prepositional phrases, that follow on ἱλαστήριον, are wholly independent of each other. They add two fresh details. Christ makes men's peace with God, provided they have faith : moreover, His 'atonement' is achieved ἐν τῷ αὐτοῦ

αἵματι. How this is so, we cannot tell.
But the Apostolic teaching reproduces
Christ's own statement in the Gospel (see
St Matt. xxvi. 28). There the "putting
away of sins"—plainly the heart of what
is expressed in the term ἱλαστήριον—is
definitely connected with the "outpouring"
of His Blood. What mysteries lie behind
that "outpouring" it is not for us to
fathom. But we must not close our eyes
to the solemn fact that Christ Himself proclaimed a 'virtue' in His death, and that
all His followers, as many as ever taught
in early days, likewise proclaimed this
thing. Though 'blood' in the ancient
world (I think, universally) was taken as
the seat of life; yet blood that is shed
stands for death—stands for life laid down
for others. As S. very justly observes, the
'idea of sacrifice' is a 'central conception'
of N. T. religion. Though we may not
see its meaning, we 'must not explain it
away'; nor regard it as 'mere metaphor.'
To this I say 'Amen,' with all my heart
and soul!

Continuing the consideration of what is said in *v.* 25, we come to the Apostolic statement of a purpose that was involved in Christ's work of propitiation. This is stated once and again; but the conception is introduced by different prepositions. The first time it is εἰς ἔνδειξιν, the second πρὸς τὴν ἔνδειξιν. Plainly the latter phrase is more definite than the former; but its larger degree of definiteness, I think, must be taken to lie rather in the addition of the article than in the change of the preposition. Subtle minds have drawn a distinction between εἰς and πρός in such connexions: but the plain man is rather tempted to doubt whether they will hold.

What St Paul desires to say is obviously this. God's ' Righteousness ' (meaning thereby—in anthropomorphic terms—His absolute sense of right) is somehow touched and affected by the act of ' passing over ' sin. The πάρεσις of sins demands, in the Apostolic thought, some sort of justification. It might have been supposed that God was not δίκαιος (that is, absolutely

12—2

'just'—that He could tolerate sin, the which, from His very nature, is palpably impossible. This desiderated 'justification' of the Perfect Justice of God is supplied by the Death of Christ. That demonstrates indisputably that sin is not 'indifferent'; not a thing which does not matter. The idea has, possibly, been over-emphasised by Puritan Divines. It is not in the Pauline scheme of primary importance. Still here it plainly is, and has to be grappled with.

For that purpose we must be clear as to how πάρεσις differs from ἄφεσις. 'Forgiveness,' as we call it, that is to say, the wiping out the memory of a wrongdoing, as one wipes out the 'score' on a slate, in such sort that the wrongful act is wholly dead and buried and the wrongdoer is restored to the position he occupied, before he did the wrong—'forgiveness,' I say, is ἄφεσις, which word we sometimes render by the Latin term 'remission' (which is not very adequate) and sometimes by our own word. Πάρεσις (which is only found

here in Biblical Greek) is a wholly different
matter.   It means a 'passing over without
notice,' a temporary disregarding.   In sense
it is akin to that ὑπεριδών, of Acts xvii.,
which our English (A.V.) renders so whim-
sically.   That πάρεσις belonged to another
age : it cannot continue for ever ; for it is
palpably derogatory to God's supreme
Righteousness.   Therefore it must give
place, and an ἄφεσις be achieved, at a cost
which will prove for ever that God does
not disregard sin, or view it as indifferent.
As for προγεγονότων (where one would
have rather looked for an aorist participle)
it should be noticed, as a fact, that the
perfect γέγονα is not infrequently employed 'irrationally.'   A concordance will
demonstrate this.   Those, who are zealous
for a 'perfect' sense in the word, can find
a loophole here, in the thought that 'sins,'
once sinned, remain 'sins' permanently (in
the absence of ἄφεσις).   Ἐν τῇ ἀνοχῇ is,
of course, a temporal expression.   Ἐν τῷ
νῦν καιρῷ recalls to the mind the distinction (in Acts xvii.) between "the time

of ignorance" and the "now," in which God bids men "everywhere repent," in view of coming judgment.

At the end of *v.* 26, I have ventured on a novel rendering. The καί I take to be 'adversative,' not 'copulative.' The problem is, how shall God be 'Righteous' in Himself, and yet accept sinners as 'i' the right.' This is what theologians commonly speak of as the reconciliation of Justice and Mercy.

S. says "righteous *and also* declaring righteous." That is precisely what 'διὰ τὴν πάρεσιν' (a thing which palpably demands excuse) will not at all permit. It should be "righteous *yet also* 'righting'." Such an adversative force in 'and' is found, one would suspect, in every language.

Τὸν ἐκ πίστεως Ἰησοῦ is sufficiently compact, regarded as a phrase. It means "anyone, who belongs to faith in Jesus." The expression is of the same pattern, not improbably, as the descriptive phrase in Galatians "οἱ ἐκ περιτομῆς." But I cannot feel certain, whether it actually signifies

"him, who rests on faith in Jesus," or,
"him, who belongs to 'faith' in Jesus,"
that is, to the company of the faithful.
Yet truly it matters little.

§ 7.   The new 'Righteousness' the
same for all

In *v.* 9 just above we met the puzzling
question τί οὖν; προεχόμεθα (which, by the
way, our English revisers rendered "What
then? Are we in worse case," whereto the
American Company appended this pithy
comment, "For 'in worse case' read
'better' and omit the margin"!). We
can now say, that any claim the Jew might
have to priority, is effectually wiped out.
To 'glory' in the privilege of Abrahamic
descent, or the possession of the 'Law,'
was peculiarly Jewish. Such glorying is
now rendered impossible, nay even inconceivable.

iii. 27. "What becomes, then, of
our boasting? It has been entirely
shut out."

Here we have a past fact simply. The tense concentrates attention entirely on the consideration that it is past. Henceforth all 'boasting' (and the article, though it may conceivably be only the article attached to 'abstract nouns,' as such, seems here to define the 'boasting' as that of St Paul's compatriots) "has been excluded," "is excluded." So far, all is 'plain sailing.' Now there are 'rocks ahead.' The use of νόμου, in the very next question, is eminently perplexing. However, we recall that in other instances, the Apostle uses this particular term with prodigious freedom. viii. 2 will illustrate.

All English versions say 'law.' What the ordinary reader may gather therefrom one hardly likes to think. S. inclines to the rendering 'system.' To my mind, in modern English 'principle' is the nearest equivalent.

Let us, then, adventure so.

iii. 27—31. "Thanks to what principle? The principle of doing things? No! the principle of believing. Our

view is, that a man is set right before
God by faith, apart from doing Law's
biddings."

" Or, can it be that God is the God
of the Jews alone? Is He not the
Gentiles' too? Aye, surely, the Gentiles' also ; if in very truth there is
One God, who will accept the Circumcision, thanks to faith, and the Uncircumcision, because they have the
Faith."

" Do we then by our faith annul
the Law? Nay, nay! We establish
it."

Viewing the passage as a whole, one
notices at once the full force of the νόμος
difficulty.   It is a class of difficulty which
dogs our steps everywhere.   To the orderly
English mind, it is barely conceivable that
a word should be employed in one paragraph in two senses.   That is, presumably,
why our Company of Revisers retained the
term ' law ' all through.   Yet the more one
peruses the sentence, the more certain one
becomes, that the νόμος of *v.* 31 has nothing

whatever to do with the νόμος of *v.* 27.
Verse 31 contains a purely subsidiary question. It does not appear to affect the section
generally, or to have any intimate relation
with it.

But, mark the baffling conciseness of
the question that follows ἐξεκλείσθη.
"Where is our boasting?   It is shut out.
By what sort of principle?"   So runs the
text.   Would it be going too far to affirm
that, when St Paul declares that "boasting"
is "shut out" by such and such a principle,
he means that none can boast, because the
'principle,' whereby a man finds favour
or mercy with God, is not 'works' but
'faith'?

"What 'principle' excludes it?" he
asks.   This must plainly be a brachylogy;
for the expanded sense should be, By
the operation of what principle is it excluded?   The answer is, Faith not works.
That is the principle which renders all
boasting impossible.   The λογιζόμεθα γάρ
—γάρ appears preferable to οὖν—represents the Pauline position.   Possibly, by

the use of the plural, he means to convey
the idea that his readers are carried with
him. On the other hand, quite as possibly,
he is speaking for himself alone. The ἤ
(in *v.* 29) introduces, as normally, an impossible alternative. If Law were the
royal road to δικαιοσύνη, Israel would
occupy a position of unfair privilege. The
Gentile would be situated, by comparison,
most unfavourably. My impression is,
that in saying εἴπερ εἷς ὁ θεός, the writer
means us to gather that God is the same
for all, as I have put it in the paraphrase.
The distinction (in *v.* 30), between ἐκ
πίστεως and διὰ τῆς πίστεως, is not very
easy to grasp. And yet we can hardly suppose the variation unintentional. Maybe,
the anarthrous form distinguishes 'faith'
as a whole from 'works' as a whole;
whereas the διὰ τῆς πίστεως refers to belief
in a specific form, that is to say, belief in
Christ. The distinction, such as it is, rests
less on the variation of preposition than on
the presence or absence of the article. In
v. 31 the writer, having dealt with the

question of 'glorying,' raises yet a further question, and answers it very briefly.   If the Law (an objector might urge) does not help a man with God, what is the use of it ?   You are emptying it of all meaning. Not so! responds the Apostle, Law becomes more real than ever.   For the explanation of this 'dark saying,' we must turn to a later passage.   From xiii. 10 we learn that Love is πλήρωμα νόμου.

St Paul's great Master Himself had expressly repudiated the charge of abolishing 'Law.'   He spoke definitely of 'the Law.' I should say it is likely enough that 'Law' means 'the Law' here too.   Νόμον οὖν καταργοῦμεν would   really   contain   no meaning, setting Jewish Law apart.

§ 8.   THE FAITH OF ABRAHAM AND
ITS LESSON FOR US

In the last section of chap. iii. it was laid down that 'boasting' is impossible. At this point we seem to hear a voice that

asks, What? had even Abraham no ground
for glorying? This opens up the theme
of the Patriarch's position, and the whole of
chap. iv. is taken up with its consideration.
In *v.* 1 a little group of manuscripts omits
the verb εὑρηκέναι. This is plainly ad-
vantageous. For the question that naturally
arises is not, What did Abraham get? but,
How about Abraham? The personal pronoun ἡμῶν has been thought an argument
for a preponderance of Jews in the Church
at Rome. But clearly that conclusion is
by no means inevitable. It may be the
writer is using the phrase of an imagined
objector, or he may be for the moment
unusually conscious of his own Abrahamic
descent. In a general way we must remember that with St Paul 'we' is used for
four separate things. Sometimes it means
'my brother Jews and I'; sometimes 'my
brother Christians and I'; sometimes 'my
fellow workers and I'; and sometimes
simply 'I.' We have to be prepared for
its use in any of these ways at any
moment.

iv. 1. "What then shall we say of Abraham, our natural progenitor? [*Cannot he glory?*] Why, if Abraham 'found favour' by things done, he is in a position to boast. But he is not as towards God. For what does the Scripture say? *Abraham believed God and it was accounted to him for righteousness.*"

Gen. xv. 6 (LXX).

Here we have the familiar citation already employed in 'Galatians' (iii. 6). There it came in somewhat suddenly, and was not discussed with the fulness we shall find in the course of this chapter. At the end of *v.* 1 I insert the words that seem to be needed by the context. For it is very plainly a question whether he ἔχει καύχημα, or no. The ascription of an actual 'δικαίωσις' to the Patriarch is not in the earlier letter. There the δικαιοσύνη (of which the quotation speaks) is not so directly identified with the theological *status* as it is here.

The Patriarchal 'belief' in question is, as this chapter tells us, the belief in the promise of a son. The same ἐλογίσθη εἰς δικαιοσύνην is used, in Psalm cvi., of Phinehas, who "*stood up and executed judgment*." From that passage we should deduce, that the phrase, taken by itself, need by no means necessarily carry all the meaning assumed by St Paul. But, even should it be argued that too much is built upon the 'text' in Genesis; yet the undoubted fact remains, that implicit trust in God is the keynote of the Patriarch's story, as told in the primitive record.

We next pass on to consider what we may call the topic of 'merit' in relation to Abraham.

iv. 4. "For one that works, his wage is not reckoned of favour, but of obligation. But for one who does not 'work'; only believes on Him whose way it is to set right the ungodly—it is his faith [and nothing else] that is 'counted for righteousness'; even as the Psalmist pronounces the felicitation of the man whom God accounteth 'right,' apart from merit,

Psalm
xxxii. 1–2.

Blessed are they, whose iniquities have been forgiven and whose sins have been covered with a veil. Blessed is the man whose sin the Lord shall not count (against him)."

In this section there is compression, which tends to some obscurity, in a language as diffuse as our own. The whole train of thought is as follows :

When a man works, he is given his wage, as a debt and not as a favour ;

When there is no work, there is no wage ;

And this was Abraham's case :

He did not 'work' (in a theological sense—that is, he did not aim at achieving God's favour by 'doing'); he only 'believed' :

It was this belief that won for him his 'righteousness'—his *status*, as a man who is 'right with God.'

We are never told, in so many words, that Abraham had no 'merit,' and therefore no ground for 'boasting' as towards

God. That we are left to infer. Instead,
we are asked to note that he attained to a
' blissful' standing (and, of course, we must
remember that the word μακάριος connotes
an altogether exceptional happiness; 'it
is gods we count μακάριοι and the most
godlike among men,' says Aristotle)—in
fact that blissful state whereof the Psalm
makes mention. Moreover, as in the
quotation of iii. 20 ἐξ ἔργων νόμου was
introduced; so here the 'blessed one,' of
whom the Psalmist tells, is identified
with the person " in whose favour the
Lord reckons 'rightness'"—in itself a remarkable phrase, no doubt framed on
the analogy of the Psalmist's λογίζεσθαι
ἁμαρτίαν, though δικαιοσύνη describes a
condition or state, while ἁμαρτίαν probably
does not.

There are one or two points of language
to be noted in the five verses.

Χάρις, to begin with, is not technical.
God is called ὁ δικαιῶν τὸν ἀσεβῆ. This
(I apprehend) must be taken as a descrip-
tion of the Divine Nature; hence the

present participle. 'The godless' one would have expected to be plural rather than singular. Λογίζεται, as a passive, strikes the reader of the classics as startling. However it is good 'Biblical.' In *v.* 6 we gather that 'δικαιοσύνη' is negative rather than positive : it represents the removal of 'sin,' not the presence of active goodness. As I have urged already, it is the condition of the man accepted by God.

'David' has spoken of a man who is μακάριος for just this reason. Such a man (St Paul argues) was Abraham. He was δίκαιος, he had δικαιοσύνη, in that particular sense.

We pass on to a further question. Granted he was so 'blessed,' in what condition did he attain to it? The question is put because it effectually disposes of the Judaistic contention that circumcision is indispensable. That is to say, the answer does.

> iv. 9. "This felicitation then does it fall on the circumcised, or on the uncircumcised? We say (you know)

his faith '*was reckoned*' to Abraham '*for righteousness.*'......"

In this verse the word μακαρισμός may conceivably have shifted its sense. It is only found three times in St Paul, and the *data* are insufficient. Better therefore keep to the sense we are sure of.

iv. 10—12. "Under what conditions, then, was it reckoned? When Abraham was circumcised, or when he was uncircumcised? Not when he was circumcised, but while he was uncircumcised. Indeed he took circumcision as an outward symbol; as a seal of the 'faith-righteousness' which was in his uncircumcision; to the end that he might be a Father of all that believe in uncircumcision, so that they too might be counted 'righteous'; as well as a Father of the 'circumcised'—in the case of such as should be, not merely circumcised, but also walking in the steps of that uncircumcised 'faith' our Father Abraham had."

In his rendering of *v.* 11 Martin Luther
is disappointing. One would have hoped
he would be bold and speak of ' Glaubens-
gerechtigheit' in one colossal term, which
would adequately reproduce τῆς δικαιοσύνης τῆς πίστεως. Unhappily he fails us.
Δι᾽ ἀκροβυστίας, in the same verse, is a
formula of *circumstance.* . The readings of
v. 12 are sadly muddled in the MSS. But
plainly we cannot read (to oblige any MS.
or group of MSS.) such a jumble of words
as this ; τοῖς οὐκ ἐκ περιτομῆς μόνον ἀλλὰ
καὶ τοῖς στοιχοῦσι. The second τοῖς must
be eliminated, though the editors are apt
to retain it. For my part, I assume that
what the writer meant to say was τοῖς
οὐ μόνον ἐκ περιτομῆς οὖσιν ἀλλὰ καὶ
στοιχοῦσιν κ.τ.λ. That is, Abraham was
to be a Father of converted Jews (circumcised, converted Jews) *but only* on
condition of their having 'faith,' as he
had.

The general sequence of the thought in
the two verses is uncertain. But presumably it runs like this ;

When Abraham was 'accepted,' was
he circumcised, or uncircumcised ?
Why, surely, uncircumcised.
Circumcision was only a 'seal,' a
'token' assumed long after.
Because then he was uncircumcised,
when he attained to 'righteousness,'
He is fit to be the 'father' of all
uncircumcised 'believers';
(For, why should they not attain to
'righteousness' just as he did ?)
And, as for those others—the Jews,
the actually 'circumcised'—
He can be their 'father' too, provided
—always provided—they have
something more than circumcision
to go upon (for that is only
σημεῖον); to wit, the 'faith' he had
in his days of uncircumcision.

For the rest, the term σημεῖον, as
applied to 'circumcision,' is found in the
Old Testament. There it is ἐν σημείῳ Gen. xvii
διαθήκης. Σφραγίς (afterwards adopted [11.]
by Christians for Holy Baptism) was a
later descriptive term.

Next we take a wider sweep. The happy position of Abraham must be wholly separated from all conditions of Law, or of outward ordinances. So we move forward with this statement;

> iv. 13. " For ' Law ' did not bring the Promise to Abraham, or to his seed, that he should be ' heir of the world'; it came by faith-righteousness."

This rendering is not convincing. For in a general way, and especially in Abraham's story, promises precede faith, instead of following after. However, we cannot be sure to which promise the Apostle refers; the ' palmary ' promise was, clearly, the promise of the "Blessing." In Gen. xv. there are three; the Land, the Nation, the Blessing. But that was before the day of the promise which evoked the particular form of faith that *was counted for righteousness*. That comes in chap. xv., where the Lord tells Abraham his seed shall be *as the stars of heaven*. There are further promises in Gen. xviii. 18 and

Gen. xxii. 17.   But it seems to be a
departure from Pauline principles to describe any 'promise' at all *as won by faith.*
It is therefore I am half tempted to regard
both the διά's here as being 'circumstantial.'
That would alter the rendering wholly.
Then, one would have to express it like
this ;

> " For Law was not the accompani-
> ment of the promise to Abraham...its
> accompaniment was faith-righteous-
> ness."

But, on the other hand, the διά with
νόμου may be the ordinary διά, expressing instrumentality.   In that case the
second might be due to assimilation, or
attraction.   It is one of those many passages which the ordinary reader 'skims
over,' wholly failing to observe what
puzzles they contain.

The next three verses state what is
intelligible enough ;

> iv. 14—15.   " If the sons of 'Law'
> are heirs, faith is emptied of all
> meaning "—(or, " rendered valueless,"

cf. 1 Cor. i. 17)—"and the promise has ceased to exist."

"For 'Wrath' is the product of Law. And where there is no Law, there is no transgression either."

The original meaning of οἱ ἐκ νόμου is not perspicuous. It is like the phrase in 'Galatians,' οἱ ἐκ πίστεως. Ἐκ might imply 'descent,' metaphorical descent (though that is not the reason why I use 'sons' in my paraphrase). But it might only express dependence. Οἱ ἐκ νόμου are the folks who look to Law for everything.

In *v.* 15 we have before us a third statement about Law. The three obviously help to interpret one another.

Gal. iii. 19 declared of Law, τῶν παραβάσεων χάριν προσετέθη ; Rom. iii. 20, διὰ γὰρ νόμου ἐπίγνωσις ἁμαρτίας. Here we read, Law brings no blessing, but only fearful consequences—the 'wrath' of Eternal God. The same ideas recur in chaps. v. and vii. So Law is plainly dismissed, as a possible source of high good, and the text continues :

iv. 16, 17.   "This is why *the thing* comes of faith, that it may be a matter of 'favour'; so that the promise may stand fast for all the 'seed'—not only for the children of law, but also for the children of the faith of Abraham (for he is Father of all of us, as Holy Scripture says; *For a father of many nations have I appointed thee*) before the God he *believed*, that maketh the dead alive, and speaketh of things non-existent, as though they were." Gen. xvii. 5 (LXX).

We are not told what is ἐκ πίστεως; but there is little difficulty in filling up the gap.   It is not so much the 'promise,' as all that great destiny, which lies before God's People.   We may call it, if we will, the κληρονομία.   Ἵνα κατὰ χάριν excludes the possibility of something earned, the possibility of 'obligation' (ὀφείλημα), in the matter.   That is why I say "favour," not "grace."   In the next clause there would seem to be reference to some definite passage in Genesis, in which mention is made of *the seed*. But it is not easy to fix upon any. There are many repetitions of the promise *to thee and to thy seed*. We have it in xii. 7, xiii. 15, xv. 18, xvii. 8, xvii. 19, xxiv. 7—not to mention xxvi. 3, and xxxv. 12, where the promise made to Abraham is renewed to Isaac and Jacob. In all of these places but one, the 'promise' is of 'the land,' for an everlasting possession. For the writer, this is a figure, pointing to a spiritual inheritance. The 'seed' here is not as in Gal. iii. 16 (where it is identified with Christ), but as in Gal. iii. 29, where all the faithful are regarded as in very truth Abraham's sons.

In *v.* 17 the ὅτι belongs to the quotation, and should be translated accordingly. Καλοῦντος τὰ μὴ ὄντα ὡς ὄντα is a rather perplexing phrase. The καλεῖν is possibly like the familiar use in Plato, 'καλεῖς τι δικαιοσύνην.' Τὰ μὴ ὄντα glances at the unborn 'promise-child' Isaac, of whom the Almighty speaks, as if he already were.

And now St Paul unfolds the full

splendour of that 'faith,' which was
"*accounted for righteousness.*"

iv. 18—22. "Who, when hope
was hopeless, hopefully believed, so
that he became *a Father of many* Gen. xvii.
nations, as the saying stands, *So shall* ⁵·
thy seed be; and without weakening
in faith, contemplated his own manhood in its deadness (for he was already
some hundred years old), and the
deadness of Sarah's womb. Confronted with God's promise he did
not doubt nor disbelieve, but was
mighty in faith, giving glory to God
by being convinced, that, what He
has promised, He is able to perform.
Wherefore, *It was accounted to him* Gen. xv. 6.
for righteousness."

The ἐπ᾽ ἐλπίδι (in *v.* 18) I do not profess
to understand; but the whole phrase is
'literary,' and the effect is as in the
paraphrase. Εἰς with the infinitive is
'consecutive,' rather than 'final.' But this
is an unusually vigorous instance. It virtually equals ὥστε ἐγένετο. Μὴ ἀσθενήσας

in classical Greek would be οὐκ ἀσθενήσας. The use of the former negative is normal in later Greek.   Indeed it must be remembered that it is οὐ, which is the intruder, and not μή (I mean in classical usage).   The signification of κατενόησεν (which is not 'notice' but 'contemplate'), as well as the story of Genesis, requires the extrusion of the οὐ before κατενόησεν. The whole point of the story is, that he did realise his 'deadness.'   Whether ἤδη is read or no makes no sort of difference. The two πίστει's (in *vv.* 19 and 20) are both 'datives of respect.'   On the other hand, τῇ ἀπιστίᾳ is 'comitative' (lit. "with unbelief"..."he did not doubt with unbelief"). Ἐνεδυναμώθη is deponent.   We need not go about to conceive of an outside influence (as in Phil. iv. 13).

'Glory' is 'given to God,' when the truth is told, as in the story of Achan, or in St John ix. 24; here however it is somewhat different.   Abraham 'gives God glory' by not doubting of His power. I assume that the καί, which couples πληροφορηθείς to δοὺς δόξαν, is a καί of identity.

Thus, having dwelt upon the details of Abraham's faith, in its most conspicuous manifestation, we turn to our own case, and see that, in effect, we also are called upon to believe in God's quickening power. Where we must 'give glory to God'—and in fact where we do give it—is in accepting unhesitatingly the crowning miracle (cf. x. 8). We too must not 'weaken' in faith; we must be 'mighty,' as our father was.

iv. 23—25. "Not for him only was it written, that it was reckoned to him for righteousness; but for our sakes too (it was written) to whom righteousness will be reckoned—because we are they who believe on Him, who raised our Lord Jesus from the dead; who *was delivered up*, Isai.liii.12. *because of* our sins, and was raised...."

The object of the scriptural record is plainly to strengthen faith. The contemplation of what it achieved for Abraham

long since, will plainly minister to us
that "encouragement of the scriptures," of
which we are told in xv. 4. Perhaps I
am mistaken, but I do not like omitting
'righteousness' in *vv.* 23 and 24. Greek is
a more elliptical language by a good deal
than English is. Therefore I have inserted
the word in either verse. The παρεδόθη
of *v.* 25 is an indubitable reference to the
closing words of Isaiah's majestic chapter,
καὶ διὰ τὰς ἀνομίας αὐτῶν παρεδόθη. If one
asks, whereto was He given up—the Innocent Sufferer, the Servant of the Highest
—the answer is simply *to death.* The prophet expressly says so. Who it was gave
Him up, is another matter. But we see
behind the event the Will of the Eternal.
The διὰ τὰ παραπτώματα tells us why He
was given up. It was in a word, because
we—we men—had sinned, with sins innumerable. What are we to say about
ἠγέρθη διὰ τὴν δικαίωσιν? Ah! what?
We know the Apostle's teaching about sin
and Christ's resurrection. From 1 Cor. xv.
we learn that, "if Christ be not raised, we

are yet in our sins." Ergo, if He is raised,
we are not in our sins. We are at peace
with God, we are 'i' the right' with God—
in one word, "we are justified." Now our
cautious English says, " Who was delivered
up for our trespasses, and raised for our
justification." And the wary English reader
can easily discern the meaning of the earlier
clause. But what does he make of the
other? If it means anything at all, it
must mean Christ was raised up to achieve
our justification. The writer of the ' Hebrews,' no doubt, pursuing the figure of
the ritual of the great Day of Atonement,
does make the ' sprinkling of the blood '
(technically the προσφορά) the crucial
point in our High Priest's great act,
thereby shifting the centre of gravity, from
the place of the Victim's death on Earth,
to the Eternal Tabernacle. But that
particular figure is not the one pursued
by our Apostle. And indeed we must
remember that Christ fulfils many types;
and it will not do to build any 'one and only'
theory of the manner of His propitiation

All we know is what He Himself tells us ; to wit, that His blood was shed " for the remission of sins " ; and what St Paul says here, "*He was delivered up because of our sins.*" To resume what I was saying a line or two above ; with St Paul our 'justification,' our 'setting at one' with God, was achieved by the Death of Christ. That is the way he contemplates it. In consequence, discarding our familiar ambiguity ("was raised for our justification "), I will make bold to suggest an alternative : "and was raised *because of our justification*" —the which I assume to mean that the Resurrection of Christ is the seal of our justification, already achieved by His death. He *said*, He died for our sins. Now we know it ; *because He is Risen.*

For choice I would wish to render ;

"Who was delivered up because we had sinned, was raised *because we are justified.*"

S. observes that the action of διά is primarily 'retrospective.' Then why not make it so ? 'Our sins,' which went before, were the *origin* of His death. All this degree of causation we cannot apply to our justification : for anyhow God's Holy One could not be holden of death. Yet some degree of causation we may leave. However that is not the most decisive reason for considering the preposition even here to be retrospective. The whole trend of Pauline teaching demands we should.

§ 9.   THE POSITION OF THE JUSTIFIED

All chap. v. (it must be admitted) is highly difficult. Any reader can pick out of it sublime ideas and inspiring 'texts,' but the connexion of the whole is exceptionally baffling. The first two verses indeed are transparent enough : but immediately after them perplexing questions arise and before we have reached *v.* 11 (beyond which, in this paragraph, I do not propose to go) one wishes with all one's heart that, either one could be certain the text is unimpaired, or else there were opportunity for asking one who knew from outside evidence, how thought follows after thought.

Consider first the five opening verses. What about the leading verb? Is it ἔχομεν (with A.V. and the American Revisers) or ἔχωμεν (with R.V. and the huge preponderance of MS. authority)? Take we comfort in the thought that copyists were highly prone to confuse the long 'o' and the short: so that after all MSS. in such a case need not count for everything. And further let us ask ourselves whether "Let us have peace" is more likely than "We have peace" in this context. For me, I should opine, that if one has not peace, it is a futile thing to cry 'Go to! let us have it.' Ἔχομεν be it then.

v. 1—6. "Being then set right with God thanks to faith, we are at peace with Him, through our Lord Jesus Christ; through whom we have also gotten our access to that favoured position in which we stand. And we exult in the hope of God's glory.

Yes, and we also exult in our tribulations, being sure that affliction en-
genders fortitude, and fortitude proved
valour, and proved valour hope, and
hope brings not to shame."

" All because the Love of God is
shed forth in our hearts by reason of
the Holy Spirit, that has been given
us ; for while we were still weak,
Christ, when the day arrived, died for
ungodly men."

In *vv.* 1, 2, 3 the American revisers
eliminate all imperatives. If any is to
stand, it would be the second καυχώμεθα.
Yet the atmosphere of the passage seems
to call for the present there, as well as in
the other two verbs. The thought of the
προσαγωγή is a link between this Epistle
and 'Ephesians.' There it is mentioned
twice, here only once. The χάρις, to which
we have access, is necessarily a 'state':
from 'Galatians' we remember wrong
faith can extrude us from it (Gal. v. 4).
The ἐπ' ἐλπίδι (of *v.* 2) gives the ground of
the 'exultation.' We cannot say 'glory'

here because of the following δόξης. The nature of the 'hope' is not very clearly defined. God's 'glory' suggests the Shekinah. On the other hand, it may be not the 'glory' which is God's, but the 'glory' He means for us—shall we say, the lost image?

The great passage about 'glory,' in 2 Cor. iii. (see especially *v.* 18), was penned before our Epistle: but I doubt if that can help us. The truth is, we cannot possibly know what our 'Hope' does comprehend. And there we must leave it.

The paradoxical 'exultation' in 'tribulations' is of a parenthetic character. Adversity has its uses. Courage, in its lower, and its more developed form (δοκιμή), is the natural fruit of it. And perfect courage strengthens ἐλπίς. The οὐ καταισχύνει here is thought to be derived from Psalm xxii. (ἤλπισαν καὶ οὐ κατῃσχύνθησαν). How the ὅτι, which follows next, and the clause which it introduces connect with the preceding matter, it were hard to say. But we can see that the Divine Law must

minister to that joyful attitude of mind, of
which the Apostle is speaking. Nor again,
are we quite at our ease in estimating the
relation of *v.* 6 to the rest of the context.
One would be rather tempted to treat as
one parenthesis all the words from οὐ μόνον
δέ as far as καταισχύνει ; and place them in
a bracket as wholly subsidiary. Then the
death of Christ would be brought into
intelligible relation with the hope of the
Glory of God.

And not only is there much difficulty
in unravelling the thought. The reading
in *v.* 6 presents a further obstacle. Εἴ γε,
εἰ γάρ, ἔτι γάρ, εἰς τί γάρ, ἵνα τί γάρ, are
all offered ; and of these it is shrewdly
supposed that εἴ γε presents most likelihood of being original. But what are we
to make of it? is the 'love of God in our
hearts' (that is, the sense of God's great
Love) emphasised by this clause with εἴ γε?
And do we not rather need εἴπερ?

I confess I cannot manage to marshal
the sequence of thought in a satisfactory
chain. All I can say is this. Clearly there

is an '*a fortiori*' contained in the ὑπὲρ ἀσεβῶν. That we should naturally link with the thought of the 'hope.' Our hope of some great good thing is obviously much strengthened by the thought of what 'Love Divine' has achieved for us already.

Let me add, that I should insert a full stop after τοῦ δοθέντος ἡμῖν, read ἔτι γάρ for εἴ γε, and cut out the second ἔτι altogether. This implies a certain lack of confidence in the MSS. But I think the phenomena will justify such an emendatory diffidence. The truth is, manuscripts have yielded up their store : now the critic's art begins—or should begin.

From all this perplexity we turn, with something of relief, to what the Apostle says of the grandeur of Christ's Love.

v. 7—11. "Why! scarcely for a righteous man is any prepared to die. I say, for your good man (maybe) a man might nerve himself to die."

"But God establishes His own love in this that, while we were yet sinners, Christ died on our behalf. Much more then, having been accepted now through His blood, shall we be rescued by His means from the wrath of God."

" If, when we were enemies, we were reconciled to God by the death of His Son, much more, having been reconciled, shall we be saved by His Life...."

"And not only so, but we exult also at (the thought of) God, through our Lord Jesus Christ ; by whom we have now gotten our reconciliation."

In chap. v. so far we have had three grounds of joyfulness or 'exultation' mentioned. The 'hope of glory,' tribulations, and lastly the thought of God. The relation of ἐν Θεῷ to διὰ τοῦ κυρίου ἡμῶν (in *v.* 11) I apprehend to be this. Man could not speak of 'glorying' in God at all, were it not for the new relation established in Jesus Christ. In other words, the relative clause (δι' οὗ ἐλάβομεν) at the verse's end explains what the writer means by " rejoicing in God *through* Jesus Christ." In *vv.* 7 and 8 one is tempted to suspect a dittographia. I do not think any distinction between δίκαιον and ἀγαθόν will help us. The same thing is said twice over; and one wonders if two separate readings can possibly have been combined. There is, to be sure, another element of repetition in the passage; for the statement of *v*. 6 is restated in *v*. 8. But that restatement is fuller.

In *v*. 9 the σωθησόμεθα (as being coupled with ἀπὸ τῆς ὀργῆς) bears the narrower sense of 'rescue': the other lower down must be taken in a larger meaning. At least, so I should say. That σωθησόμεθα appears to me to look forward to the final redemption. The 'dying' Christ brought the first one; the eternally 'living' Christ will bring about the other. The 'saving' from the wrath, in a sense, *is yet to be*; so is this other. They have neither to do with the 'now.'

The third ground of 'glorying'—introduced by a participle, not an unusual phenomenon in the Pauline style—is, as it were, an afterthought.

§ 10. THE παράπτωμα OF ADAM AND
THE δικαίωμα OF CHRIST

And now comes a wonderful passage,
very full indeed of difficulty, linguistic and
other, but also richly full of suggestive
thought. It is true that, for the writer,
Adam was a veritable person ; whereas,
for many moderns, he is not. We all know,
know only too well, our dismal liability to
fall into acts that shame us. Some modern
thinkers tell us, that these tendencies do
not matter ; that they are mere survivals ;
that by slow yet sure degrees they will be
eliminated, and so the race will attain to a
state of moral perfection. But Christians,
for 'reasons and reasons,' are unprepared
to accept this latterday message of comfort.
Instead they are very sure that things are
somehow wrong, and that it is not to racial
evolution we must direct our gaze to save
us, but to moral regeneration, acting upon
the individual. Therefore, even if we
do not accept an historic 'Adam,' yet we

know what the name 'Adam' means for us. His story typifies the mystery of sin —of wedded sin and death. It will be said, if we give up 'Adam,' as an historical personage, we make the section meaningless. But that we cannot help. Anyhow we can study it as it came from the Apostle. The attempt to master his meaning is prodigiously worth the effort.

Let us paraphrase some verses and pass to their interpretation.

v. 12—14. "And so, as through one *Man* Sin entered into the world, and Death through Sin—and so death made its way to all mankind, because that all have sinned...sin, mark you, was in the world before Law came, though sin is not laid to men's charge where Law exists not; notwithstanding Death did reign from Adam until Moses even over those that had not sinned precisely as Adam did—Adam, who is the type of Him that was to come."

The connexion of the διὰ τοῦτο is of

the very vaguest. I have therefore employed the formula which seemed to me
to reproduce such vagueness most naturally.
Ἀνθρώπου, I should say, might be spelt
with a capital : to one versed in Hebrew
speech it recalled the idea of Adam, as
'man' cannot do for us. Sin and Death
(as S. observes) are both personified. We
are moving in the realms of 'myth'—the
acknowledged vehicle of religious truth, as
the Greek sage taught long since. 'Death'
is to be taken as physical death. For that
is linked with sin, in some mysterious way,
in the teachings of O.T.; and so St Paul
conceives of it. The διά (in διῆλθεν) means
'all about,' 'in every direction.' The 'sin'
spoken of in ἥμαρτον may be mystical, or
literal. It may be part and lot in Adam's
transgression or it may be individual erring;
in the latter case, not uninfluenced by
hereditary taint; for Adam's sin is plainly
regarded as worldwide in its effect. This
latter explanation is the likelier. There is
an undeveloped antithesis latent in the first
two lines. We can follow its general trend

without any difficulty : 'as one man's sin brought death, *so one man's holiness brought life for all.*' It disappears because the writer suddenly realises the importance for his argument of the worldwide pheno-menon of death. Death and sin go together : the fact that all men die, is a *proof* that all men sin—though truly responsibility is not perfectly developed until the coming of Law. Ἐλλογᾶσθαι must be distinguished from the more general λογίζεσθαι. It is a definite bookkeeping metaphor. There-fore 'imputed' is perfectly fair (if one knows what 'imputed' means). St Paul in 'Phi-lemon' says τοῦτο ἐμοὶ ἐλλόγα "please put that down to me." Ἄχρι νόμου is an odd expression; but it can only have the meaning I have assigned to it.

The sin of Adam, *ex hypothesi*, was not a sin of innocence; it was a sin of knowledge, an act of flat disobedience. That is what is meant by speaking of folks "who had not sinned exactly as he did." The last clause of *v.* 14 is, as we should say, 'dragged in.' It is owing to the Pauline habit

of constantly letting the thought outrun
the pen. For the idea is not wanted
here.

       v. 15. " But not comparable to
the transgression is the gracious gift
of God. For if by the sin of the one
the many died, much more has the
grace of God and the free gift, that
came by grace—the grace of the one
man Jesus Christ—abounded unto the
many."

We shall see directly what is meant by
the opening statement in this great verse.
The Apostolic writer is grappling with a
question which many a man must have
asked (at least one would so suppose) in
Rabbinical schools. That is, how does it
comport with the infinite justice of God,
that one man's error should have effects so
wide in extent, as to involve the whole
race in death? It is indeed a natural
question. St Paul answers it by bidding
us note that the righteousness of Christ (I
am not speaking in accurate terms) was
infinitely more far reaching for good than

Adam's transgression was for evil. That
every man's death is due to the influence
of the latter, in ways we cannot apprehend,
was plainly part of his creed. In this he
was a man of his age. The belief, no
doubt, troubled him (or, at least, had
troubled him, in his pre-Christian days) as it
troubled others, his countrymen. But now
he sees light on the difficulty and hastens
to set it before us. "The many" (that is,
the world at large) do die, because they
have sinned. One sin will involve them
in death, any sin at all; for death is the
inevitable concomitant of sin. But, contemplate on the other hand Christ and what
He has achieved. God's 'grace'—His
free undeserved love—is pitted against
'Adam's' sinfulness. This goodness, this
royal bounty (δωρεά is more than mere
'gift'), operating in the sacred person of
the one man Jesus Christ (for the 'grace'
in a sense is His, as well as the Father's),
has likewise affected 'the many,' but in a
vastly higher degree—as we shall proceed
to understand.

The next phrase needs much of expansion; I will venture to supply it. The lines on which expansion must proceed are laid down in the latter half of the verse.

v. 16. "Moreover *the transgression was* with one man sinning once. Not so was the glorious gift. For judgment proceeded from one sin, and ended in condemnation; but the free gift came after many sins, and ended in full acquittal."

Here, as δικαίωμα balances κατάκριμα, it should bear a 'forensic' sense. The full text I postulate, would run as follows,

καὶ οὐχ ὡς δι' ἑνὸς ἁμαρτήσαντος ἦν τὸ παράπτωμα, οὕτω δι' ἑνὸς ἁμαρτήσαντος ἦν τὸ δώρημα.

Also, I assume that δι' ἑνὸς ἁμαρτήσαντος is a 'circumstantial' expression. Διά must not be rendered 'by' or 'through,' but merely 'with.' One sin once sinned brought judgment upon all—and judgment of the most serious; nothing short of κατάκριμα. When the reign of Grace arrived, *sins were infinitely multiplied,* yet Grace notwithstanding availed for worldwide 'acquittal.' With ἐξ ἑνός we must of course supply παραπτώματος, from the following παραπτωμάτων. With regard to the term itself, Thayer very justly remarks, that it differs from ἁμάρτημα 'not in force, but only in metaphor.'

> v. 17. "For, if through the sin of the one Death reigned, by means of the one, much more they who receive the abundance of the grace—that is, the gift of 'righteousness'—shall reign in life through the one, through Jesus Christ."

This, I think, will speak for itself. It is surely amply plain. The καί before τῆς δωρεᾶς is a καί of identity. The 'royal gift of *righteousness*,' in the technical, theological sense, constitutes the χάρις. There is but one thing more to remark before passing from the verse. It is this. Death has reigned in 'the many'; we should anticipate that St Paul would declare, by way of antithesis, that Life will reign in those who are described as οἱ λαμβάνοντες

—a term, be it remarked, susceptible of two meanings : it may be either, "those who take," or, "those who are given" : for everyone is aware that λαμβάνειν and δι-δόναι are regular correlatives. But he does not. It is his way to vary his antitheses, and here there is special reason. The idea of the believer 'reigning' with Christ was a favourite one with St Paul. To reign ἐν ζωῇ, again, might signify more things than one. I incline to the belief it means in this place, 'reign and live.' The διὰ τοῦ ἑνός appears in either clause. There is no 'man' in either member ; in the second in this verse it would not have been desirable, in connexion with the Glorified Jesus.

We may now push on to the end of this deeply interesting chapter.

v. 18. "So then, as with a single act of sin all mankind were affected, to the extent of condemnation ; so also with one *righteous deed* a life-giving acquittal extended to all the race."

Here, once again, I would take the διά as 'circumstantial,' though I conceive it is less necessary so to do than in *v.* 16 above. Ἑνός is probably neuter. One cannot imagine διὰ ἑνὸς παραπτώματος meaning "thanks to a sin of one." The elliptical form of the sentence is highly singular. But the gaps are easily filled. Only I doubt if it be wise to fill them with terms as definite as 'judgment' and 'free gift' (with our English versions). However Luther does the same. The imperturbable Vulgate passes grandly on its way with a literalness that makes the Pauline sentence more bald than ever. What is anyone to make of such a verse as this;

Igitur sicut per unius delictum *in omnes homines in condemnationem*; sic et per unius justitiam *in omnes homines in justificationem vitae* ?

Could one wish for a more convincing proof of the sacredness that attached to the letter of the New Testament from very early days?

The sense in which δικαίωμα is used in

the verse is unexampled. Yet our Revisers
adopted it, and I think with justification.
The truth is, we must have a concrete
term to balance παραπτώματος. What
the δικαίωμα may be is another question.
The next verse leads us to see in it that
'obedience' of the Only-begotten, which
stands out in absolute contrast to the disobedience of 'the man.' One thinks of
the famous quotation in 'Hebrews' from
Psalm xl.,

> "*Then said I, Lo I am come...for
> to achieve, O God, Thy will.*"

But that is not a Pauline quotation.
Some justification perhaps for this bold
use of δικαίωμα may be found in the well-
known term employed by the Stoical School
to describe a perfect act. That term is
κατόρθωμα. We need not 'righteousness,'
but a 'piece of righteousness'; seeing that
in the former member we have not 'sinfulness' but a single 'sin.' Besides, in 'Revelation,' which I had for the moment
wholly forgotten, the word is found in the
plural for the " righteous acts" of the

saints (Rev. xix. 8). Aristotle apparently
draws a distinction between δικαίωμα and
the word δικαιοπράγημα. But I doubt if
that throws any light on the passage before
us. Δικαίωμα, he says, is ἐπανόρθωμα ἀδική-
ματος. This definition, one suspects, is
due to the sage's belief as to the meaning
of δικαιοῦν. He takes it as meaning a
'setting right.'

The astonishing freedom wherewith
the Apostolic writer handles vocabulary
is shown by his employing δικαίωσις here,
whereas in *v.* 16 above he said δικαίωμα.
Moreover the employment, in the course
of a single verse, of δικαίωμα and δικαίωσις
in wholly different senses is ἀνδρείας οὐ
τῆς τυχούσης.

Perhaps one ought to say that the
Vulgate version is evidence for an early
belief amongst Christians that the ἑνός in
either case in this verse is *masculine.*
Here is precisely one of those points which
latterday translators will have to consider.
The tradition of early versions is a thing
which has to be weighed. *Per unum*

delictum (plainly) is what we should have anticipated, seeing the general tendency exhibited in the Latin.

> v. 19. " For as through the disobedience of the one man the many were constituted sinners; so also by the obedience of the one the many shall be constituted 'righteous'."

In classical Greek παρακοή means 'mishearing.' Here and in Heb. ii. 2 (where it is coupled with παράβασις) and 2 Cor. x. 6 it is used for 'disobedience.' The verb in the Greek O.T. means to 'disregard,' as in Is. lxv. 12. It belongs to the later books only. Heb. v. 8 gives us an instance of ὑπακοή applied to Christ. In 'Philippians' St Paul himself subsequently spoke of Him as "obedient unto death." The use of καθίστασθαι in the section is well illustrated from St James' Epistle. Jas. iv. 4 is an excellent instance. Δίκαιος, it will be noticed, means here the opposite of 'sinner'—*a person who is not a sinner*, nothing more. It is not 'righteous' positively, but only negatively, i.e. destitute of guilt. That is why I place the word in inverted commas.

v. 20, 21. "Law entered in by the way, that the transgression might multiply. But where sin multiplied, Grace altogether surpassed (it). That, as sin had reigned and men died, so Grace might reign by 'righteousness,' and the end be life eternal, through Jesus Christ Our Lord."

St Paul's position with regard to Law we partly know already. Law is in no sense σωτήριος. It came in at a late date in the economy of God. Its purpose and aim we trace as the definition of sin. Here the παρεισῆλθεν emphasises its 'episodic' character. The verb is not so invidious as it is in Gal. ii. 4. Τὸ παράπτωμα must, I think—that is, if any regard is to be paid to its form at all—be taken in a concrete sense, as pointing to the primal sin, the sin of Adam. We are not grammatically permitted to view it otherwise. In the very next clause we pass from the concrete to the abstract. Ἁμαρτία is 'Sin,' with a capital 'S.' Ὑπερεπερίσσευσεν here must mean "abounded *more*."

In *v.* 14 above, it was 'Death' that reigned. In this verse it is 'Sin'; but the two are so close a pair, that the one's reign is the other's. "In death" should not be taken by any means as 'local.' It might, perhaps, express union; but it probably is just 'instrumental.' Δικαιοσύνη (in *v.* 21) is the antithesis of ἁμαρτία. That means 'sinfulness,' δικαιοσύνη means simply the opposite state—the state of folks not 'sinners.'

"So Grace might reign through righteousness, and the issue be life eternal" is not an easy clause. The *status* expressed by δικαιοσύνη corresponds in the spiritual sphere to death in the physical. Yet not altogether. For, in the Pauline thought, there are, so to speak, two 'lives,' corresponding to two 'redemptions.' The first redemption brings 'life,' as opposed to the 'deadness' of sin. So a man becomes καινή κτίσις. But it is the second 'redemption' (the ἀπολύτρωσις yet to be) which leads on to "life eternal."

In the comparison here there are two terms in the one member and three in the other.

There is 'Sin' and its issue 'death'; set against these there is 'Grace,' which operates through 'righteousness' (the abolition of sin) and so finally leads on to ζωὴ αἰώνιος. But how are we to marshal this two, and this three? If Χάρις, Δικαιοσύνη, Ζωή are A², B², C², is Ἁμαρτία to be A¹ and Θάνατος B¹, or should they be B¹ and C¹? That is to say, is θάνατος opposed to ζωὴ αἰώνιος? or is it to be taken as expressive of that condition of moral death, in which all 'sinners' lie? Take it as you will, it is certain that θάνατος is not here so decisively physical, as it was in *v.* 14. From that we cannot get away.

There are yet two more things to say. The one is that he must be indeed a stickler for grammar on the lines of classical Greek, who sees in these two ἵνα's a 'final' force. St Paul cannot have meant that Law came with the purpose of multiplying transgression. He is stating not an

intention, but a result. A result inevitable,
if you will—as inevitable indeed as the
result of the Incarnation in dividing the
sons of men—but still only a bye product.
Law came to make clear to men what was
right and what was wrong. By the way
—only by the way—it tended to heighten
guilt, and so intensify ' sin ' (not but that
the sense of πλεονάσῃ is actually literal).

The second of the ἵνα's is even further
removed from the region of the purely *telic*.
It introduces a remoter consequence. We
are not required, I think, to imagine the
Deity as having this double purpose in
His thought when the Law was given to
man. We are only to regard it as an
edifying exposition of the results directly
flowing from the function Law discharged.
Guilt was multiplied on the one hand; and
on the other hand the rich harvest of God's
Grace was enhanced beyond all measure.
Man's necessity (as the old proverb has it)
is God's opportunity. Homely though the
proverb is, there lies in it real truth.

And again we must note in passing

the doxological force of the mention of Jesus Christ in the closing words of the chapter. St Paul himself was not one to forget, or let others forget, the personal obligation. I remember an old saint said (a Bishop of our Church, not long since gone to his rest) that he could not away with a sermon, in which there was no mention of the holy Name of Jesus.

So was it with the great Apostle. The Lord Christ was first in his thoughts, and also first on his lips. Symmetry or no symmetry—and the pupil of Gamaliel never troubled himself to excess about literary artifice—he could not end this section without one grateful word to His honour, who has done it all. Διά—yes, διὰ Ἰησοῦ Χριστοῦ it comes. That is the Pauline 'Gospel,' the only Gospel that counts.

Already we have had at the end of *v.* 11 a similar recognition welling up spontaneously from an ever-grateful heart.

§ 11. Δικαιοσύνη IN RELATION TO THE
LIFE OF ACTUAL HOLINESS

"Life-giving acquittal" (*v.* 18), we have
seen, is the prime fruit of our Redemption.
The believer is δίκαιος; he is 'right with
God.' He has attained through the grace
of God and the work of Jesus Christ to an
entirely new relation. At this point there
must needs crop up the problem of anti-
nomianism.

That problem is faced forthwith. Let
us hear the Apostle explain why 'believers
in Jesus Christ,' who technically are not
'sinners,' may not be 'sinners' *in fact*.

Τί οὖν ἐροῦμεν (with which we start) is
a mere formula of transition.

vi. 1—4. "And what shall we
say (about this)? Are we to stay on
in sin, that Grace may have more
scope?"

"Out upon the horrid thought!
People who have died to sin...how
shall we any longer live in it? Can
it be you do not know, that all of us

who have been baptised into Jesus
Christ, were baptised into His death?
By baptism into His death we shared
His burial. That, just as Christ was
raised from the dead by the Glory of
the Father, so we too should make
our walk in a life completely new."

The transition is abrupt but (as I
suggested above) the question inevitable.
If "righteous" meant 'righteous in fact,'
it could hardly arise at all. It is just
because it does not, that we have to put
the question. Before we were 'justified,'
we were in 'sin'; now that we are 'justified,' are we to "stay on" (Phil. i. 24 will
illustrate this meaning) in sin "that Grace
may multiply"? Up till now we have
never heard of 'grace' as 'multiplying.'

That was what Sin did, not Grace, in
chap. v. Yet we can easily understand
why πλεονάζειν is used here. Grace
περισσεύει *per se*; it ὑπερπερισσεύει, contrasted with multiplied transgression. It
is not that it becomes more rich—
for it is supremely rich anyhow: it only

gains more scope (or, at least, might be so regarded, on this very impious hypothesis).

Something has been said already on this topic in chap. iii. 8.

The first answer the Apostle makes is that the thing is inconceivable. In his phrase we have " died to sin "; just as in Gal. ii. 19 he spoke of having " died to Law."

This is a figurative way of saying that, so far as sin is concerned, we are no longer existent. It has nothing to do with us, nor we with it. That being so, that we should ' continue' in sin is flatly impossible.

This conception of ' death to sin' is worked out upon new lines.

Our ' death to sin' is associated with our mystical union with Christ.

The pathway to this union is the rite of Baptism. The ϵἰς Χριστόν (to be distinguished very carefully from the ϵἰς in ϵἰς τὸ ὄνομα) must be taken as implying the idea of incorporation.

The expression ἐβαπτίσθημεν εἰς τὸν

θάνατον is difficult, all will allow. The
whole point of Baptism is to denote that
we have a share in the death of Christ;
that is to say, in the merit of it. But this
is hardly what the Apostle is saying here.
The conception of 'burial,' and of 'resurrection to new life,' is of course familiar
enough, in connexion with the sacrament;
and while in warmer climes the practice
of immersion obtained, the symbolism was
speaking. The difficulty of attaining to
any clear conception of the meaning of our
passage lies in the fact that Christ's own
death and Christ's own resurrection were
actual, historical: while the 'death' and
'resurrection,' wherein we partake by
baptism, are ideal, mystical. If it had
been "were baptised into death," we should
have felt no perplexity. For if Baptism
implies new 'life,' it must imply 'death' as
well. It is the αὐτοῦ which contains the
whole of the difficulty. And we cannot
comfort ourselves with the thought that it
only means " were baptised into a share in
what His death achieved "; for that would

not be 'on all fours' with the purely
mystical burial and mystical resurrection
whereof we go on to speak.

We must leave it, then, uncomprehended;
or only dimly grasped. As for *v.* 4, the
εἰς τὸν θάνατον must be taken as depending
on the διὰ τοῦ βαπτίσματος. The idea of
the Christian's death and the Christian's
resurrection, mystically shared with Christ
in Holy Baptism, recurs in Colossians ii.

It is only in this passage that the
resurrection of Christ is said to be the
work of the 'Glory of the Father.' We
should notice, as I hold, the tense of περι-
πατήσωμεν.

In the section that follows next, we are
conscious of the interweaving of two
mystical deaths, for us, and also of two
resurrections. It makes the thought hard
to trace; but that cannot be helped. Let
us do what we may with it.

Verse 5 is so very puzzling that before
I attempt a rendering I should like to
discuss it a little. To start with, σύμφυτος
is only here in N.T.; and that makes it

difficult to be certain as to its meaning. It
ought to mean 'born with,' or else 'akin
to' (to judge by classical usage) ; but there
is large probability that the notion of
'birth' has receded, as ideas often do in
compounds, and that the notion of 'union'
or 'oneness' is really prominent.   The
Vulgate renders the term by '*complantati*.'
*Si enim complantati facti sumus similitu-
dini mortis ejus* is the very curious version
it presents.   This '*complantati*' has made
its way into our English.   "For if we
have been *planted together* in the likeness
of his death..." is what 1611 says.   Tyndale however used 'graft,' instead of 'plant.'
But all our renderings are almost as obscure
as the venerable Latin.   Contemplate the
Vulgate's dative '*similitudini*'! Whatever
can it mean? and what can be its construction ?

If σύμφυτος means 'one with,' as seems
not improbable, it must be wholly out
of the question to couple it directly with
τῷ ὁμοιώματι τοῦ θανάτου αὐτοῦ. One
cannot be 'one with a likeness of death,'

even if one paraphrases the 'death likeness,'
so as to make it in itself convey some
significance. It remains, apparently, that
ὁμοιώματι should be either a dative of
manner or a dative of respect. That is,
we must render it either ' by the likeness '
or ' in the likeness.'

Suppose we put it thus :

vi. 5—7. " For if we have become ' one with Him,' *by a death that
is like His death*, then so shall we
also be, by a resurrection like His
resurrection. For this we can apprehend, that our ' old self ' shared
His crucifixion, to the end that the
sinful body might wholly be made
away with ; that so we might no
longer be thralls of Sin. For a man
that has once died has paid his penalty
—Sin has no more claim on him."

This paraphrase conveys what I *think*
to be St Paul's meaning. I dare not even
say ' what I believe.' For truly a man
must be exceptionally self-confident to be
sure about the matter.

With regard to ὁμοίωμα, it might be worth while observing that in N.T. Greek it seemingly represents what we may call a *substantial likeness*. I mean it is no faint shadow, but a something which is really 'like.' What 'death' it is that is meant, one can only guess. Is the ὁμοίωμα a reference to the 'symbolical' death of Baptism—the act, that is, of immersion? Or is it to the mystery of our union with Christ on the cross (St Paul's familiar conception, as in συνεσταυρώθη below)? Moreover, must we carry on the idea of ὁμοίωμα to the Resurrection too? Or is it, as it were, a sort of 'zeugma'? and are we to suppose that the genitive ἀναστάσεως depends upon some idea of 'partnership,' conceivably latent in σύμφυτοι? For this last there is much to be said. It would give a good sense:

"For if we have been one with Him in a death that is like His death, so shall we also be 'partners' in His resurrection."

Yet again (to return once more to the

thought of the ὁμοίωμα) could such a term as ὁμοίωμα, by any chance, apply to the mystical association of the believer in Christ's crucifixion? It hardly seems possible.

We cannot (do what we will) avoid some sense of perplexity; for, as I said just now, there are two 'deaths,' the death of the Font, and the mystical 'con-crucifixion' (if I may coin a word); and also two 'resurrections,' the rising to new life now, and the rising to new life hereafter; all four of them present together before the Apostle's thought. And it is very hard indeed to disentangle them.

Verse 5, accordingly, I must leave unsettled: I do not know whether the words should be expanded thus:

εἰ γὰρ σύμφυτοι γεγόναμεν τῷ Χριστῷ, τῷ ὁμοιώματι τοῦ θανάτου αὐτοῦ· ἀλλὰ καὶ σύμφυτοι αὐτῷ ἐσόμεθα, τῷ ὁμοιώματι τῆς ἀναστάσεως αὐτοῦ...

or whether it should be thus:

εἰ γὰρ σύμφυτοι γεγόναμεν τῷ

Χριστῷ, τῷ ὁμοιώματι τοῦ θανάτου
αὐτοῦ· ἀλλὰ καὶ (κοινωνοὶ αὐτῷ) ἐσόμεθα τῆς ἀναστάσεως αὐτοῦ...

where the words in brackets are to be
regarded as derived from σύμφυτοι. Only,
one thing I cannot believe—I cannot believe
that St Paul could talk of us as being
"*united to the likeness of His death.*"
For, frankly, it would not be sense.
And Holy Scripture cannot gain by being
presented to readers in an unintelligible
form.

The next verse we might render as
follows ;

> vi. 6.   " For this we can see, that
> our old self shared His crucifixion, that
> the sinful body might be done away ;
> so that we should no longer be slaves
> of Sin. For he that has died the
> death has paid the penalty ; Sin
> touches him no more."

In τοῦτο γινώσκοντες (which is equivalent to τοῦτο γὰρ γινώσκομεν) we have
a Pauline participle of a kind that is not
uncommon.   The peculiar force of the

present stem, which does not mean 'know'
of course, must be carefully preserved.
The 'old man' is the 'unregenerate self';
that 'self' that is, or was, before the καινὴ
κτίσις came. Συνεσταυρώθη calls to mind
the great saying in 'Galatians,' Χριστῷ
συνεσταύρωμαι (Gal. ii. 20). "The body
of sin" is a striking phrase. We have
another very much like it in the very
next chapter (vii. 24). Philippians iii. 21
and Colossians ii. 11 afford other like
locutions. Sin, after the words τοῦ μηκέτι
δουλεύειν (how well the old schoolmaster
recalls the Thucydidean instance in the
Grammars of that infinitive with τοῦ introducing a purpose!) must be spelt with
a capital. Verse 7 is of exceptional interest. Death cancels all obligations. S.
quotes a Rabbinical saying, 'When a man
is dead, he is free from the Law and the
Commandments.' And this, no more, may
be the meaning here. But I am half
inclined to suspect that ἀποθανών is really
passive, and that it ought to be rendered
"he that has died the death." Plainly,

when the penalty of sin is paid, Sin can
have no more claim. In that case, in
ὁ ἀποθανών we should see a reference to
ὁ συνεσταυρωμένος (to any convinced believer). Then would the 'forensic' sense,
which must be detected in δεδικαίωται, be
strikingly brought out. What a curious
thing it is to think that in good Scots the
familiar term for execution is 'justification'!
'He was justified yesterday' meant 'He was
hanged yesterday.' The ἀπὸ τῆς ἁμαρτίας,
which closes the verse, must be taken in
a 'pregnant' sense, "He is quit, and
safe from Sin."

What St Paul says in this verse, and
indeed in somewhat more than this verse
only, is very aptly illustrated by 1 St Peter
iv. 1. "Forasmuch then as Christ has
suffered in the flesh, arm ye yourselves also
with the same mind: for *he that hath
suffered in the flesh* πέπαυται ἁμαρτίας"
(some MSS. read ἁμαρτίαις, which—I
should fancy—must be wrong).

There is just the same appeal to the
death that is shared with Christ; to the

mystical participation in the great event of Calvary.

vi. 8—11. " But if we died with Christ, we believe we shall also share His life ; being sure that Christ, raised from the dead, is subject to death no more. Death is no more His lord."

" Because the death He died, He died for Sin once for all ; whereas the life He lives, He lives for God."

" So do you also reckon yourselves as dead to sin, but alive for God in Christ Jesus."

These verses open with a characteristic variation. It might very well have been συναπεθάνομεν...συνζήσομεν. Observe how in this sentence the mystical joint-death of the Cross is coupled with the 'real' joint-life we anticipate through union with the Ever-living. S. says, and truly enough, that 'different senses of life and death lie near together with St Paul'; mentioning 'physical' and 'ethical.' But it is even more than that. There is 'mystical' death and moral 'death,' and the 'death' which corresponds to 'life eternal.' And the ideas are interwoven, as if the three different 'deaths' (and also different 'lives') were all upon one plane. Εἰδότες means rather more than "knowing." I believe "being sure" is about right for it. Intuitive knowledge is the root idea of the word. "Being raised" is incorrect, but virtually inevitable. "Dieth no more" will not do for οὐκέτι ἀποθνήσκει. It means "is no more *one who dies*." Compare the use, in Heb. vii. 8, "for here tithes are taken by men liable to die" (ἄνδρες ἀποθνήσκοντες). "Death is no longer His *master*." The idea of bondage underlies. While the Lord Christ was on earth, as 'Son of Man,' 'Sin' was, in a sense, His master. Not that He sinned Himself; but that in Him was fulfilled the mysterious prophecy of Isaiah liii.

It was because 'Sin' was His master that the Lord Jesus had to die. For Sin and Death share one throne. The curious ὃ γὰρ ἀπέθανεν (in which it would appear that the ὅ is a sort of 'cognate,' or 'internal,' accusative) can be illustrated from ' Galatians,' ὃ δὲ νῦν ζῶ ἐν σαρκί (Gal. ii. 20).

There "the life I now live in the flesh" is a perfectly sound rendering. R.V. reproduces it here, a manifest improvement on the old and familiar version. The ἐφάπαξ (as in Heb.) carries the idea of 'never again.' And now what about the dative (τῇ ἁμαρτίᾳ)? How is that to be understood? Christ might have 'died to sin,' in the same sense that we should 'die to it'—that is, have done with it for ever.

But it seems more reasonable (though it cannot be considered certain, with an author like St Paul) to take τῇ ἁμαρτίᾳ as being the same sort of dative as the τῷ Θεῷ just after. I have rendered "He lives for God." The plain person might be puzzled to explain what that might mean. I think it does mean this : that He lives eternally, as it were, *for the Divine pleasure*. He died accordingly to gratify Sin ; He lives because God so wills it. For the moment we lose sight of the thought of

His own Godhead; of Himself as being
'the Life.' But then, we have to bear in
mind that regularly in N T. the resurrection is described both by a passive verb
ἐγείρεσθαι (where the Power of the Father
lies behind), and a neuter verb ἀναστῆναι.
So we need not be surprised at the Life of
the Everliving being here attributed to
a 'something not Himself.' St Luke xx.
38 may illustrate the dative. There, in
Christ's ever memorable dictum, we are told,
"God is not the God of the dead, but of
the living; πάντες γὰρ αὐτῷ ζῶσιν." That
dative does not mean, at least I think not,
"All live *by Him*." For that would be
a transgression of grammatical decorum.
The Deity may not be spoken of in the
special form of speech which belongs to
instruments—just instruments. It must
mean "live, *because He will have them
live*."

So in the passage before us the idea
presented is this. Said Sin (to the Sinless
One) "You shall die; I will have you die;
it is my right you should." Thereon the

Innocent Sufferer bowed His head, and died—only ἐφάπαξ. Then came the voice of God; "You shall live, live eternally; so is My will." And He lives for evermore. That is how I take the passage. Right it may be, or may not be. But, at least, it is coherent.

In *v.* 11, inevitably, the meaning of our dative shifts. *Do what you will you cannot keep one 'dative sense' all through.* As in words there often is a *double entendre*; so is there in cases also. It may be reproduced here, by the retaining of 'for' throughout. We are to reckon ourselves as "dead for sin," in the sense "dead, so far as sin goes" (that is, non-existent for it, or him). And as for the words "for God"; while it is conceivable that *we* 'live,' as Christ 'lives,' because it is God's will; I think it is more likely we live in a different sense. We live to do His will: we live for His service. And this 'life' (the whole-hearted Apostle will never let us forget), this life is ἐν Χριστῷ Ἰησοῦ. There the ἐν is not instrumental. It is the

ἐν of the 'Vine and the Branches,' the ἐν
which signifies the vital union.

We pass on naturally :

vi. 12—14. " Let not then Sin
be king in your mortal body so that
you should obey his desires ; neither
hand over, I crave you, your members
to sin, as tools of unrighteousness.
But present yourselves to God, as
men risen to new life ; and your limbs
(hand over) to God as tools of righteousness. For Sin must not be your
lord. You are not under *law*, but
under Grace."

The moral here enforced applies to the
life of the world that is. It is for the
θνητὸν σῶμα. There, if anywhere, Sin
might easily 'be king': 'reign' is not
decisive enough. 'Lusts,' to our modern
ear, goes something too far.

The ἐπιθυμίαι of Sin are like the
ἐπιθυμίαι of anyone else (even the Lord
Jesus Christ says ἐπιθυμίᾳ ἐπεθύμησα).
But they are such desires as are proper to
one's nature. Sin's 'desires' are, from his

nature, desires that are wholly evil.   The
verb παριστάνειν is used with some range
of meaning. 'Set beside,' 'show,' 'lead
up to' (in 1 Cor. viii. 8 even 'commend')
are some of its significations. The παρὰ
suggests a 'presence'; the ἰστάναι means
'set.'   I have Englished it differently in
the two members of the sentence.   The
truth is, the change of the tense makes it
all but inevitable.   Here, as in Rom.
xii. 1, we have the peremptory tense linked
with the Name of God.   It is just conceivable that a semi-ritual flavour attaches
to the word in that connexion. The word
might mean '*admovere.*' However, I cannot find any trace of such a sense in LXX.
The μὴ παριστάνετε invites the believer
not to do what is so natural.   The tense
in κυριεύσει has an imperatival force.   Yet
grammarians, we must admit, only allow
that with the second person.   To us, the
last words of the section sound somewhat
oddly.   But they are not any stranger than
the well-known saying that strikes so
curiously on our ears, in the familiar Funeral

Lesson. "The sting of death is sin; and
the power of sin is the Law." In a
way, barely intelligible to us (who have
no acquaintance with Law, in the sense
in which St Paul knew it), the notions
of Law and Sin were coupled in the
Apostle's mind. Where Law is, Sin must
be. In the benignant realm of Grace
there is no Law : it simply does not exist.
That is the teaching of 'Galatians'; κατὰ
τῶν τοιούτων οὐκ ἔστιν νόμος (Gal. v. 23),
"In face of things like this Law does not
exist." But let us make no mistake about it.
The deliverance from 'Law' does not mean
'lawlessness' in the sense of iniquity (ἀνομία).

vi. 15—23. "What then? Are
we to sin, because we are not under
Law but under Grace? No, no, no!
Do you not know, that when you yield
yourselves as 'slaves' to anyone, to
obey his orders, you are his slaves
whom you obey—whether it be the
slaves of Sin, to end in death, or the
slaves of (*God's*) obedience, to end *in
his acceptance*?"

" Now God be thanked, that slaves you were once of Sin, and had obeyed, with all your heart, that kind of teaching to which you were given over ; but having been freed from Sin you became slaves to Righteousness. I use a human analogy, because you are weak and carnal. As, I say, you yielded your members slaves to uncleanness and iniquity to become ever more and more wicked ; so now yield up your limbs as slaves to Righteousness to grow in holiness. For when you were Sin's slaves, you were free in regard of Righteousness."

"For what profit had you then from those things, cver which you now blush to think of them ? Why, they all end in death. But now, being freed from sin, and become the slaves of God, you have your profit in growing holier, and it will end in life eternal. Sin's slaves get nothing but death : whereas God's gracious gift is life eternal—in Jesus Christ our Lord."

In all this we can find nothing of any especial difficulty. In 16, we must observe how δικαιοσύνη is the antithesis of θάνατος. It follows, that the former carries its technical significance. 'Death,' in the spiritual sense, connotes exclusion from God. Those who have δικαιοσύνη are they who are not so excluded. They are 'right with God.' In v. 17 is presented (what I had for the moment forgotten) a highly puzzling phrase.

It is "you obeyed, from the heart, the τύπος διδαχῆς *to which you were given over.*" Much as I should like to render it, as if it were ὑπηκούσατε ὃν τύπον διδαχῆς παρεδόθητε, i.e. "you became obedient to the type of teaching which was delivered you"—on the οἰκονομίαν πεπίστευμαι principle ; it does not seem to be possible. It is the ' εἰς ' that bars the way. With the ἦτε we should like a μέν (which we perforce must do without). Yet even so we are left with a choice of the particular point at which the apodosis shall begin. No doubt the obvious thing is to make it begin at ὑπηκούσατε δέ. In that case the ἐκ καρδίας would exhibit that same confidence in the sincerity of converts, which St Paul for the more part shows. My difficulty is, that I can very well imagine a man being 'handed over' to 'sin,' or to false ideas; but I cannot imagine him being *handed over* to a Gospel. The Gospel is given to him; not he to it. Against that you have to put the fact, that τύπον διδαχῆς would naturally be referred to some definite kind of teaching—though we need not disturb our minds with that curious Teutonic fancy, that St Paul is in saying so 'giving away' the early faith by admitting there were, so to speak, different 'brands' of Christian doctrine, Petrine, Pauline and what not.

It is Scylla and Charybdis. Translate it either way, and you find that you are open to destructive criticism.

If only you could ὑπακούειν εἰς τινά! Or, if only you could regard the εἰς as introducing the thing which you obey; not that to which your obedience, taking shape,

would lead you on!   There presents itself,
to be sure, a method by which we may cut
the Gordian knot.   We might eliminate
the εἰς, and declare that inconvenient preposition due to a copyist's misunderstanding
of the ὃν παρεδόθητε τύπον διδαχῆς, a phrase
which in itself is perfectly simple.

Then 'ἐκ καρδίας' we could render:

> "You were the slaves of Sin, but
> with heart and soul you believed the
> teaching that was delivered you."

Thus all would be plain and straightforward; and indeed I am not sure that, in
the end, it would not be wiser and better,
either to strike out the εἰς, or to treat it as
non-existent, simply as a solecism—which,
to be sure, is far from impossible.

The Vulgate bravely reads; "Gratias
autem Deo, quod fuistis servi peccati,
obedistis autem ex corde *in eam formam
doctrinae,* in quam traditi estis."   It does
not even trouble to say, "ei formae doctrinae, in quam...."   But that is the
Vulgate's way. Ὑπακούειν, in N.T., is
always followed by the dative: so we dare

not here assume that εἰς with the accusative could represent the dative.

In ἀνθρώπινον λέγω, on the strength of Gal. iii. 15 (where a similar apology is attached to the employment of the 'will' analogy), we must see an excuse for the figure of 'slaves.' Yet it seems a little odd that the excuse should come in now; in view of the fact that we have had a good deal of figure before. Yet a distinction, no doubt, might be found. In μέλη and ἀκαθαρσία we must detect a definite reference to characteristic heathen vices.

I have translated εἰς τὴν ἀνομίαν "to become ever more and more wicked," because it is balanced by the words εἰς ἁγιασμόν; and ἁγιασμός certainly is a word that describes a *process*. It is not ἁγιωσύνη Δικαιοσύνη, when contrasted with ἁμαρτία, very naturally means 'righteousness,' in our ordinary sense; when set in contrast with death, the sense it bears is technical. The καρπός of sinfulness, though it is not expressly stated, is moral deterioration, leading inevitably to death. The καρπός of righteousness is just the opposite, amelioration of character, till 'holiness' is attained. "Wages" is, if it be not pedantic to say it, incorrect for ὀψωνία. The Vulgate says 'stipendia'; our versions 'wages,' or 'reward' (Tyndale). What slaves have from their master is 'rations.' They may be well fed or ill fed. It makes a good deal of difference to a slave, what kind of a master he has. It was not at all a happy thing to be Cato's slave, or Lucullus'. 'Sin' in this figure does not *earn* death. It inevitably brings death. The touching and time-honoured antithesis in our English is not to be found in the Greek—unless indeed we make χάρισμα (a word employed deliberately of God's good 'giving') extend a backward influence upon what has gone before it.

With the mention of 'soldiers,' of course, ὀψωνία could mean 'wages'; not in the case of 'slaves.'

Mark, how the "In Christ Jesus" comes again! It is a refrain never long time absent. There is held to be a

significance in the order of the names.
"Christ Jesus" represents the 'Glorified
Christ.' Notwithstanding our Revisers
would have been wiser to abstain from any
alteration. The rhythm is totally ruined
by so doing. And rhythm is of worth in
holy writ.

§ 12.   THE BELIEVER AND THE LAW

We now approach a question, which
was very much to the front in the Apostle's
mind at this period; the question of Israel's
Law and the believer's relation to it.

Let the great Evangelist speak:

vii. 1—3. "Can it be, you do not
know, my brothers, for I speak to those
that can understand Law, that Law is
master of a human being, as long as
ever he is alive? The wedded wife, Cf. 1 Cor.
you see, is absolutely bound by Law vii. 39.
to her living husband. But if her
husband shall die, she is altogether
released from the law of the husband."

"Accordingly, while her husband

lives, she shall pass for an adulteress,
if she become mated to another. But,
if her husband shall die, the law has no
hold on her; so that she is no adulteress,
though she be mated to another."

Γινώσκουσι νόμον (v. 1) must be taken
in a general sense. We are not to deduce
therefrom a preponderance of Jews in the
ranks of the Roman Church. "The law
of the husband" may be like 'the law of
the Nazirite,' or 'the law of the leper,' in
the Pentateuch. On the other hand, seeing
that adultery is an offence recognised by
all human codes, the phrase may only be
equivalent to 'husband-rule.' If the former
is the case, we need only suppose that the
Apostle is using a form of speech familiar
to himself from early associations. The
curious locution καταργεῖσθαι ἀπό is found
also in Gal. v. 4. Χρηματίσει is used as in
Acts xi. 26. In v. 3 " she is free from the
Law" means, "she is free; the Law cannot touch her." All this is simple enough.
When we come to apply the figure, we find
ourselves in rather deep waters.

vii. 4.   "And so, my brothers, you too have been made dead to 'the Law,' in the body of Christ ; so that you pass to another mate, to Him that was raised from the dead, that we (all) may bear fruit to God."

In the figure just above, we had a wife and a husband: the latter dies, and the former may legitimately mate again.   The phrase γενέσθαι ἀνδρὶ ἑτέρῳ (*v.* 3) is intentionally vague; it covers all sorts of 'mating,' legitimate or other.   Θανατοῦσθαι does not mean 'die,' it means 'be put to death.' This consideration directs our thoughts to the death by which Christ died.   In that the believer mystically had part and lot : or, if preferred, we may say 'has.'   As for διὰ τοῦ σώματος, one cannot feel sure exactly what it does mean.   The σῶμα of Christ (one knows) in Col. i. 22, and in 1 Pet. ii. 24, is the medium of reconciliation.   "And you once alienated...now hath He reconciled ἐν τῷ σώματι τῆς σαρκὸς αὐτοῦ διὰ τοῦ θανάτου" ; so says 'Colossians.'   It follows, that the 'body'

here may be intended to be taken as recalling the 'broken' Body of the Crucified.
If so, we should be half tempted to render
it "in the person of Christ." Yet 'person'
is a dangerous term and more wisely left
alone. Another very possible way of
understanding the 'body,' is as the mystical body, in which we are 'incorporate.'
Then we might paraphrase, "because you
are one with Christ." Between these two
ideas "because you died with Christ" and
"because you are one with Christ," the
true interpretation probably lies. The
change of person exhibited in καρποφορή-
σωμεν is difficult to account for. Had the
first person been emphasised, by the addition of a personal pronoun, our thoughts
would have flown back to i. 13. But it is
not, as it happens. It remains that we
should account for it, by that tendency of
the Apostle to associate himself with others
whenever he is saying a thing which might
be possibly construed as conveying a reproach. He will not speak of καρποφορεῖν
unless he unites himself with those who are

required καρποφορεῖν by the necessities
of the faith.   All Christians, whether
Roman or other, must (whether they will
or no) be fruitful in their lives.   The
association with ' marriage' makes one
wonder, for one moment, whether the
' fruit' in question be children—that is,
spiritual children.   But that use of καρπός
is rare ; it is not in LXX at all.   Besides
the whole context declares for the 'fruit of
holy living.'   It will be noted, that the
figure and the application of the figure
do not exactly square.   The ' Law' (in
the application) should be the 'husband' ;
it was to the Law, that in old days
the believers were united.   But it is not
the Law that dies : they die themselves
mystically, and are wedded to another
Bridegroom.   It is the whole Church that
is the ' Bride,' not individual believers.
However, it might be said that the image
is but half pursued : it is not worked out
at all in full detail.

       vii. 5, 6.   " In our unregenerate
days the demoralising sins that come

by Law were set working in our
members. They would have borne
fruit by death. But now the Law has
become nothing at all to us; for we
have died to that, wherein we were
(once) held fast; so that now we can
be slaves, not *to* an antique letter, but
with a spirit wholly new.”

Cf. viii. 6.   Εἶναι ἐν τῇ σαρκὶ is the exact antithesis
of ‘being in the spirit.’ In the ‘body’ all
must be; none need be in the ‘flesh.’
The antithesis here presented is found as
early as the famous saying of Our Lord
(St Mark xiv. 38).

Τὰ παθήματα τῶν ἁμαρτιῶν is easier to
paraphrase, by a good deal, than to trans-
i. 26.   late. The πάθη ἀτιμίας (perhaps) may help
us to the idea. But the whole expression
seems to point to definite sins, under the
image of disease. Τὰ διὰ τοῦ νόμου is the
strongest statement we have had, as to
Law’s relation to sin. Here it positively
makes sin.

Ἐνηργεῖτο I think to be passive. A
something evil is behind, some demoniacal

power, which sets them working. Εἰς τὸ
καρποφορῆσαι denotes what grammarians
often call the 'conceptual' result. In
this case, the result never came, for the
process was stopped in good time. Τῷ
θανάτῳ is ambiguous. It might mean 'for
Death'; but I believe it is 'by death.'
An accusative in such a case would have
been conceivable, but I do not think
St Paul would use it. Therefore he employs a 'modal' phrase. We have elsewhere
καρποφορεῖν ἐν ὑπομονῇ (' by resolute fortitude'), and καρποφορεῖν ἐν ἔργοις ἀγαθοῖς.
But this is different from either.

In *v.* 6 it makes no difference whether
we read ἀποθανόντες or ἀποθανόντος. In
any case, the Law is that in which we once
were held. Above we died 'to it': and
the best editors, here also, read the
nominative. I have ventured to reverse
the phrases at the end of the sentence; and
that, because one feels that it would be
very helpful indeed to have a dative after
δουλεύειν of the thing which is actually
served. We used to serve the Law—the

Law written in black and white (γράμμα)
—worn out although it was. Now we
serve the 'spirit,' which is altogether
new. Maybe, however, the writer shrank
from talking of δουλεύειν καινότητι πνεύματος. Hence the insertion of the preposition.

In what he has been saying of Law
(especially in *v.* 5) the Apostle lays himself open to a charge of speaking of Law
with disrespect and even irreverence.

This charge he now hastens to meet :

vii. 7—10. " What am I saying ?
Is the Law sin? No! No! of course it
is not. But I should not have known
sin, except by the aid of the Law.
I knew nothing of wrong desire ; only
the Law said, Thou shalt not covet.
And Sin, seizing an advantage, thanks
to the commandment, produced in me
every kind of wrong desire. For,
apart from Law, Sin is dead."

" Time was, when I was alive, before Law came. But when the commandment came, Sin sprang into new

life, and I—I died! So the commandment that was meant to be life-giving,
for me was found to be death-bringing.
For Sin, seizing an advantage, by
means of the command beguiled me,
and thereby slew me."

The formula of transition (see vi. 1)
almost suggests an opponent's objection.
'What? do you mean to say that Law is
Sin?' The formula of rejection, μὴ
γένοιτο, is Pauline altogether; and very
largely confined to 'Romans.' The οὐκ
ἔγνων presents that well-known figure of
language by which what is really 'potential'
(as here, 'I should not have known') is expressed as an absolute fact, qualified by
what comes after. Οὐκ ᾔδειν, of course, is
the same. The word ἐντολή describes a
distinct commandment, such as one of the
Ten Words. Διὰ τῆς ἐντολῆς (in *v*. 8) may
be attached to κατειργάσατο or to ἀφορμὴν
λαβοῦσα. Lying as it does between the
two, it will go very well with either; or
even with both. Νεκρὰ describes what
we in modern speech should call a

state of suspended animation. 'Sin' was not actually dead. She existed merely potentially, till an ἐντολή came. Then, forthwith, she sprang into life and baneful energy. In *v.* 9—11 the writer palpably has before his mind the earliest instance there is in Holy Writ of the coming of ἐντολή, and sin's disastrous re-animation ('animation,' if you will).

The story of Eden provides the setting of the figure. Man is happily alive in perfect innocence. But alas! there is an ἐντολή—a something which may not be done. Here is Sin's 'opportunity.' Sin may be compared to the 'Serpent.' It is the serpent who 'beguiles,' in the story of Genesis. On the other hand, it is the woman who gives the fatal fruit. But, be it by serpent or woman, poor man is beguiled, and dies.

Thus Law (and its component elements, the ἐντολαί) are fully vindicated.

vii. 12. "And so, the Law for its part is holy. The commandment too is holy and just and good."

The antithesis of the μέν is only latent.
It is a case of '*honi soit.*'

'Holy' stands in complete and absolute
antithesis to 'sinful,' as its very antipodes.
'Just' is in contrast with 'unfair,' 'inequit-
able.' 'Good' means 'kind,' designed
to help and not to hurt. As with the
'help-meet,' in the old-world story, so was
it here. What God designed for good (the
warning ἐντολή) somehow engendered
harm.

Where did the fault lie?

It is thus the Apostle makes answer:

vii. 13. "Did then the thing,
that was good, prove to be my death?
Nay, nay! But it was sin, that its
sinfulness might be displayed; because
that it used what was meant for my
good to bring about my death—to the
end that through the commandment
sin might be proved superlatively sinful
...(*It was Sin that was my death*)...."

This verse, in all its intricacy, is highly
typical of Pauline style. There is no
predicate at all. 'Sin' is marshalled in

the foreground, and we anticipate such a pronouncement as, ' No, it was Sin that was my death.' But not at all! The sentence is diverted into quite another channel, and (instead of telling us that it was sin that was to blame) the Apostle passes on to explain, what purpose lay behind this malevolent activity ; or rather, how sin's malevolence only resulted in making clearer sin's horrid sinfulness. The ἵνα we must not press. I mean, we must not attribute such a purpose to the Deity. Evil defeats itself. We do not, and cannot, conceive of the All-Holy as engaged in outwitting wickedness. Therefore ἵνα is for us, and probably for the writer, at least as much 'consecutive,' as it is 'final.' The turning of good into evil is obviously a note of highly developed depravity.

The reading in *v.* 13 varies between γέγονε and ἐγένετο. As I have said (I think) before, the perfect of this special verb is often used aoristically. Therefore either reading would do ; though ἐγένετο is more in accord with normal Greek. If one

was permitted to suggest emendations in
the text—and nowadays amongst scholars,
I should say, there is a feeling that the
critical instinct must be allowed, at least
occasionally, a little scope in that direction
—I think I should be tempted to say, that
the text would be more straightforward,
if we might make an alteration and read
ἀλλ' ἡ ἁμαρτία ("no, it was sin that proved
my death"); ἵνα φανῇ ἡ ἁμαρτία κ.τ.λ.
(" that sin *might be seen using*, what was
for my good, to bring about my death").
It is true that in St Matthew vi. 5 it is
said, of the hypocrites, that they stand
praying in prominent places, ὅπως φανῶσι
τοῖς ἀνθρώποις. But that is not quite the
same, for one naturally supplies the necessary participle, "that they may be seen of
men *praying*": and that we cannot do
here. The adverbial phrase καθ' ὑπερ-
βολὴν comes five times in this group, and
nowhere else in St Paul. Every writer has
favourite phrases, which vary at different
times of his life. This is sometimes forgotten by persons who lay much stress

on vocabulary, as a never failing test of authenticity.

And now St Paul says a thing, which occasions us some surprise, as a something unexpected.

vii. 14. "We know" (he says) "that the Law is a thing of the Spirit...."

Then, what (enquires the reader) about that παλαιότης γράμματος, of which we heard just now? Ah! but that is precisely it. We are not concerned with γράμμα. We want—and the Apostle intends—to point out that *in essence* the Law is a thing of πνεῦμα. It is so for one great reason ; that it has enshrined in it the holy Mind of God. It is His 'Law'; and He is πνεῦμα. This we must not forget. No spoken word of man is an adequate vehicle of this transcendent thing. But every word that has in it an element of 'spirit,' or is recognised as coming of the Spirit, must be treated with all reverence. The spirit in things spiritual needs spirit for its discernment

The Law, a thing (in itself) corresponding to its high origin, was simply too
good for man. Man could not rise to it.
So is the view of this passage;

> vii. 14 (continued). ..."whereas
> I am wholly 'fleshly,' in utter bondage
> to Sin."

There is another place in St Paul, where
our better MSS. read σάρκινος (instead of
σαρκικός) as the antithesis of πνευματικός.
The ordinary distinction is familiar to all
students. If we are to keep σάρκινος, in
1 Cor. iii. 1 and here, we must suppose that
it denotes a high degree of 'fleshliness'—
a complete predominance of the lower
nature in a man. Πεπραμένος ὑπὸ τὴν
ἁμαρτίαν ("the thrall of sin, bought and
sold") is an unexampled expression. St
Paul goes on to explain the nature of this
awful bondage.

> vii. 15. "For the thing I am
> bringing about, I cannot see. For,
> not what I want, do I do; but what
> I loathe, that I do."

In this verse we have three words, all

of which might simply mean 'do.' Two
of them, I imagine, are very nearly syn-
onymous. Between πράττειν and ποιεῖν
it seems a futile thing to discriminate.
Κατεργάζεσθαι, however, stands upon a
different footing. That contemplates result. A man, an immoral person, can see
(γινώσκει) only too well what he is doing;
but he cannot see, with sufficient clearness,
whereto it tends. Οὐδεὶς ἑκὼν ἁμαρτάνει,
said the sage of old; and there is a good
deal of truth in it. Inadequate faculty of
γινώσκειν accounts for very much of human
weakness. Maybe (but I think it unlikely)
the first clause should be interpreted on
other lines: "for what I am bringing
about, I do not *intend*." The idea of
'determination' belongs to the verb sometimes, but not in the present-stem forms.
Therefore we cannot entertain this interpretation seriously.

> vii. 16. "And, if I do what I do
> not want; I agree, that the Law is
> admirable."

Literally it runs; "I agree with the

Law, that it is (an) excellent (Law)." The
Law is pictured as commending itself. It
proclaims itself as God's Law, and such 'I'
feel it to be.

vii. 17—20. " That being so, it
is not I, that perpetrate the thing, but
the sinfulness, that dwells within me.
For I know that there dwells in *me*,
that is, in the *lower me*, no good at
all."

" As for the wanting (to do good)
that is ready to my hand; but the
achieving the good is not. For I do
not do the good I want to do; but the
evil I do not want to do, that I do.
And if I do what I do not want;
then it is not I that achieve it, but
the sinfulness that lives in me."

The οὐκέτι's in the passage are of an
idiomatic character. " So now it is *no
more* I " (our Version) is not adequate.
'Sinfulness' is more correct in the idea
it conveys than 'sin.' We are working
onward to the doctrine of the two 'men'
in the 'man.' There is a lower self and

a higher self; the ἐγώ in this passage is
the higher, better self. But the σάρξ,
or lower nature, prevails in unregenerate
days.

Θέλειν (as is well known) has attached
to itself by now a far stronger signification
than it had in earlier days. It means definitely ' want.' Παρακεῖσθαι is used of
a thing to which you can ' help yourself ';
you have only to reach out your hand, and
there it is! It is rather an odd thing to
say, ' I can want, as much as I like'; but
that is what he does say. In *v.* 19 (as
compared with *v.* 15) we can certainly detect
the indiscriminate use of ποιεῖν and πράσσειν. In a general way St Paul has a well-
marked tendency to deliberate variation.
We have the same thing in English. Our
earlier translators were well aware of this,
and literary instinct made them shun,
amongst other things, the Revisers' principle of ' one word for one.'

In *v.* 15 we read ἀλλ' ὃ μισῶ, τοῦτο
ποιῶ : in *v.* 19, ἀλλ' ὃ οὐ θέλω κακόν, τοῦτο
πράσσω. The conclusion is inevitable,

that the writer used which verb he chose,
and whenever he chose.

vii. 21—23. "Accordingly I find
the rule; when I want to do the good,
it is the evil which is ready to my
hand. You see, in my inner self, Cf. 2 Cor.
I cordially assent to the Law of God. iv. 16.
But I am conscious of another principle,
(established) in my members, waging
war on the Law I approve, and trying
to make me captive to the principle of
Sin, that is in my members."

Could one wish for a better instance of
the difficulty involved, for the man who
wants to understand, by the habit the
writer has of using a single word in several
senses? Contemplate νόμος here! Of
course it is perfectly true that νόμος can
be affirmed to be not one word, but two ;
for we can effect a discrimination by attaching the definite article. But the aid
of the definite article (its aid to the interpreter) is more apparent than real. Our
revisers (no doubt, believing that ὁ νόμος
must mean "*the* Law") inserted in their

margin, "with regard to the Law." But
it is not possible. The sentence before us
is not of a form in which the accusative
could be so interpreted. Their text ("I
find then the law that, to me, who would
do good, evil is present") is not unduly
lucid. St Paul is here using 'law' in a
sense familiar to us in connexion with
'laws of nature.' A 'Law of Nature' is a
statement of what is observed to happen.
Such is this 'law' St Paul finds. It is
the way things always go. In the very
line below, we have "the Law," to all
intent, identified with the familiar Law of
Holy Writ. About that we can make no
mistake; for the 'Law' is qualified as
"the Law of God." Still it is the second
sense, in which we have νόμος used. The
third sense is in the next line; three
meanings in three lines. Another νόμος
is perceived, residing in the 'members'
(an expression used for choice apparently,
instead of σῶμα, when the thought of sin
is present) and engaged in constant war
with "the law of my mind" (that is, of

course, the law the thinking part of me
approves—for practical purposes the 'Law
of God'; but not entirely the same : for
I can only approve such part of the ' Law
of God,' as is fully made known to me).
The eager reader will say, Why! of course
this ἕτερος νόμος is the law opposed to
God's, the law of Sin.   But it is not; it
is a ' νόμος '—an indeterminate ' tendency '
residing in the lower ' me '—always employed in the hapless task of bending my
better will and better judgment to the
'law of Sin' (likewise "seated in my
members"). It is not too much to say,
that here we have one Greek word, that
must be supplied and equipt with three
equivalents in English. First it is only a
'rule'; then it becomes a definite 'law';
anon it is a principle—or, if you will, a
' tendency ': last of all, it returns to the
sense of a law, which is definite law;
yet not so definite, as the Law of God
above.

Moreover, in between, we have the
'law of my νοῦς,' which cannot (strictly

speaking) be identified with any one of the
other four, though it is a real 'law'—what
we should call a 'law' in English.   Maybe
this confusion is due to mere paucity of
vocabulary.   Yet it is very hard to believe
that the resources of a Plato, or the resources of an Aristotle, would not have
coped with the emergency.   There is a
flexibility in the language, that makes it
possible to express the most complex ideas
with perfect facility, in spite of the com-
parative insufficiency of vocabulary.   But
this glorious flexibility we do not find in
our Epistles.

The pureness of Pauline Greek was
possibly not unaffected by 'Hebrew' influences.   Perhaps we should not complain.
But the man, who has spent his days in
teaching classical Greek, cannot but feel,
what a mystery it is in the Providence of
God, that a teacher like St Paul, so
splendid and so fruitful on the 'Spirit'
side of him, should have been by comparison (especially in the argumentative
parts of his writings) so deficient on the

side of the letter. ' If only he could have written like Plato!' one finds oneself saying.

Anyhow a wooden literalness is the very last thing desirable, if the meaning is to emerge for modern readers.

Only what is the translator to do in a paragraph like this? In a paraphrase one may say ' tendency,' ' principle,' what you will! In a definite rendering such devices are altogether impossible.

vii. 24, 25. " O! hapless man that I am! Who shall rescue me from this death-bringing body?"

" Thanks be to God (*there is deliverance*) through Jesus Christ, our Lord."

" So then, the unaided ' I ' serves God's Law with the reason; but with the lower nature I serve the law of sin."

These two be glorious verses. All can draw hope from them and splendid inspiration. Yet, even so, a prodigious conflict of tongue and wit alike has raged, and will rage, around them in every period.

Χάρις τῷ θεῷ (S. finely says) is just a 'sigh of relief.' The agonising question has found an answer. One need only say *Deo gratias!*'

But what precisely was the question? "Who shall deliver me from..." what? Is it "this deadly body"? or is it "the body that is linked with this death"? The 'body,' in itself, is not 'death-bringing.' It has a glorious destiny. But, in its present 'fleshly' state, it falls a ready victim to sin; and sin leads on to death. My own feeling is for taking τούτου, not with θανάτου merely, but with the whole expression.

The cry appears to me to be, 'Who will deliver me from this body, which is always dragging me down'? For in the verses above, the 'principle' of evil, and the very 'law' of sin, have their stronghold in 'the members.' But we cannot say with certainty which is the more likely view.

And then again, what about διὰ Ἰησοῦ Χριστοῦ? The Holy Name might be the medium through which the Apostle offers thanks. " I thank God, through Jesus Christ." That is very plainly conceivable. On the whole, however, one inclines to side with the view, which attaches the words to the unexpressed ' redemption.' ' Thank God! *I am delivered*, through Jesus Christ our Lord ' (that is to say, through what He brought).

But there are several questions more (and questions hotly disputed) connected with the verses. Αὐτὸς ἐγώ does not mean 'I myself,' but 'I of myself' (as the American Revisers have it) or ' I by myself.' Let that be granted. When we view the whole of the last sentence, we ask ourselves in perplexity, assuming that ' I by myself' is the proper meaning, to what stage in a man's experience, to what stage in the Apostle's experience, does it refer ? Is it the despairing cry of the unregenerate ? or is it the cry that goes up from each and every Christian in the

time that is? Both opinions have been
held by large sections of the Church. The
latter would seem the likelier. Then what
about the χάρις τῷ Θεῷ? May we put it
in this way? May we say, 'you must
observe that St Paul does not plainly tell
us what it is he thanks God for'? There
is a deliverance; there is a redemption.
To be accurate, there are two. There is
the redemption of δικαιοσύνη (or, if you
will, of δικαίωσις) which puts us in the right
with God, and further, and most important,
unlocks for us on earth the treasure house
of the Spirit. But, when all is said and
done, it is the ' soul' alone which enjoys
that ' redemption,' not the ' body.' The
ἀπολύτρωσις τοῦ σώματος (which I would
identify with the ἀπολύτρωσις τῆς περιποιή-
σεως, "the redemption of realisation," in
Ephes. i. 14) is yet in the far future.

Redeemed in part, anon to be redeemed
in full—that is the position of man. Yet
God may be thanked for this, "through
Jesus Christ our Lord," that the full
and absolute redemption is potentially

achieved by Christ for all already. It only remains to live 'in the spirit' now. Still, one believer will view it one way, and one another ; and none will be wholly right. For truth is many sided, and further our intelligence, however illuminated, can never be capable here of grasping things as they are.

For the rest, in the understanding of this verse, the more a man is inclined to the sterner western view, the more he will believe that the conflict is here and now, though the victory is sure. St Paul was assured of the victory ; but there were times and times when he doubted of himself—though of Christ he doubted never.

§ 13. The new life of the 'Justified'
and their splendid destiny

The redemption of which we spoke just now, the redemption which evokes the outburst of thankfulness, though in one aspect 'potential,' in another is 'actual' exceedingly. Right relation is restored between God and the believer. Thereby the believer passes from the peril of condemnation.

This freedom from condemnation appears in the very opening of the memorable viiith chapter. The last clause of chap. vii. might have suggested that the peril still exists. But it ought not so to be. After all, it is only if the 'flesh' is allowed to prevail that any danger arises. And it need not be allowed ; it must not be allowed. For hear what St Paul has to say!

> viii. 1, 2. "There is then no condemnation for them that are ' in Christ Jesus'; for the rule of the Spirit of Life hath freed thee, in Christ Jesus, from the rule of Sin and of Death."

The 'then' does not refer to what has gone just before. It looks further back— maybe to the end of chap. v. The form of the word κατάκριμα may possibly be

taken as individualising the result. It is
not οὐδεμία κατάκρισις, which would be a
general phrase stating an universal result,
but it is οὐδὲν κατάκριμα, none for 'you'
and none for 'me.' The σε (which I believe to be right, as in the older MSS.)
tends likewise to the same conclusion. Τοῖς
ἐν Χριστῷ Ἰησοῦ covers the thought of
mystical incorporation. In *v.* 2, νόμος is
used with the same wide-ranging freedom
as in the last chapter. "The 'Law' of
Sin and Death" does not mean the 'law'
they impose, but the *rule*, the authority
they exercise. We live under a new regime.
Not Sin, not Death is master. There is
another prevailing power. It is "the rule
of the Spirit of Life." In this last phrase
it is possible that the two nouns are in
apposition. For the Spirit is the Life.
But a more probable explanation would
be that "the Spirit of Life" is a phrase
akin to "the Body of Death." He is
called "the Spirit of Life" because He
gives new life, and makes a man καινὴ
κτίσις.

Next follows a well-known *crux*. I would render it freely like this:

> viii. 3.   "For what the Law could not do—where the Law was weak through the 'flesh'—God, sending His own Son in the likeness of sinful flesh, and indeed for sin, *achieved*... He condemned sin in the flesh."

Here be difficulties truly! not indeed in the two opening clauses; for they are plain enough. They are appositional phrases, the second explaining the first, to be taken in relation to the main pronouncement of the sentence. The Law would have 'condemned sin' (how, we will discuss directly), only human frailty stood in the way. It was the σάρξ that baffled the 'Law,' from this point of view.

"What the Law could not do..." suggests, as a contrast, "*God did.*" I venture to supply it. For, without some slight expansion, the sentence, to English ears, would tend to become meaningless. But the trouble does not end there. The sudden turn of the sentence, to be found in

the word κατέκρινε, has this of awkward-
ness in it; to wit, that the act described
by the word κατέκρινε was really the
work of the Son, and not of the Father,
unless we have recourse to the dogma of
'coinherence'—which. I take it, we shall
not do.

But we have not yet arrived at κατέκρινε. There is a phrase which comes
before that. God is said to have "sent
His own Son in the likeness of sinful
flesh." The word ὁμοίωμα is used in
Phil. ii. 7 in speaking of the Incarnation.
There it runs ἐν ὁμοιώματι ἀνθρώπου γενόμενος. As I have remarked before, in
ὁμοίωμα there seems to lie an added idea
of 'reality.' So here, Christ came "in the
likeness of frail humanity." The 'likeness'
was real, complete; but it did not extend
to the frailty, for frailty is not of the
essence of humanity. Σάρξ does not here
connote, in itself, any such conception: it
is as in Col. i. 22.

About καὶ περὶ ἁμαρτίας there is large
controversy. Our revisers say "and a

19—2

an offering for sin " : the American Committee, who frequently are right when they differ from our own body, very cautiously prefer "and for sin." But what does it mean ? If one refuses to believe in the 'LXX' usage here (περὶ ἁμαρτίας for 'sin offering' : cf. Heb. x. 3), the least that one can do is to say something which has a meaning. It might be "and with sin in view." That would give the degree of vagueness, that is obviously desiderate, if ἐν τῇ σαρκί is explained as I for one think it should be.

And now comes the greatest difficulty of them all; the interpretation of κατέκρινε τὴν ἁμαρτίαν ἐν τῇ σαρκί.

Here S. says "condemned Sin by His flesh." In the first place, that emphasises the point I remarked before as touching κατέκρινε, that it was the Son who κατέκρινε, strictly speaking. Or rather, it aggravates the difficulty of Persons : for 'his' must needs refer to the subject of the sentence; and that is the Father. Next, "in (or by) His flesh" would naturally mean "in His Life," "by His Life," on Earth. There would be no plain reference to death upon the cross. And that, I think, would destroy the explanation of S., that Christ 'non-suited' sin, for evermore, *by His death.* His idea is that Sin has no claim against a believing man, inasmuch as he shares Christ's death. Because I cannot believe in this explanation of ἐν τῇ σαρκί—the explanation of κατέκρινε, by itself, would undoubtedly do admirably—I incline to another view.

It was not 'sin' Christ condemned, it was '*sin in the flesh.*' That is, He demonstrated, for all eternity, the *needlessness of sin.* Up till then everyone had urged '*humanum est errare.*' There are scores and scores of proverbs which condone all sorts of wrongdoing. '*Ils le font tous,*' I have had said to me. But they do not! Christ did not! He lived in utter sinlessness. In a word, " He condemned *sin-in-the-flesh.*" It is not a question of 'sin' (that needs no condemnation) it is a question of sin in man. Is that excusable or

is it not? Christ showed that it is not!
What was the importance of this? It is
very plain to see. As long as ever man
held sin to be only natural : so long there
was small chance of humankind attaining
to aught of holiness. But 'what man has
done, man can do.' And, at least, we
cannot say, 'It is hopeless for a man to
try to live in holiness.' Christ rises up
before us in all His perfect innocence.
He "condemned" sin. He condemns us
too if we give way to it.

The upshot (if you will, the upshot
that was intended by the 'Divine Love'
which sent the Son) is set forth in the very
next verse :

> viii. 4.   "To the end that the
> claim of the Law might be fulfilled in
> the case of us that walk not after the
> flesh but after the Spirit."

The δικαίωμα of the Law is what the
Law demands as right. One would have
looked for a plural here. It may be there
is reference to some comprehensive precept, such as Levit. xi. 45. If it were not

for the manner in which the sentence ends, a wholly different sense might attach to the word. The δικαίωμα of the Law might be the death of the sinner ; and that would have been 'fulfilled' (ἐν ἡμῖν) by the death of the Crucified. But plainly the δικαίωμα has to do with righteous living, and not with sin's punishment. Δικαίωμα we have already had with manifold significations. In i. 32 it stood for 'just decree'; in ii. 26 (plur.) for 'ordinances'; in v. 16 for 'verdict of acquittal'; in v. 18 for 'act of righteousness'; and here for 'just demand'—a sense nearer i. 32 than any other. So the word is used five times, and *always* with a different meaning. Yet all are intelligible and readily derived from the root meaning and the formative element.

Πληρωθῇ reminds us again of xiii. 10. To "walk after the flesh" is a phrase that is fragrant of its origin. In our everyday speech it would be 'live the lower life.' In περιπατεῖν κατὰ πνεῦμα, the question suggests itself, what πνεῦμα? Having regard to κατὰ σάρκα (which must mean our lower nature) one would say, the 'spirit' is ours; it stands for the higher part of us, that part, 'thanks to which we enjoy our contact with the Divine; that part in us, which alone can be influenced by the Divine.

> viii. 5—8. "For they that are 'after the flesh' are fleshly minded; and they that are 'after the spirit' are spiritually minded. The mind of the flesh means death; contrariwise, the mind of the spirit means life and peace. The mind of the flesh, you see, means enmity towards God. For it does not submit itself to the Law of God; indeed it cannot: and they that are 'in the flesh' cannot please God."

In this there is little to trouble us. "After the flesh" and "in the flesh" are phrases both expressing surrender to the lower nature. The second is probably the stronger. In the one case the figure would seem to be that of following a guidance;

in the other it is utter absorption. When you are "in the flesh" the lower nature masters you altogether. Φρονεῖν is a difficult term, and φρόνημα even harder— I mean, to render in English. As S. observes, the terms connote very much more than 'reason.' 'Affections' too and 'will' are covered by them. For the phrase φρονεῖν τὰ τῆς σαρκός, compare St Matt. xvi. 23 (οὐ φρονεῖς τὰ τοῦ Θεοῦ), and Phil. iii. 19 (οἱ τὰ ἐπίγεια φρονοῦντες). The φρόνημα of the flesh is that general attitude towards life, and all that is in it, which stamps the lower nature. It is identified with 'death' (in very much the same manner as 'the rock' in 1 Cor. is identified with Christ), because it leads to death unfailingly. It is also said to be ἔχθρα εἰς θεόν. That and death are, in the end, the same. God is Life; and that which is ungodly is *ipso facto* 'death.' Οὐχ ὑποτάσσεται (v. 7) describes the normal state of the 'fleshly mind.' As a habit, it does not bend or bow to the will of God. The verb one would call 'deponent.'

'Αρέσαι does not mean 'please once,' but simply 'please.'

The Apostle now gladly leaves the saddening contemplation of the ill case of the ungodly and turns to a brighter picture :

> viii. 9, 10.   "But *you*, you are not 'in the flesh,' but 'in the spirit'; so surely as God's Spirit dwells in you. But if anyone hath not the Spirit of Christ, he is none of His. On the other hand, if Christ be in you, although the body be dead, because it is sinful, the spirit is life indeed because...."

It will be noted that though περιπατεῖν κατὰ πνεῦμα is to "live after one's own higher nature," in the expression εἶναι ἐν πνεύματι (seeing that ἐν πνεύματι undeniably signifies a dominating influence) the πνεῦμα is not our πνεῦμα, but the 'Spirit' which comes from God and in a sense is God. Εἶναι ἐν πνεύματι means to have God's Spirit in one ; or, in another form of speech, to have Christ in one. Πνεῦμα

Θεοῦ, πνεῦμα Χριστοῦ, Χριστός, all three express the same thing. It is what we commonly call the 'Indwelling Christ.' The latter half of *v.* 10 is highly obscure. The 'body' is, we can understand (because it was and remains the σῶμα τοῦ θανάτου, owing to the σάρξ of it), 'dead,' in a mystical sense. There is nothing obscure in that. It sins; it has sinned; it is always liable to sin. We are here not very far from the ' σῶμα σῆμα ' conception ; though that is, to be sure, in no wise Pauline teaching. The 'body,' *ex hypothesi,* is our body ; is the 'spirit' also our spirit ? And if the body be νεκρός, because it has sin in it, is our spirit more than living, positively a source of life (ζωή), because the taint of sin in it has disappeared (διὰ δικαιοσύνην)? It is conceivable, but not likely.

If this idea is dismissed we have to face the plain alternative, which involves an awkward phenomenon. The 'body' remains your body, but the 'spirit' is no longer your spirit—even vitalised by God's

Spirit. It is now the Spirit of God which is 'life' essentially (even as Christ said of Himself, "I am the Life"); and the change from the thought of 'you' to the thought of God is somewhat startling in its very abruptness. Nor are we finished with questionings even now. The Spirit of God is Life; none questions that; but why "Life διὰ δικαιοσύνην"? Is it because, in Himself, the Spirit is altogether Holy? or, is it because His gracious influence makes you 'holy'—or even in a lower sense 'righteous' (that is, keeps you right with God)? It is plain to see one could argue long about it. Anyhow, consideration calls for some revision of our paraphrase. Shall we alter it, and say this?

viii. 10 (*bis*). "And if Christ be in you; for all the body is dead, because it is sinful; yet the Spirit" (which is Christ) "is a source of Life...."

Up to this point all goes smoothly. Then we have to make our choice, I should hold, between three renderings:

(1) "because He is wholly

righteous"; though I believe that 'righteousness' is only a quality of God in a somewhat narrow range,

(2) "because He will make you righteous,"

(3) "because *you are at peace with God."*

The third I hold to be right. The thought of the sanctifying power, which we associate with the Holy Spirit, is contained here in the word ζωή—and not in δικαιοσύνη. The believer can be sanctified because he is quit of guilt; because he is δίκαιος. That is a necessary foundation for the Spirit's further work.

"The body is dead, because of sin; the spirit is life, because of righteousness"; so says our English. And I think it will have to stand. Yet, beyond all manner of doubt, it lies in very great need of explanation. Plain people clamour for more. They say, What does it mean? Or, worse still, they make haste to decide all unaided what it means; and are very likely wrong. But it may be said in reply, Well, so are

so-called scholars. And that is also true :
but at least they try to weigh conflicting
theories.

And the Spirit which is Christ's, or
Christ, is more than life-giving now. It
brings with it the splendid promise of life
surpassing life.

And so we proceed :

viii. 11. "And if the Spirit of
Him, who raised Jesus from the dead,
do dwell in you ; He that raised the
Christ from the dead shall also
quicken your mortal bodies, through
His indwelling Spirit in you."

Here we notice how the Risen One is
named by two several names. The first
time He is Jesus (a name full of hope for
us, for it is His human name) ; the second
time He is God's Christ (and, as such,
our Redeemer). It is curious that our
MSS. have, some διά with the accusative,
others διά with the genitive, at the end of
this statement of hope. The latter is clearly
preferable. It is not owing to the Spirit's
mere Presence, but because of His *potent*

Presence, that we can look for resurrection.
The authority of MSS. is said to be 'evenly
balanced.'

If then the πνεῦμα in us is so vitally
important ; if our very resurrection wholly
depends on it; the moral is obvious. We
must live 'by' and 'in' the πνεῦμα. All
our actions must ever be subjected to His
guidance, directed to one great end. Long
ago in 1 Thess. the Apostle had given
warning τὸ πνεῦμα μὴ σβέννυτε. That was
in a narrow sense. Expand it to the fullest
and you are in possession of life's secret.
There is no other. This is set before us
now in language most plain and direct.

> viii. 12, 13. "Accordingly, my
> brothers, we are debtors, not to the
> flesh, to live after the flesh—for, if you
> live after the flesh, you are on the
> road to death ; but if by the spirit you
> slay the evil deeds of the body, you
> shall live."

Once more we have a sentence broken
off at the very start. "Not to the flesh,"
it says. Then to what ? We are never

told. Engrossing ideas crowd in, and we
have to tell ourselves—in this case an
easy matter. Μελλετε ἀποθνήσκειν is no
easy phrase to render. I have given what
I think its force. Πνεύματι, brief as it is,
really covers no less than this, "by living
the spirit-life." A somewhat similar instance occurs in Gal. v. 5. Πρᾶξις bears
in other places the sense of 'nefarious
doing.'

Looked at from another point of view,
the 'spirit-life' not only carries with it the
promise of deathlessness, but is also the
title to sonship.

viii. 14—17. "For, all that are
led by the Spirit of God, they are the
sons of God...."

(*And sons you are.*)

"...For you have not received the
slave-spirit, to relapse into craven
fear; but you have received the spirit
of sonship, whereby we cry, Abba,
Father. The very Spirit of God joins
in witness with our spirit, that we are
the children of God. And if children,

also heirs—God's heirs and Christ's
coheirs; if so be we share His
sufferings, that we may also have a
share in His glory."

The 'slave-spirit' in this place is contrasted with the 'spirit of sonship.' The
former is the mind with which the bondsman
is forced to regard his master. The 'son-
spirit' is something more. With regard
to *υἱοθεσία*, it may be said: it comes five
times in St Paul and never appears to carry
any special sense of '*adoption.*' Of course,
we are not 'sons,' as Christ is Son. Yet
υἱοθεσία means no more than 'sonship.'
There is no other word, so far as I am
aware, to express the idea. Plato would
have coined *υἱότης*; and that would have
been useless here; for it would have meant
a different thing. What we want is the
'*status* of son': the *πνεῦμα υἱοθεσίας* is
the 'spirit' (it is almost the *φρόνημα*) of
folks who have that *status*. The Jews
knew nothing of adoption; and, I think,
in our translations 'adoption' might well
vanish. 'Fear' was our old condition, the

fear of the 'wrath' of God. It does not comport with 'sonship'; but only with the 'slave *status.*' Πάλιν εἰς φόβον is highly irregular; but S. is plainly right in taking it as equivalent to ὥστε πάλιν φοβεῖσθαι. Κράζειν connotes passion. Such an appeal was made by Christ in the Garden to His Father. I mean the writer of 'Hebrews' denominates it κραυγή.

The cry, that is our cry, is the very cry of Jesus, ᾿Αββά, ὁ Πατήρ. In St Mark we have the same form. Christ was, all but certainly, bilingual Himself. It is difficult to account for the disappearance from our Liturgies of this traditional appeal. It plainly should be there. In *v.* 16 the sense would seem to be, our own spirit tells us we are God's 'children'; God's Spirit, present in us, bears out our spirit. We have, in common English, no word that quite expresses the tender beauty of τέκνον. 'Bairn' does; but 'bairn' alas! has never won its way into 'classical' acceptance. But it is just the right word, precisely parallel.

The members of the family—the τέκνα or the υἱοί (which indeed is the usual term, when legal rights are in view)—are *ipso facto* 'heirs.' 'Heirship,' associated first with the 'land,' is a common O.T. idea, endorsed by the usage of Christ. The 'joint-heirship' seems to draw no distinction in 'kind' of heirship as between the 'Son' and the 'sons.'

Συνπάσχομεν might refer to the mystical union in Christ's Passion. However probably it does not. It speaks of that ὑπομονή by which 'souls' must be won. The 'glory' of Christ is regarded as one supreme event in which we may have a share. By contrast, the tense of συνπάσχωμεν describes a way long and hard —the path of the bitter Cross.

Yet why need a Christian man take any thought of suffering? With this inspiring thought we pass into that great passage which, in its majestic working up to a climax truly magnifical, may very well be regarded as the most splendid in all the Epistles.

viii. 18—21. "For I reckon that (all) the sufferings of the time that is now are nothing worth, compared with the glory that shall be revealed—aye, reach to us."

"For the earnest expectation of all creation is eagerly looking for the revelation of God's sons. Creation was made subject, you know, to disappointment; not of its own free will, but because of Him who subjected it, with a hope that creation itself shall be freed from the thraldom of constant failure, and enter on the glorious freedom that belongs to the children of God."

One hardly likes to comment at all on a passage like this. Τὰ παθήματα τοῦ νῦν καιροῦ indicates that the suffering of συνπάσχομεν, just above, is literal hardship, such as falls to the lot of sincere believers in most ages. The order of the words that come at the end of the sentence is strictly 'classical,' save for εἰς ἡμᾶς. That is an appendix. Its addition and its form are both characteristically Pauline. Καραδοκεῖν (a curious formation) means to 'watch intently.' The compound noun is said to be common in later Greek. How far the force of the term has worn away with years, we cannot tell. Both times it occurs in St Paul it seems to carry an intense meaning. The κτίσις is the creation (by which St Paul probably meant our world), in the Vulgate *creatura*. This creation has had a 'fall': it has been condemned to in-effectiveness. The teaching is derived from the story of Genesis. Ματαιότης, in English, would be represented by 'futility.' '*Vani-tati*' is again Vulgate. The conception is that the world is ashamed of its ineffective-ness; it would like to be vastly better. But it cannot; it may not be so. The Will of the great Creator has said 'no' to its ambition. And it did do better once, before it was 'cursed.' Time was when its Maker pronounced it 'very good.' But this doom imposed upon it is neither imposed capriciously, nor bars the door to hope. Ἐφ' ἐλπίδι—the spelling is familiar in the Catacombs—goes, of course with ὑπετάγη, which it happily modifies. Man is the firstborn of nature. He has anon his redemption (reserved to the 'sons of God' who are ἀπαρχή τις τῶν αὐτοῦ κτισμάτων, Jas. i. 18); and when that redemption comes, the poor world's will come as well. For man's sake the earth was cursed; but when man is redeemed and enters once for all upon his glorious freedom, then all reason for earth's curse will have disappeared and she will have her δόξα. The coming of the glory of God's redeemed is called a 'revelation,' an 'unveiling.' It is then the 'image of God' will stand out unmistakeable.

Meanwhile there is eager waiting for man and all creation, waiting and even groaning. The δουλεία of φθορά is not very happily rendered by the 'bondage of corruption.' 'Corruption' suggests putrescence. This φθορά is merely 'spoiling,' the deterioration which disappoints a happy promise—for the earth does promise well.

viii. 22—25. " For we are sure

the whole Creation groans together, aye travails together, and always has. Yes, and also we ourselves, though we enjoy the Spirit as a firstfruit, I say we ourselves groan within ourselves, looking forward to the sonship, the redemption of the body."

"*For hope* it was we were saved. Now a hope that is realised is not a hope. For none hopes for what he sees. But if we hope for that we do not see, we have courage in the waiting."

When the whole Creation is said to "groan together," it means that there goes up from it an universal groan. Συνωδίνει may describe any agonising pain : here however the 'birth' metaphor (as in Jesus Christ's own saying) is not improbably present. In *v.* 23 'the Spirit,' that is, the gift of the Spirit to man, which came after Christ's Ascension, is said to be an ἀπαρχή of our future inheritance. In 2 Cor. i. and v. it is called an ἀῤῥαβών. The phrase there is just as here. In the one case we have 'a firstfruit in the Spirit'; in the other 'an earnest in the Spirit.' In either case the πνεύματος is an appositional genitive. In Ephes. i. 14 the Holy Spirit is called the "earnest of our inheritance." It is a pledge and proof that one day we shall have it all.

Creation groans ; we groan. It is the full 'sonship' that we want ; for that 'sonship' brings with it the 'bodily redemption.' It is then, as we conceive, that the body, in Pauline phrase, will become πνευματικόν.

In *v.* 24 we find theological doctors differing not a little with regard to τῇ ἐλπίδι. The old view was solid for "by hope." But that is hardly defensible. 'Faith' or 'grace,' as you chance to regard it from man's side or from God's, is the medium of 'saving.' And moreover this act of faith, or this giving of God's grace, is a something now behind us. The 'hope' must lie in front, if it is to correspond to St Paul's statement just below. Therefore "*by hope*" it cannot be. "*In hope*" enjoys the preference of the American company. "*With hope*" might, perhaps, be better—a 'comitative' dative. "*For hope*" has a good deal to be said for it. In Gal. v. 1 we have a similar dative : and there, as well as here, the rendering 'for' suits best. It appears to be employed, as if it were ἐπ' ἐλπίδι, like ἐπ' ἐλευθερίᾳ. The latter is actually found in Gal. v. 13. The ἐσώθημεν refers to the earlier 'redemption,' the redemption of δικαίωσις.

Ἐλπὶς βλεπομένη I have made bold to paraphrase by "a hope that is realised." In English we cannot 'see' a 'hope': we can 'see' the thing we hope for. The variants in this verse do not affect the sense in the least. I have followed the R.V. reading. It matters not whether one says "none hopes for," or "there is no need to hope for." And that represents the amount of divergence in the readings.

In *v.* 25, I should say, the stress must lie not on ἀπεκδεχόμεθα, but on δι' ὑπομονῆς. I have rendered it accordingly. One can afford to wait; one can afford to show courage in waiting, if one has a real 'hope'—a hope like the Christian one.

Ὑπομονή, by the way, is the Christian form of ἀνδρεία. The latter word does not occur in the whole of N.T. Maybe it was rejected from the faith's vocabulary because of its arrogant sound. St Paul does use ἀνδρίζεσθαι in one place, but only once.

We now pass into a section of a highly esoteric character, in the course of which we first touch on one especial way in which the Spirit helps us; and shortly after deal for a time with the puzzling problem of predestination. Let us take these two topics separately.

viii. 26. "And, acting as we act, the Spirit also lends His aid to our infirmities. For how we should pray aright, we are not sure: but the Spirit Himself intercedes on our behalf, with groanings not in words."

It may well be thought that here there is some sort of reference to the strange gift of 'glossolaly.' When that was displayed 'in Church,' mysterious sounds were poured forth, sometimes intelligible, and also sometimes not. These may have been sometimes of the nature of στεναγμοί. Ἀλά-λητος is a hard word. It is only here in N.T. (Liddell and Scott in their Lexicon give one reference from the Anthology.) It ought to mean 'past telling,' and the Vulgate in this place says *inexenarrabilibus.* The natural rendering, therefore, is " with groanings terrible." And indeed it is easy to see that there would be a something terrifying in a paroxysm of 'glossolaly,' in which the unwitting speaker should outwardly seem to be in a very agony of fervent supplication.

In a general way, however, the reference is thought to be to ' unuttered,' or ' mute,' pleadings, of which man has, and can have, no cognisance whatever. Or again, there are who think that these groanings of the Spirit are called 'unutterable' because they may not be uttered. This seems to me most unlikely : for, plainly, from *v.* 27, if anybody heard them, he did not understand them. Only " He that searches the hearts " could fathom that potent pleading. On the whole then I suspect that there is a reference to something of which they knew the secret, but we do not. Yet, truly, the view which supposes a pleading of the Spirit, all unbeknown to us, is far more attractive really, and withal far more encouraging. Perhaps there may be on earth 'pneumatic' persons still, who could throw real light upon it. For commentators cannot. Mere language we can understand: and therefore I will say that συναντιλαμβάνεσθαι is equivalent to our English 'lend a helping hand.' It belongs to everyday speech. In the Gospel of St Luke it is what the busy Martha desires Mary to do. "Our weaknesses" represents "us, weak in our different ways." The singular notwithstanding would have been more intelligible. For the 'weakness' in this case would seem to be well defined—a weakness in laying needs before Our Father in prayer.

viii. 27.   "And He that searcheth men's hearts knows what the mind of

the Spirit is.   For in a way divine
He intercedes for Saints."

Ὁ ἐραυνῶν τὰς καρδίας may be a re-
miniscence of a curious phrase in Proverbs,
xx. 27, ὃς ἐραυνᾷ ταμιεῖα κοιλίας.   But in
Rev. ii. 23 the Son of God declares to the
angel of the Church in Thyatira, "I am He
which searcheth reins and hearts"; and conceivably Christ Himself, when on earth, said
some such thing.   The Fourth Gospel undoubtedly claims for Him some such power
in earthly days.   Yet in this case, one would
suppose, ὁ ἐραυνῶν must be the Father.

It does not appear to me wise to make
the clause ὅτι κατὰ Θεόν κ.τ.λ. depend too
immediately on that which goes just before.
A colon would seem desirable directly after
πνεύματος.   The great God, to whom prayer
is addressed, knows what we cannot know,
the 'intent,' or 'mind,' of the Spirit.   The
term is anthropomorphic, but that cannot be
helped.   The reason St Paul seems to give
for this intuitive knowledge is that the
Spirit's supplication is of itself κατὰ Θεόν.
He that prays and He that hears are more

than *en rapport*; they are actually One. The passage in 1 Cor. ii. (about the spiritual 'wisdom') has certain statements in it, which offer analogy.

The following verse is important because it forms a bridge to the 'predestination' teaching. In itself it but carries forward the idea of the Spirit's aid. That aid is in our prayers. But it really extends to all life. Moreover not only the Spirit is a helper of God's people. Everything helps them; everything must.

> viii. 28. "We are sure, that for those who love God, He makes all things work together for good—for those that are the 'called,' in accordance with His purpose."

The reading in 'W. H.' commends itself, as providing the sense we desiderate. It is God and the purpose of God behind all things that are, that make the believing man's position impregnable. Συνεργεῖν, to be sure, elsewhere is a neuter verb. But it is not unreasonable to suppose that, on occasion, it might be used in a manner corresponding to its sister verb ἐνεργεῖν. And, if it be active here, there is no reason I can see for 'refining' in our rendering. Why imagine a brachylogy? Surely there is meaning enough in the words as they stand.

The κατὰ πρόθεσιν starts a whole new train of thought. It is the spark which fires a whole train, as we shall see directly.

Before I venture on any sort of rendering of the next two verses, let me say something about words. Πρόθεσις is an ordinary late Greek term for 'purpose.' Προγιγνώσκειν is a 'classical' word; it means to 'know beforehand' (to know as a bird, for instance, knows that spring is coming); or, to 'determine' or 'judge' beforehand. In N.T. it occurs four times. First, in Acts xxvi. 5, where St Paul affirms that his fellow-countrymen could bear out what he was saying, if they chose, προγιγνώσκοντές με ἄνωθεν ("because from of old they have knowledge of me"): there the πρό- in προγιγνώσκοντες is practically obliterated

by the ἄνωθεν. In 'Romans' we have it
twice; here and in xi. 2, "God hath not
cast from Him His people, ὃν προέγνω."
That instance, I think, stands apart. It is
found also in 1 Pet. i. 20, where Christ is
spoken of as προεγνωσμένου πρὸ καταβολῆς
κόσμου (which can hardly mean " fore-
known," but must mean "foredetermined"
for that particular service, the redemption
of men with His blood). 2 Peter also
contains it, in the primitive, simpler sense
"having foreknowledge, beware" (iii. 17).

Προορίζειν is non-classical. Further, it
is not in LXX. It is 'N.T.' and later
only. It is read in the notable prayer
(Acts iv. 28): "all the things that Thy
hand and Thy counsel foreordained to
come to pass." It occurs here in this
section twice. Again, in 1 Cor. ii. 7,
where the Apostle speaks of the heavenly
σοφία, he says that God had "foreordained
it (προώρισεν) before the 'world' (πρὸ
τῶν αἰώνων) for our glory." In 'Ephesians' we have two instances; i. 5 (προ-
ορίσας ἡμᾶς εἰς υἱοθεσίαν διὰ Ἰησοῦ

Χριστοῦ) and i. 11. The latter is a passage
very analogous to this in 'Romans.' It
is part of that weighty sentence with which
the Epistle opens. The words are; "according to His good pleasure (εὐδοκίαν),
which He purposed (προέθετο) in Him,
εἰς οἰκονομίαν τοῦ πληρώματος τῶν καιρῶν "
—a very difficult clause, which I conceive
to mean, "to be worked out, when the
right time came," the εἰς being 'temporal'
—"to sum up all things in Christ, the
things in the heavens and the things on
the earth; in Him, I say, in whom also
we were made God's own (ἐν ᾧ καὶ ἐκληρώ-
θημεν), προορισθέντες κατὰ πρόθεσιν τοῦ
τὰ πάντα ἐνεργοῦντος κατὰ τὴν βουλὴν
τοῦ θελήματος αὐτοῦ (foreordained *thereto*
according to the purpose of Him who
maketh all things work to suit the counsel
of His will)."

Here we have four nouns in all to set
forth the conception of the Heavenly Purpose; εὐδοκία, πρόθεσις, βουλή, θέλημα;
together with two verbs, προτίθεσθαι and
προορίζειν. It is neither possible nor of

any profit, I think, to endeavour to discriminate between the 'nominal' terms.
And further, I should say that, in regard
to the verbs, προτίθεσθαι bears the simple
meaning 'propose,' or 'purpose'; while
προορίζειν means 'to appoint beforehand'
—no more. The statement in 'Ephesians,' and the statement in 'Romans'
here, we shall not do amiss to regard as
containing part of that σοφία, of which
mention is made in 'Corinthians.' Of
that wisdom the Apostle says, ἡμῖν ἀπε-
κάλυψεν ὁ θεὸς διὰ τοῦ πνεύματος. And
the question is, what does this mean? and
further, who are ἡμῖν? Does it cover
all Christians together, or does it mean
St Paul himself?

There remains yet one more word to
be briefly discussed. That is εἰκών. In
the incident of the tribute money, εἰκών
means merely 'likeness.' In 'Revelation'
it occurs pretty frequently, to describe the
"image" of the "beast." In St Paul it
is clearly a term covering more than ex-
ternality (as also in Heb. x. 1, where

αὐτὴν τὴν εἰκόνα τῶν πραγμάτων apparently means "the things, as they actually are "). For instance, while in 1 Cor. xi. 7 the male is said to be the εἰκὼν καὶ δόξα Θεοῦ (from Genesis, of course) ; in 2 Cor. iv. 4 the Son Himself is said to be εἰκὼν τοῦ Θεοῦ. The same descriptive phrase is applied to Him in Col. i. 15. In Col. iii. 10 we read of the "new man," who is "renewed...κατ᾽ εἰκόνα τοῦ κτίσαντος αὐτόν" (Genesis, once again). It would seem that the Pauline doctrine is, that our 'manhood' is to be substantially as Christ's 'manhood,' when the day of its perfection comes, at the second Redemption. It will be more than mere 'resemblance'; very much more.

And now let us face the two verses :

viii. 29, 30. "For those whom He 'foreknew,' He also appointed of old to attain to the intimate likeness of His own Son ; that so He might be the firstborn in a family of many Cf. Heb. brethren. And whom He appointed ^{ii. 11.} of old, them He also 'called'; and

21—2

whom He 'called,' them He also
'justified'; and whom He 'justified,'
them He also 'glorified.'"

From the very nature of God—from
our bare conception of Him—it follows,
of necessity, that His 'knowledge' is absolute. It transcends all bounds of time
and bounds of space. This 'foreknowledge' we must assume; we cannot help
it. At times St Paul loves to dwell on
the amazing comfort that lies, for every
humble believer, in the idea that his
own 'call' is part of an eternal purpose.
But how did he come by the thought?
Did he deduce it, as we should do, from
the definition of Godhead? Or does he
claim in his statements about it a 'plenary
inspiration'? On them, as everyone knows,
stupendous superstructures have been upreared. Ruthless logic has divided mankind not only into σωζόμενοι and ἀπολλύ-
μενοι, but even virtually into σεσωσμένοι
and ἀπολωλότες. And, no doubt, some
have gone so far as to see the futility of
any preaching at all in a world where

some are doomed everlastingly to death
and others, equally certainly, to everlasting bliss.

In our age we have come to understand that such conclusions will not hold.
We cannot let the concept of God's 'foreknowledge'—inevitable as that is—conflict
with that other concept of His unending
Love. In consequence, we refrain from
pushing to their logical issues any apostolic pronouncements, however they may
help to strengthen faith. We may be
sure he did not mean or desire that any
rigid system should be raised upon what
he has said. Our own 'Church of Eng-
land' Article on this topic is a marvel of
cautious statement; especially considering
the age in which it was penned. Then
religious 'determinism' (as fatal to morality
as any other 'determinism') was fairly
rampant. Now it is well-nigh dead. The
swing of the pendulum is all the other
way. Maybe it has swung too far.

For the rest we must remember that
the very term 'foreknowledge'—or indeed

'fore-' anything else—is bound to lead us astray. For the existence of God is time-less. Moreover, the Apostle—whatever views we may hold of the nature of in-spiration—in speaking as he does, was plainly a man of his age.

But let us return to his words. In προέγνω there may be, as S. maintains, a flavour of O.T. usage. In Amos iii. 2 we read, "You only have I *known* (ἔγνων) of all the nations of the earth." There 'known' means 'accepted,' 'recognised,' even 'chosen for mine.' There may be a similar ἔγνων in St Matthew vii. 23. But I rather doubt it. Nor am I clear about this 'peculiar' usage in Romans viii.; though in xi., I must admit, it seems de-cidedly likely. For there the ὃν προέγνω ("whom He 'knew' of old") may very well re-echo the ἔγνων of the Prophet. Here I should be content with a very general sense, "had in His mind of old" (keep-ing, of course, the translation "foreknew"). The 'προ' travels back in thought to the time before all time. In the other προέγνω

it is a matter of earthly history. Προώρισεν
(Vulg. *praedestinavit*) is adequately rendered by 'foreordained' or 'appointed of
old.' '*Praedestinavit*' itself was once a
harmless word. Now, as 'Ian Maclaren'
might say, it is dark with the accumulated
darkness of ages of theology. The phrase,
which sets before us what we are 'appointed' to be, needs very careful handling. We are to share the μορφή of the
εἰκών of God's Own Son. It is plain
'man' cannot share the μορφή of God
(especially if μορφή is—as Lightfoot vows
it is—a term that is consecrate to express
'essential being'). What we can share
is Christ's 'Sonship.' The reality of sonship, as perfected and consummated in
the very 'Son of sons'—that we may well
attain. We are beyond dispute to be
like Him, very like Him, for the idea is Cf. 1 John
emphasised by the intentional reiteration. iii. 2.
And there we must stop. Only, as St Paul
declares, this likeness one day to be must
be recognised and cherished, as in accordance with a 'purpose,' that was before

time was. Still, here we do not find any
phrase like πρὸ τῶν αἰώνων. However, in
the end, that matters not. The general
issue is this; we are to look forward to a
day when Christ will be indeed the 'Eldest
Brother' in a mighty family.

Verse 30 marks the stages in the
evolution of the believer. First, in the
far-off past, in the abysm of eternity, the
everlasting 'purpose'; then, on the stage
of earth, the 'call'; the 'call' once welcomed by 'faith,' succeeds the δικαίωσις,
the 'acceptance' as God's own. Here we
look for another term, which is not present. After δικαίωσις, normally, would
follow ἁγιασμός. But that we overleap,
and pass to the final stage of all, the stage
represented by ἐδόξασε. Here again we
should have looked for δοξάσει. But
not so; the thing is conceived as potentially accomplished. In the mind of God
it is.

The thought that underlies the pair of
verses is predominantly of that stupendous
destiny (reaching forward and reaching

backward beyond all flight of thought) which belongs to the people of God. It is *just because they are His*, they may assure their hearts all is absolutely true.

In view of truths so stupendous, what confidence should be ours!

viii. 31, 32. "This being so, what shall we say? If God be for us, who is against us? *He* spared not His own Son, but delivered Him (to death) on behalf of us all! How shall He not then with Him freely give us everything?" Cf. Psalm cxviii. 6. Cf. Gen. xxii. 16 (LXX).

The 'gift of all gifts,' obviously, is pledge of all other 'givings'; that they cannot and will not fail.

There follows a well-known problem, and a very hotly argued one, in textual punctuation. This is the method I would follow:

First comes a general question, τίς ἐγκαλέσει; This question is not answered. Instead it is contemplated in the light of two great facts. Not only God, but Christ as well, are the champions of the elect.

No accusation then; no assault in any form;
can conceivably prevail.

> viii. 33—35. "Who shall impeach
> God's elect?"

> "God is He that acquitteth : who
> is it that condemns ? Christ it is, who
> died—nay rather, who was raised, and
> is at God's right hand; who also inter-
> cedes for us. Who is it, that shall
> part us from Christ's love?"

The first question merely repeats, in a
more special form, and under a particular
figure, the question of *v.* 31, τίς καθ' ἡμῶν ;
The 'elect' (who are the same people, in
St Paul, as the κλητοί, though viewed from
a different standpoint) do not lend themselves to accusation. For why? God
"acquits" (the forensic sense is demanded
by the context) ; then who is like to "condemn"? Aye, speaking even more broadly (for now we seem to bid farewell to the
question, τίς ἐγκαλέσει;), have we not a
'rock of defence' in the Person of Jesus
Christ? He "died" for us—there is proof
of love supreme. He was "raised," He is

"at God's right hand"—there is proof of
infinite power. He "makes intercession
for us"—there is proof of effectual aid.

Is it conceivable any person can sever
us from that love? or even any *thing*?

viii. 35—39. "Shall pressure, or
straitness of circumstance, or persecution, or famine, or peril, or the sword?
As it stands in Holy writ, *For for* Psalm
Thy sake we are slaughtered all the xliv. 23 (LXX).
day long; we are counted as sheep for
the knife."

"Nay, in these things, all of them,
we are more than victorious, through
Him that loved us. For I am convinced, that neither death nor life; nor
angels, nor principalities, nor powers;
nor things present, nor things to come;
nor height nor depth, nor any other
created thing, shall be able to sever us
from the Love of God in Jesus Christ
our Lord."

The Apostle himself had had (as 2 Cor.
xi. testifies) no small experience of the
thousand and one hardships that may beset

a Christian man, especially a missionary.
In all the long catalogue there is only one
thing he knew not; and that he was to
know before the end. The ὅτι in *v.* 36 is not
'recitative'; it belongs to the quotation.
Our splendid "are more than conquerors,"
which I do not like to degrade by insertion
in my paraphrase, is a legacy from the
Genevan Version. The Genevans may
have darkened counsel with their predes-
tinarian tendencies, but we owe them
much for this. In *v.* 38 the word δυνάμεις
seems somehow to have got misplaced.
It appears to belong to the group with
ἄγγελοι and ἀρχαί. Πάσης ἀρχῆς καὶ
ἐξουσίας καὶ δυνάμεως come together in
Ephes. i. 21, all being appellations of the
angelic hierarchy. In Col. i. 16 we have
a somewhat different nomenclature, θρόνοι
...κυριότητες...ἀρχαί...ἐξουσίαι. This an-
gelology (covering apparently malignant
powers as well as beneficent) belongs to
Jewish thought. It is no necessary part
of a Christian man's belief. A ὕψωμα
is really 'a high thing,' a thing that is

uplifted; βάθος correspondingly 'a low thing'
(only by analogy). Maybe, the two terms
cover ἐπουράνια and καταχθόνια. In 2 Cor. Phil. ii. 1c
x. 5 we have "and every ὕψωμα that up-
lifts itself against the γνῶσις of God."
There the "high thing" is different; it
seems to stand for "arrogant thought."
In *v.* 39 οὔτε τις κτίσις ἑτέρα covers any
conceivable thing that may exist, though
it be beyond our ken. In ἑτέρα there lies
the meaning 'different in kind.' Just now
the question was "Who shall sever us
from the love of Christ" (*v.* 36, where our
oldest MSS. read 'God,' as they do here):
now it is "from the Love of God," but
this love for man all centres in the Person
of the Crucified.

§ 14. ISRAEL AND THE MYSTERY OF
ELECTION

With the end of chap. viii., as S. remarks, we have reached the end of the
main argument. But there still is much

to discuss. The writer still had in mind things he desired to say. For instance Israel—what about Israel? To the student of the Old Testament, it is a highly absorbing question; above all, to a Jew. Taking accordingly a new start (there is no connexion whatever, such as Greek usage insists upon, between this chapter and the last), St Paul says what he has in his heart about the matter. Incidentally we have given us that list of Israel's "advantages" we looked for in chap. iii.; but then were disappointed.

ix. 1—3. "I speak truth, as a Christian man, I do not lie; my conscience bears me out, in the Holy Spirit. I have great pain and unceasing anguish in my heart. For I could have wished to be myself 'cut off' from Christ, for my brothers' sake, my kinsmen 'after the flesh'...."

Cf. Exod. xxxii. 32.

The ἐν Χριστῷ and ἐν πνεύματι ἁγίῳ of this solemn opening are very hard to define and also to reproduce in straightforward English. The συνείδησις, it will be seen, is detached from the man, as is only natural; seeing it is the faculty which passes judgment on his actions. The form ηὐχόμην implies that the wish is impossible. But the spirit of the Apostle is as the spirit of Moses. He is fain to sacrifice himself for the good of his countrymen. Ἀνάθεμα in LXX (especially Joshua vi., vii.) is the accepted rendering for the '*accursed* (or, '*devoted*') *thing*.' This term has already appeared in Pauline Scriptures (Gal. i. 8; 1 Cor. xvi. 22) in the same sense it bears here, "Let him be devoted to destruction." In later days it became only too freely used in the Church. Ἀνάθεμα...ἀπό... means, literally, "accursed and cut off from." Now follows the full list of Israel's exceptional privileges, setting off in heightened colour the amazing paradox of the Nation's apparent rejection:

ix. 4, 5. "...people, who are Israelites; to whom belongs the Sonship, and the Presence, and the Covenants, and the Law-giving, and the Ritual, and the Promises; whose are the

Cf. Exod. xvi. 10.

Patriarchs and of whom in earthly descent is God's Anointed One— He that is God supreme, blessed to all eternity. Amen."

In their own speech Jews were called the *'Sons of Israel'* (represented by Ἰσ- ραηλῖται). Now 'Israel' was a name of solemn significance, closely associated with one of the Nation's most cherished traditions. *Thy name shall be called no more Jacob, but Israel* (Gen. xxxii. 28); so had said the mysterious stranger that wrestled at Peniel. And 'Israelite' is surely a name of unique significance. The 'Sonship' of Israel is stated, in very decisive language, in the prophecy of Hosea, *Out of Egypt have I called my Son*, ἐξ Αἰγύπτου ἐκάλεσα τὸν υἱόν Μου; though that is not the form preserved in LXX: for there it is not *My Son*, but *his children*; μετεκάλεσα τὰ τέκνα αὐτοῦ. From which we may perhaps conclude that the words so familiar to us from the quotation in our first Gospel were not in the writer's mind. However, more striking still is the statement in

Exodus iv. (to which a reference is all
but certain). In that passage it runs;
*And thou shalt say to Pharaoh, Israel is
my firstborn son ; and I have said to thee,
Send forth my people, that they may worship Me. If then thou wilt not send them
forth, lo, I will slay thy firstborn son*
(LXX). The Δόξα is, of course, the
Shekinah. The plural 'Covenants' covers
the various covenants with Abraham, with
Isaac, with Jacob, as well as the national
covenant of which Moses was 'mediator.'
In regard to ἡ λατρεία S. quotes a
Rabbinic saying of much interest. The
'Promises' reach their climax in the Mes-
sianic hope. For us, the foremost of all
is that one which affirms, *And in thy seed
shall all the nations of the earth be blessed*
—interpreted, be it understood, on LXX
lines ; for of the meaning of that version,
as distinguished from the Hebrew, there
can be very little doubt ; καὶ ἐνευλογηθή-
σονται ἐν τῷ σπέρματί σου πάντα τὰ ἔθνη
τῆς γῆς, Gen. xxii. 18.

The question that arises with regard to

the application of the closing words of *v.* 5
is discussed by S. with a lucidity altogether
admirable. His conclusion is that they do
refer to the Lord Jesus Christ Himself.
At this, he says, he arrives 'with slight
hesitation.' St Paul's teaching about
Christ's Person is unmistakeable. He was
always ἐν μορφῇ θεοῦ (Phil.) ; He is εἰκὼν
τοῦ θεοῦ τοῦ ἀοράτου ; He is πρωτότοκος
πάσης κτίσεως. But is He ever called
distinctly 'God'? The Vatican MS. has
a colon here. That would make the clause
a doxology. On the other hand, in Rabbinic use, a doxology of the kind is properly
employed *only after the mention of God* ;
so that this would be abnormal, if it were
indeed a doxology. Moreover this very
verse was quoted by Cyril Alex. in answer
to Julian's avowal that St Paul never called
Christ 'God.' Again, an ascription of
glory to Christ, not unlike this in general
character, is found in 2 Tim. iv. 18.

Moreover grammar lends her aid, and
suggests that, had the words been a doxology addressed to the Father, their form is

unusual. The ὤν should be omitted. As it stands, it would naturally be taken as equivalent to a relative clause, ὅς ἐστιν ἐπὶ πάντων θεός. The probabilities are very nicely balanced. On the whole, however, the evidence bears out the rendering of our own English versions, which take the words as belonging to Christ, and not to the Father. Compare the Johannine statements; θεὸς ἦν ὁ λόγος and ὁ λόγος σὰρξ ἐγένετο. The κατὰ σάρκα here seems to call for a like antithesis. All this (the student will know) is just abbreviated 'S.'

For the rest, Israel's grandest privilege is unmistakeably this. From Israel was to come the Hope of the world.

Was there, then, no hope for Israel? To that topic we shall return in the course of argument. Meanwhile there are other ideas that must engage attention. For instance, this one. There is 'Israel' and 'Israel.'

The formula introducing *v.* 6 is wholly unexampled. To say so is to put it mildly. There is no other use of οἶος even remotely analogous. The neuter singular οἷον is found in no other place. Accordingly we must guess what it may mean. At first one wonders whether a classical οἷόν τε may be lurking in hiding. But such a use is wholly unknown to the New Testament. The Vulgate says, *non autem quod exciderit verbum Dei*, which at least possesses the merit of being even more unintelligible, if possible, than the Greek. Our English is probably right; " But it is not as though...."

ix. 6—9. " Of course, I do not pretend that the Word of God has failed. Not all that are from Israel, you know, *are* Israel. Nor, because they are Abraham's 'seed,' are they all 'children.' No! *In Isaac shall a seed be named thee.* That is to say, not the children 'of the flesh' are the children of God; but the children of the Promise are reckoned as the 'seed.' For this saying is matter of promise, *About this season will I come, and Sarah shall have a son.*"

Ἐκπίπτειν (in LXX) is a word that is

Gen. xxi. 12 (LXX).

Cf. Gal. iv. 28.

Gen. xviii. 10—14 (exact LXX).

employed especially of flowers. As in
Isaiah xl. 7, 8 ἐξηράνθη ὁ χόρτος καὶ τὸ
ἄνθος ἐξέπεσε, τὸ δὲ ῥῆμα τοῦ θεοῦ ἡμῶν
μένει εἰς τὸν αἰῶνα (the quotation of 1 Peter).
This is the only use of the kind in N.T.
In 1 Cor. xiii. it should be ἡ ἀγάπη οὐδέποτε
πίπτει. The Isaianic passage probably
suggested the word. Κληθήσεται (in *v*. 7)
means little more than ἔσται. In classical
Greek κέκλημαι sometimes means only
'I am.' The point of the citation from
Gen. xviii. we must take to be, If you come
to think of it, even Isaac was not born
naturally. He was not a τέκνον σαρκός.
From the beginning of the race mere
'natural' descent was thus depreciated.

However another idea is contained in
the section also, though it is not emphasised.
Abraham had another son; he had Ishmael.
But Ishmael was set aside; he was not
recognised as being the σπέρμα. Here
we see 'election' working. It is even
more prominent in the instance that follows
after.

ix. 10. "Not only so, but Rebecca

also, brought to bed *at one time* of Isaac our father...."

At this point the sentence breaks off, and when Rebecca next reappears, she is in the dative (αὐτῇ). The word κοίτη in N.T. is always suggestive of marriage. But κοίτην ἔχειν is apparently unique. Ἐξ ἑνός, one would imagine, must be corrupt. The idea that underlies must be not *one* husband, but *two* children at *one* birth.

ix. 11—13. "For the children being not yet born, and having done nothing good or evil, that the purpose of God might abide, which works by election—not depending on things done, but on (the will of) the Caller—

Gen. xxv. 23 (LXX).

it was said to her, *The elder shall serve the younger.* As it stands in Holy

Mal. i. 2.

writ, *Isaac I have loved, Esau I have hated.*"

The word ἐκλογή is not in LXX. But the idea of 'choosing out' is everywhere. In N.T. only in 'Romans' has ἐκλογή this meaning. 'Conduct' (ἔργα), the Apostle avers, has nothing to do with 'election.'

There is no 'merit' in it (in modern phrase);
it rests wholly on God's will. This conception appears to us a somewhat perilous
doctrine : but, as S. points out, St Paul was
controverting the contemporary Rabbinic
notion that somehow Israel was chosen for
exceptional worth in him. For us the
' Jacob' type, if we stop to think, commends
itself conclusively, as compared with the
' Esau' type ; and we feel that, though the
creature must not argue with the Creator,
it is only on the assumption that He is
holier and wiser and more just in every
way. If you push the Pauline conception,
set forward in this passage, you will find
yourself with a God on a level with
Mahomet's—a God for whom right and
wrong simply do not exist, a Being of
unlimited power and measureless caprice.
Yet, plainly, when man claims 'merit,' he
must be put in mind that *before God* he
can have none.

The passage, cited from Malachi, contains a late conception in its attitude to
Esau' or 'Edom.' In Deut. xxiii. it is

expressly said, *Thou shalt not abhor an Edomite, for he is thy brother.* But the famous Psalm bears witness to a growing enmity of Israel towards this 'brother,' based upon unbrotherly conduct (Ps. cxxxvii. 7).

St Paul has now stated the dogma of 'election,' in its naked simplicity. He forthwith proceeds to reply to the objection that arises unbidden.

ix. 14—16. "What then are we to say? Is there injustice with God? Nay, nay, impossible!"

"To Moses, He says, you know, *I will pity, whomsoever I pity; and will have mercy on whomsoever I have mercy.*"

Ex. xxxiii. 19 (LXX).

"So then, it is not a matter of human wish, nor human exertion, but of the pity of God."

For ἀδικία the Vulgate very rightly says *iniquitas.* Why our version has "unrighteousness," I cannot tell. The quotation from Exodus is curiously used. The emphasis is laid on the '*whomsoever*';

in the original it lies on the futures ἐλεήσω
and οἰκτειρήσω. Whom God pities, He
will pity; to whom He shows mercy, He
will show mercy. It is really a proclamation of the essential 'graciousness' that is
Jehovah's attribute. In *v.* 16, so far as
I know, no adequate explanation of τοῦ
τρέχοντος has been discovered. 'Running
a race,' or 'a desperate race,' is an idea
familiar enough. But to 'run' for to 'exert
oneself' is a wholly different matter.
Maybe, if the word is correct, it is merely
due to assonance.

ix. 17, 18. "Why? The Scripture
says to Pharaoh, *Just for this I have* Exod. ix
raised thee up, that in thee I might 16 (not
display my power, and that my name LXX).
might be noised abroad in all the
earth."

"Accordingly, whom He will,
He pities; and whom He will, He
hardens."

Reference to the text of Exodus will
show that the message of the Almighty to
the proud king of Egypt (of the North

land and of the South) is that, whereas he
might have been slain outright with the
sword of pestilence, he has been, for God's
own purpose, allowed to recover from the
evils, with which his people have been
plagued. This is, in the original text, the
nature of the 'raising up.' Our R.V. says,
have I made thee to stand. The A.V.
rendering is apparently affected by the
citation of St Paul. Such another use of
'raise' we have in St James v. 15. The
compound verb is used in Habakkuk and
Zachariah in the sense which the writer
postulates. In any case, Pharaoh is a
mere instrument in God's hand.

The σκληρύνει of *v.* 18 is the LXX
term for 'harden.' S. is plainly very right
in declaring too much must not be built
up on the handling by the Apostle of his
citation. Here the school of Calvin errs.
At this point the figure of Pharaoh recedes
into the background. We have instead
the petulant objection of some unknown,
arraigning in general terms the Providence
of God. To this the Apostle makes reply

that God is God, and men are but His
creatures.

ix. 19—21. "You will say then
to me, What fault does He find now?
No one withstands His will! Nay,
but who art thou, O man, to bandy
words with God? Shall the thing Cf. Isai.
xxix. 16.
moulded say to the moulder, Why
hast thou fashioned me so? Can it
be the potter has not full power over
his clay, to make out of the selfsame
lump one vessel for honour, another
for dishonour?"

The thought in *v.* 19 is that man must
be irresponsible. He is as he is made.
The good are good, because He made
them good; the evil likewise evil. The
suggestion is that the maker must bear the
blame and not the made. The answer is,
in effect, that all such talk is blasphemous.
The idea of 'vessels for honour' and
'vessels for dishonour' reappears in 2 Tim.
ii. 20. But there it is implied that it rests
with a man's own self, which sort he is.
Here the Potter's power is unlimited. All

depends upon His will. It is futile and irrational for mere man to dispute His power, His knowledge, or His wisdom.

This hard doctrine is modified, in part, by what comes next. There may be a gracious purpose concealed from us, in what to us might seem to be unfair dealing.

ix. 22—29. "Suppose God, wishful to display His wrath (at sin) and to make known His power, has borne with much long-suffering abominable things, right fitted for destruction; as well as to make known the riches of His glory, in the case of things He pities, which He prepared long ago for glory...."

"Even us, whom He hath called, not only from among the Jews, but also from the Gentiles; as indeed it says in Hosea, *I will call my 'not-people,' my people; and her that was not beloved, beloved. And it shall be in the place, where it was said to them, Ye are not my people, even there they*

Hos. ii. 23 (freely cited).

Hos. i. 10 (the 'there' inserted).

shall be called the sons of the Living God."

"Isaiah cries touching Israel; *If* Isai. x. 22
the number of the children of Israel (possibly
the correct
shall be as the sand of the sea, it is the LXX
text: our
remnant that shall be saved. For a reading
being
word complete and concise shall the corrupt).
Lord bring about on the earth."

"Indeed, as Isaiah has said before,
Unless the Lord of Hosts had left us Isai. i. 9
behind a seed, we should have become (LXX).
*as Sodom and been likened to Go-
morrah."*

In all this there is very much to puzzle
and divide interpreters. Plainly, the absolute will of God destroys man's will
altogether. On the other hand, if it belongs
to the very nature of God to be 'wrathful'
against sin, it is conceivable we must
postulate the existence of sinful persons.
But that does not condemn any given
person 'A,' to be one of these σκεύη
ὀργῆς. It is not said (as S. remarks) God
made them to be so. It only says, He
bore them.

The truth is, *v.* 21 introduces the un-
compromising image of the potter and his
clay. The potter makes out of his clay
precisely what he likes. We have, most
of us, seen him doing it; and in the East
it is a sight of every day. There could be
no more apt illustration of power entirely
unlimited. If it were not for the σκεύη
ὀργῆς and σκεύη ἐλέους, we might have
thought that in *v.* 22 we had left the potter
behind. However in actual experience
some are 'bad' men, some are 'good'; and
it is God that made them all. That is *ex
hypothesi.* In *v.* 22 a reason, a theory, is
put forward. It is not stated as fact, but
as throwing light on things. The sentence
containing this 'theory' (if a theory it be,
as the εἰ would seem to indicate) unhappily is highly intricate, not to say entirely
entangled, and we cannot unravel it. The
first verse of the section perhaps is intelligible as it stands; Suppose God put up
with σκεύη ὀργῆς, for a twofold purpose, to
display His wrath at sin, which is one
aspect of His Holiness, and to make knowr

His Power. This is thrown out as a
suggestion. The view of Aquinas (see S.)
appears to state plainly and well the gist of
it. The next verse (*v.* 25) has no construction, and we cannot be sure at all
what St Paul intended. We can only
assume it is this; As bad people exist, for
the twofold purpose stated ; so there are
people who exist, that on them God may
display the wonders of His Mercy. Only,
the writer has not said so. His thoughts
are carried off to identify the σκεύη ἐλέους
with the people of the Lord Jesus Christ
(ἡμᾶς), some of whom are actually Jews
and some are Gentiles.

High Calvinism depends on a rigorous
interpretation of σκεύη ὀργῆς and σκεύη
ἐλέους, as human beings made by God, in
His rôle as the Mighty Potter, *expressly*,
in each case, for 'wrath' and for 'mercy.'
The Apostle, I repeat, does not say so.
They are all σκεύη, to be sure, for they
are all of the Potter's making. But we
need not assume they are made to be
respectively σκεύη ὀργῆς and σκεύη ἐλέους.

That goes too far. Free will wholly disappears, and all created Mankind is reduced to a mere collection of hopeless automata. How Greek and Latin Fathers —how Origen and Chrysostom, or Augustine and his followers—have taken up the cudgels on the one side or the other of the endless controversy, can be seen excellently set forth in the pages of S.

All that we are concerned with here is the plain statement of what the writer does actually say. For that, what is needed is a more or less adequate rendering, together with some indication of the gaps in the original.

A reverent modern mind would be inclined to urge that the image of the potter and the clay cannot cover the facts of creation ; where the Creator is a Being of perfect Love and Holiness, the 'Father' that Christ revealed : and the creature is 'rational,' with power of free choice between good and evil. It only exhibits the truth of things as they are in part.

If one should say, ' But I cannot accept

your illustration as adequate,' what is the answer? Is it, 'Accept it, or burn'? I do not think so; nor do I believe that St Paul has either said it, or would have said it.

Towards the close of the chapter his thought is entirely diverted to prophecies foreshadowing a partial rejection of Israel. The first, in *v.* 25, is from Hosea ii. 23. The οὐ λαός μου, in the original, does not mean 'heathen' people, but *the ten tribes* who will be restored. As S. says, 'the writer applies the principle underlying the words.'

The next is from the same prophetic writer (Hos. i. 10). The original reference and the Pauline application are the same as in the other.

These two citations are employed to indicate the readiness of the All Father to accept as His children those who are not so by birth and begetting.

The other quotations are brought forward to support the idea that all 'Israel' is not 'Israel'; that it is only in some of the Nation that the promise will be realised.

In the ' LXX ' text, the first quotation runs ;

Καὶ ἐὰν γένηται ὁ λαὸς Ἰσραὴλ ὡς ἡ ἄμμος τῆς θαλάσσης, τὸ κατάλιμμα αὐτῶν σωθήσεται· λόγον συντελῶν καὶ συντέμνων ἐν δικαιοσύνῃ, ὅτι λόγον συντετμημένον ποιήσει Κύριος ἐν τῇ οἰκουμένῃ ὅλῃ (Isai. x. 22, 23).

The reading of the quotation in our text of Romans is compact and much more intelligible than the LXX text we have.

Ἐὰν ᾖ ὁ ἀριθμὸς τῶν υἱῶν Ἰσραὴλ ὡς ἡ ἄμμος τῆς θαλάσσης, τὸ ὑπόλιμμα σωθήσεται —so far it is plainly a citation from memory—λόγον γὰρ συντελῶν καὶ συντέμνων ποιήσει Κύριος ἐπὶ τῆς γῆς. An 'only' is wanting, to be sure ; even badly wanting. But otherwise the sense is plain enough. In the latter part of the LXX is a palpable dittographia. In St Paul this disappears. How it ever got there, it is for LXX critics to say. Obviously λόγον συντέμνων ποιήσει Κύριος and λόγον

συντετμημένον ποιήσει Κύριος are the same
Hebrew text, *rendered in two ways*.
The second quotation is from Isaiah i. 9.
The προείρηκεν would seem to refer to its
earlier position in the writings of the
prophet. Isaiah i. portrays a lamentable
picture of desolation, which has overtaken
the land. It is almost as completely de-
stroyed as Sodom was, or Gomorrah.
Here is not the quotation we should have
chosen, to illustrate the 'remnant' doctrine.
Indeed, the 'LXX' text departs from the
Hebrew in reading σπέρμα instead of
"*remnant*." And no intelligible explanation
of the citation appears unless 'remnant'
was originally part of it *as it left the
writer's hand*. Therefore one would suspect
that our σπέρμα is the correction of a
Pauline ὑπόλιμμα.

ix. 30—33. "What then are we
to say? *Why, this.* Gentiles that
followed not after 'righteousness,' Cf. Phil.
have attained to 'righteousness'—the iii. 12.
righteousness that comes by faith.
Whereas Israel pursuing a Law to

lead to 'righteousness,' has not suc-
ceeded in getting to its goal. Wherefore? Because they did not follow
the way of faith, but the way of legal
doings. They stumbled at the 'stone
of stumbling'; as it says in Holy

Isaiah
(a conflate
quotation).
Writ, *Behold, I lay in Sion a stone
of stumbling and a rock of offence;
and everyone that 'believeth' on Him
shall not be put to shame."*

Verse 30 contains a statement, not a
question. 'Righteousness' is technical
throughout. It stands for 'acceptance
with God.' The νόμον δικαιοσύνης (in
v. 31) is very odd. We should have expected the two cases to be exactly reversed,
νόμου δικαιοσύνην. That it is not so makes
the latter clause exceptionally obscure.
What can it signify to say in English
"they did not reach the Law that leads
to righteousness"? No paraphrase can
be suggested for νόμον δικαιοσύνης which
would make the matter really clear. Yet,
"the law of righteousness" is the uniform
rendering of our English versions. R.V.

says "a law of righteousness"—which
does not mend things much.

There are two Isaianic passages, worked
in together, at the end of *v.* 32 and in *v.* 33.
Isaiah, viii. 14, speaking of the God of
Israel, says, *Let him be your dread....And
he shall be for a sanctuary; but for a stone
of stumbling and for a rock of offence to
both the houses of Israel....*

In the second chapter of 1 Peter we
have all the three "stones" of prophetic
writ combined together: the *precious
corner stone* of Isaiah xxviii. 16 is identified with the *stone which the builders
rejected* of Psalm cxviii., and also with
the λίθος προσκόμματος of Isaiah viii.
Our Lord Himself claimed to be the
rejected "Stone" of the Psalm. It was
inevitable the recognition should be extended by His followers to those two
other "stones," Isaiah's "*costly stone*"
and the same prophet's λίθος προσκόμματος. In 1 Peter the Isaianic citations,
though close together, are carefully kept
distinct.

Here they are worked up together into one 'conflate' quotation.

Behold!   I lay in Sion
>
> (Isaiah xxviii. 16, but not clear LXX)

a stone of stumbling and a rock of offence
>
> (Isaiah viii. 14 : in LXX λίθου προσ-κόμματι and πέτρας πτώματι)

and he that believeth
>
> (Isaiah xxviii. 16, LXX)

(on Him)
>
> (a Pauline interpretative comment)

shall not be ashamed.
>
> (Isaiah xxviii., but not in the LXX form.)

It is well known our English says, "*He that believeth shall not make haste.*" At first sight it seems a far cry from "not being ashamed" to "not making haste." Cheyne rejects "shall not make haste" in favour of "shall not give way." I think I

have heard it suggested that it is not impossible to bring into line the Hebrew and
the Greek. But the method of it I only
half recall. The explanation presented the
LXX as being an interpretative paraphrase of the metaphor ('slipping away,'
or the like) contained in the original. All
we have now to note is that the two
'stones' are identified with one another,
and with Christ: that the ἐπ' αὐτῷ is inserted by St Paul to bring this teaching
out—the teaching that Christ is the "precious stone" laid by the Lord in Sion :
and, lastly, that ὁ πιστεύων, which need
mean no more than "he that trusteth," is
definitely associated with the theologic
virtue 'faith'; faith having been mentioned just above, in *vv.* 31 and 32. S.
remarks there may have been an early
Christian *catena* on which both writers
were drawing. That seems probable
enough.

For the rest, Christ clearly was a very
real '*stone of stumbling*' for the Jews.
The great mistake made by Israel is

developed in the next verses. But first the Apostle sets on record once again his bitter sorrow at it all.

> x. 1, 2. "Brothers, the desire of my heart at any rate, and my supplication towards God (are) for them, that they may be saved. I bear them witness they have a zeal for God; but an unintelligent zeal."

When a μέν has no answering δέ the omission of the antithesis is often expressed in English as above. The εἰς σωτηρίαν, which must mean what our version says, is without any parallel. Ἐπίγνωσις is not now thought to bear the 'intensive' sense that Lightfoot attached to it. Here such a sense is not required. What they lacked was *spiritual discernment*, nothing more. They simply did not understand things.

> x. 3. "Not knowing about God's 'righteousness,' and going about to compass a 'righteousness' of their own, they failed to yield themselves to the 'righteousness' of God...."

"God's righteousness" is the method, of winning acceptance with God, Himself has appointed. In effect it was simply Christ. As Christ said, *He* is the "Way." And so St Paul says here, but in other words ;

      x. 4. "For Christ is the goal of Law; *He is 'righteousness'* for every believer."

My interpretation is that the 'end' of 'Law' is that, at which Law aimed. It aimed at securing God's favour by the merit of perfect obedience. For men this was impossible : it could not be achieved. Only the Lord Jesus, of all mankind, ever compassed it. But the thought of His perfect obedience is not here. "Christ is Law's end" means, I think—I cannot see how any other meaning carries quite enough—"*Christ is 'Righteousness.'*" Εἰς δικαιοσύνην may only imply "so far as acceptance with God goes." But, con-sidering that, in Greek, things end 'into' and not 'in,' I suspect it is something more. Other interpretations of τέλος are ;

" end " (historical termination) of Law, as
a system ; or even " consummation," " perfection." Both are true, but neither is
adequate.

If the sense of τέλος I would maintain
is viewed as impossible, my alternative
would be to paraphrase as follows :

" For Christ ends Law for ever,
in regard to winning God's favour,
for everyone that believes."

That is to say, the way of Law, so painful
and so ineffectual, is for all time superseded by the new way, which is Christ.
Further, this ' way ' is a very near way
(μάλα δ' ἐγγύθι ναίει).

Cf. Gal.
iii. 12.

      x. 5.   " For Moses writes of the
' righteousness,' that comes by law ;
It is the man, that has achieved them,
that shall live by them...."

' Life ' and ' righteousness,' of course,
are here identified. The man who achieves
the commands in every particular is δίκαιος ;
he is in God's ' favour ' ; his name is written
in God's Book. The citation is from Levit.
xviii. 5.

x. 6—10. " But the ' Righteousness,' that comes by faith, speaks in
another tone ; *Say not in thy heart,*
who shall ascend into Heaven (that is,
to bring Christ down) ; *or who shall*
go down into the depth (that is, to
bring Christ from the dead). But
what does it say ? *Nigh thee is the*
word, on thy lips and in thy heart
(that is, the message of faith which
we proclaim). For if thou shalt confess with thy lips Jesus as Lord, and
if thou shalt believe in thy heart, that
God raised Him from the dead, thou
shalt be saved. For with the heart one
believes, and is '*justified*' ; and with
the lips one confesses, and is '*saved.*'"
This passage is palpably based on a
passage in Deuteronomy (xxx. 11—14).
Literally rendered that passage runs :
> *for this command, that I command thee,*
> > *is not exceeding burdensome,*
> > *nor is it far from thee.*
It is not in the heaven above,
> *crying* (λέγων), *Who will ascend*

Cf. 1 Pet.
i. 25.

for us into heaven, and get it for us?
   and having heard it,
      we will do it.
No, nor is it beyond the sea, crying,
   Who shall cross over for us
      to the far side of the sea,
   and who is to get it (λάβῃ) *for us,*
   and make it audible for us?
      and we will do it.
The Word (ῥῆμα) *is very near thee,*
   on thy lips and in thy heart
   and in thy hands to do it.

Our own 'R.V.' is very near this, save
for the omission of '*and in thy hands.*'
Otherwise the variation is exceedingly
small. The writer applies the language
to set forth the simplicity, the exceeding
nearness, of his 'righteousness'—the new
and only way of finding peace with God.

He represents the new 'righteousness'
as speaking for itself. The very curious
λέγων in LXX (which has no particular
grammar; for it ought to refer to ἐντολή)
perhaps suggests this personification. The
explanatory notes are unexpected. The

simple questions, "Who shall ascend into heaven?" and "Who shall descend into the deep?" would have been enough by themselves. For the 'Way' is not hidden high overhead; nor is it deep underfoot. At first sight, one almost wonders if they can be 'glosses.' Yet such allegorical interpretations are not alien from the Pauline manner.

The question " But what does it say?" (St Paul's words, not Deuteronomy's) introduces a close citation of the latter part of the same Pentateuchal section. But the ῥῆμα of LXX, the message of Moses to Israel, becomes the new ῥῆμα, the Gospel message of Jesus Christ. The mention of 'lips' and 'heart' the apostolic writer developes. Each member has its special part to play, its function to discharge. The 'lips' are for 'confession'; the 'heart' is the seat of 'belief.' In *v.* 9 the single blessing, achieved by the double work of 'heart' and 'lips,' is given as σωθήσῃ. In *v.* 10 this one idea is presented in two forms. 'Belief' leads to 'righteousness'; 'confession' is the pathway to 'salvation.' Are they then one thing or two? One, I should say, distinctly. But there is room for difference of opinion. The verbs πιστεύεται and ὁμολογεῖται are, of course, 'impersonal passives.' The importance of 'faith' in the matter is enforced and emphasised by a second reference to Isaiah xxviii. 16. Only now we have a πᾶς added, as well as an ἐπ᾽ αὐτῷ.

x. 11—13. "For the Scripture says, Everyone *that believeth* on Him *shall not be put to shame.* You see, there is no distinction between Jew and Gentile; for the same Lord is Lord of (them) all, 'rich' towards all that call upon Him. For *Everyone that shall call upon the Name of the Lord shall be saved.*"

Cf. Ephes.
iii. 8.

Joel iii. 5
(ii. 32).

The first πᾶς is St Paul's insertion; so that it might almost seem he himself had brought about unsupported that abolition of all distinction of which he speaks. But as we pass on we find that the 'open door

for all' rests on Christ's universal Lord-
ship for one thing, and on the Prophetic
promise for another. And the Pentecostal
promise *has its* πᾶς. There is no mistake
about that.

We have seen there is one 'way,' one
only way to σωτηρία, for Jew and Gentile
alike. The question next arises, Have
the Jews then had a fair chance? Has
the message been made plain to them?
The Gentiles' turn will come; but the
Jews' comes first of right. Not till they
have rejected God's plan can the Gentiles
be given their turn. They have had it, is
the answer, couched in prophetic language.
They have heard; the testimony of Holy
Writ has been amply borne out in fact:
they have 'heard,' but, with characteristic
'hardness of heart,' they have not 'obeyed.'

    x. 14, 15. "How then shall people
call on One, on whom they have not
believed? And how shall they believe
in Him, *of whom* they have not heard?
And how shall they hear, apart from
a preacher? And how shall folks

Isai. lii. 7
(not close
to LXX).

preach, except they be sent—as it
stands in Holy Writ, *Hvw beautiful
are the feet of them, that preach good
news of Peace, that preach good tidings
of good things."*

Verse 14 enumerates the conditions of
effective 'hearing' which obtain in all cases.
What we want to know is this, have all
these conditions been fulfilled in Israel's
case? Whether we read ἐπικαλέσονται or
ἐπικαλέσωνται makes very little difference.
Οὗ οὐκ ἤκουσαν ought to mean *Him, whose
voice they have not heard.* But, I suspect,
it does not here. Therefore, I should keep
"*of whom.*" Ἐὰν μὴ ἀποσταλῶσιν in the
Vulgate merely becomes *nisi mittantur.*
But the sense of legitimate 'mission,' of
apostolic commission, is discovered in the
text.

The citation of Isaiah lii. is brought
forward as a general answer to the question
'Have they heard?' It agrees closely
with the Hebrew text, and is associated
originally with the deliverance from Cap-
tivity. But the Rabbis (S.) applied it to

Messiah; and Christian folk with reason
apply it to the Redemption of all redemptions.

Yes, there can be no doubt they have
all been told. "This thing was not done
in a corner." Indubitably the message
of Christ was fully made known to His
Nation. Many did not 'heed'; and their
failure is set forth in sundry prophetic sayings. There are five of these in all. We
will take them in due order. The first,
from Isaiah, follows closely on the assumption, based on the last citation, that there
has been no defect in the 'telling.'

x. 16—21. "But they have not
all heeded the Gospel..."

[*It is to-day as it was of old.*]

"...Isaiah says, you know (*Lord*), Isaiah liii.
who has believed what he has heard 1 (LXX).
from us? Belief, then, comes by
hearing, and hearing comes through
the message of Christ."

"But, again, can it be they have
not heard? Nay, indeed, *Into all the* Psalm xix.
land the sound of them has gone forth, 5 (LXX).

*and the words of them unto the utmost
ends of the world.* Once more, can it
be that Israel never knew? First of

Deut.
xxxii. 21
(LXX).

all then, Moses says, *I will kindle you
to jealousy over a nation that is none;
over a nation void of understanding
will I anger you.* And Isaiah is very

Isaiah
lxv. 1
(LXX, but
clauses
reversed).

daring and says, *I was found of them
that never sought Me; I became manifest to them that asked not after Me.*
And, with regard to Israel, he says,

Isaiah
lxv. 2
(LXX,
with
slightly
altered
order).

*All day long have I spread out my
hands towards a disobedient and gain-
saying people.*"

The ἀκοή, in Isaiah liii. 1, means 'hearing,' i.e. message; the Apostle takes it up
in its other sense, the exercise of the gift
of the ear. The ῥῆμα Χριστοῦ is the
message, of which Christ is the subject.
The αὐτῶν of the Psalm, in *v.* 18, refers to
God's great ποιήματα. Such an universal
proclamation as they give forth is the
telling of the Gospel. The Scripture from
Deuteronomy, in *v.* 19, tells how the God
of Israel, provoked by His faithless people,

will surely deal with them as they have
dealt by Him. They have forsaken Him
for a '*not-god*'; He will forsake them for
a '*not-people*.' It is ample testimony to
Israel's disloyalty and consequent rejection. The last two citations are from
Isaiah. The two verses come close together. They speak plainly for themselves
and present no difficulty.

§ 15.   ISRAEL'S FINAL DESTINY

There remains but one more section in
the doctrinal portion of 'Romans.' With
this too let us deal and we shall be ended.
It is true its teaching has no direct bearing
on 'justification.' On the other hand, it
has very much indeed to do with the
general Pauline conception of the will or
purpose of God.

We saw in the last section that Israel
has been evangelised, but, true to its history, has not heeded nor believed. They
are, as Isaiah declared, λαὸς ἀπειθῶν καὶ

ἀντιλέγων. 'Stiffnecked' is now, as ever, the epithet to describe them. Does then this disregard of God's great message carry with it the Nation's rejection? That is the first question we have to ask ourselves.

Cf. Psalm
xciv. 14
(LXX).

xi. 1—6. "I ask then, Can it be God has rejected His people? No, no! Why, I am a son of Israel myself, of Abrahamic descent, of the tribe of Benjamin. God has not re-

Cf. viii. 29.

jected His people, whom He knew of old. Or, is it that you do not know what the Scripture says, in the story of Elijah, when he pleads with God against Israel ; *Lord, they have*

1 Kings
xix. 10
(rough
quotation
of LXX).

slain Thy prophets and digged down Thine altars, and I only have been left, and they seek my life? But what does the solemn answer say to him? *I have left for myself seven thousand*

1 Kings
xix. 18
(wide
variations
from
LXX).

men, folks that have not bowed the knee to the shameful god."

"So, in the present time too, there is a 'leaving,' by gracious election. And if it be by grace, then is it not

by works ; otherwise grace ceases to
be itself."

In a definite 'rejection,' then, the
Apostle will not believe. Holy Writ declares it impossible. Twice over it is said,
in Psalm xciv. and 1 Samuel xii., that God
will not reject His People. In both of
these places LXX employs the same verb
as here. Moreover, St Paul himself is a
son of Israel ; and, seeing he is so, the
idea of such a 'rejection' is to him in-
tensely abhorrent. Does he not belong
indeed to the loyal and royal tribe of war-
like Benjamin ? Here, as in Philippians iii.,
he plainly lays much stress on this gene-
alogical fact : and surely the tribe of his
lineage is a highly appropriate one for the
dauntless missionary. The προέγνω, in *v.*
2, may carry that special sense of 'know'
—'recognise,' to wit, almost 'choose'—
that is seen in the Prophet Amos, though
there the verb is not compound. Ἐν
Ἠλείᾳ means, in the whole section which
tells the prophet's story. There is a Homeric ring about the title. Ἐντυγχάνειν is

neutral ; the sense of it, hostile or friendly,
depends on the preposition, whether ὑπέρ
or κατά (in ' Acts ' once περί), that follows
after. Of the two quotations from 1 Kings,
the first varies a good deal in the language ;
the second is widely different from LXX
text. That reads, *And thou shalt leave
behind in Israel seven thousand men, all
the knees that have not bent the knee to
Baal* (τῷ Βάαλ, not τῇ Βάαλ as here), *and
every mouth that hath not worshipped him.*
The suggestion in LXX is that these
seven thousand only are intended to escape the slaughter to be achieved by the
chosen avengers. The Hebrew declares
Yet I will leave me. I should gather that
the ἐμαυτῷ in our text is distinctly a Pauline
addition : yet it has, or seems to have, an
important place in the argument, as rein-
forcing the notion of the ἐκλογὴ χάριτος.
However on this we clearly must not lay
any undue stress. The τῇ Βάαλ of our
text is said to be due to the fact that in
the Greek αἰσχύνη was substituted for
' Baal.' But our LXX text has τῷ.

Λεῖμμα is only here—I cannot away with λίμμα—and the spelling of ' B,' at least, is not a thing to trouble about.

The conclusion we have so far reached is that here is no *rejection* : the discerning eye only notes the working of that ' election,' of which we have spoken before. Verse 6 is one of those ' appendix-like' statements of which St Paul is so fond. The οὐκέτι ἐξ ἔργων, one would say, applies far more definitely to the ἐκλογή that is now than to that which we may find in 1 Kings xix. For there the ' seven thousand' were *left behind* precisely for this, that they had not been false to their God or forsaken Him for Baal. However, the κατ' ἐκλογὴν χάριτος may only belong to the ' now' and not to the ' then' at all. The resemblance may lie merely in the smallness of the number of the ' faithful' who are ' left.'

We proceed to apply the analogy afforded by the O.T. ' remnant' to the conditions now obtaining with regard to Israel and the new revelation.

xi. 7, 8. "How then? What Israel seeks after, that they did not attain. It was the elect attained it; the rest were hardened (in heart), as it says in Holy Writ, *God has given them a spirit of confusion; eyes that cannot see, and ears that cannot hear, until this very day.*"

The ἐκλογή means the body of people 'elected.' The scripture referred to in *v.* 8 appears to be a blend of several passages. In Deut. xxix. 4 there is something like it.

And the Lord our God hath not
given you
an heart to understand and eyes to see
and ears to hear
until this day.

Here however is no mention of the πνεῦμα κατανύξεως. That is derived from Isaiah xxix. 10, *For the Lord hath made you drunk*(?) *with the spirit of* κατάνυξις (in our English, *the spirit of deep slumber*); and Psalm lx. 3, '*thou hast made us drink the wine of* κατάνυξις' (in the English,

wine of staggering or *astonishment*). There
seems to be a possibility that κατάνυξις
was confused with the verb κατανυστάζειν.
Its own peculiar verb is only found in the
passive in LXX. It seems to mean 'be
paralysed.' In Acts ii. 37 "were pricked
to the heart" is clearly wrong. It obviously
means "were astounded." Ὀφθαλμοὺς τοῦ
μὴ βλέπειν means, I think, "eyes of not
seeing." It may, of course, be the common
infinitive of purpose with τοῦ. Our Lord
Himself quoted Isaiah (vi. 9, 10) to the
same general effect as the 'conflate' quotation here. The citation from 'David'
which follows appears to centre round
one special phrase, '*Let their eyes be darkened.*'

xi. 9, 10. "And David says, *Let* Psalm lxix.
their table become a snare and a θήρα 23, 24
and a trap and a recompense for them. (exact LXX).
*Let their eyes be darkened, that they
may not see ; and their back bow thou
down continually.*"
Originally it is spoken of the enemies
of God's servant. Spiritual blindness is

the penalty which invariably waits upon the unfaithful heart.

At the opening of the chapter the question was "Has God rejected His people?" The answer to that was Nc, only the unfaithful. All the time there has been a 'remnant,' and a 'remnant' there still is. This 'remnant' is the 'election.' The rest have been punished with blindness.

Now another question is asked which is closely akin. If they have fallen, as they have, is it with a fall irreparable? To this again the answer 'yes' is as impossible as to the other. After all, they are God's people. Moreover, behind their 'fall' can be seen a gracious Purpose. Their calamity has been the Gentiles' opportunity.

xi. 11. "Again, can it be they have stumbled to their fall? Oh, surely not! Rather by their stumbling has come salvation for the Gentiles—with the result of arousing them to jealousy."

Cf. x. 19.

If the ἵνα, in ἵνα πέσωσι, expresses a
purpose, it ought to be the purpose of the
subject of ἔπταισαν. We shall do well,
then, to regard it as 'result'—call it 'ec-
batic' if you like—and not confuse our
minds with the thought that a 'purpose'
lurks behind everything that is. Παράπτωμα plainly is correlative to ἔπταισαν,
whereas πτῶμα would answer to πεσεῖν.
That is, παράπτωμα signifies something
less than a fatal 'fall.' Though the syntax of the verse is obscure, the meaning is
plain enough. The subject of παραζηλῶσαι
one would apprehend to be the σωτηρία of
the Gentiles. The next verse is rendered
difficult by questions of vocabulary. Ἥττημα is not easy, but πλήρωμα is bewildering. The perplexity culminates in this;
are ἥττημα and πλήρωμα balancing terms?
Is ἥττημα, that is to say, "shortage," and
πλήρωμα the antithesis of "shortage"—
whatever that may be? Or, does ἥττημα
simply mean "failure" (cf. 1 Cor. vi. 7,
which is not exactly parallel), and is πλήρωμα itself entirely independent of it?

Ἥττημα may be in line with παράπτωμα or
with πλήρωμα. But who shall decide with
which ? For myself, I am inclined to the
latter alternative.

    xi. 12. " If the stumbling of Israel
be the great gain of the world, and if
the Gentiles are enriched because Israel fell short ; how much grander
shall it be when their numbers are
full ! "

Πλήρωμα means 'completion,' the 'completion' of a definite number. In this sense
we could have it in the plural ; it belongs
to the form of the word to be susceptible
of that. In the Gospels each basket has
its separate πλήρωμα. But we have no
English word that I know of to represent
it adequately. Nor have we for this πλήρωμα. Our rendering will be at best but
a bungled matter.

    xi. 13, 14. "It is to you, Gentiles,
I am speaking. So far as I am, I say,
Apostle of the Gentiles, I make the
most of my ministry, in the hope I
may rouse to jealousy my own flesh

and blood, and may save some of them."

If any passage in the Epistle be decisive for a Gentile preponderance in the Church at Rome, it would be this; ὑμῖν... τοῖς ἔθνεσιν. I do not think the μὲν οὖν is 'corrective.' St Paul is not only a missionary to the Gentiles but to Israel as well. The μέν regards that. The οὖν is, I think, of the resumptive type. A 'ministry' δοξάζεται, not when one exalts its dignity and importance, but when one makes the most of it. It is not before the world the office is made much of, but in the speaker's mind. He sets store by it; he works at it; he gives himself to it: but all the while he knows in so doing he is not untrue to his nation. It will all tend to hasten on the glorious consummation for which he yearns. Israel was set aside for a time; and the Gentiles gained greatly by it : some day he will be taken back—clasped to God's heart—and what will that imply ? Here once more the vocabulary is fruitful in questionings.

Obviously ἀποβολή is not ἄπωσις—for that idea we have definitely set aside. In Acts xxvii. 22 it merely means 'loss.' The verb means to 'throw aside' (of a cloak), and to 'lay aside' (of a quality, παρρησία). The Vulgate says *amissio*, which possibly signifies 'loss.' Both ἀποβολή and πρόσληψις are from the point of view of God. Ζωὴ ἐκ νεκρῶν, again, is a highly doubtful phrase. I should say it must be figurative. After all, the Gentiles' salvation in no way depends upon Israel : but it will be inconceivably enhanced and glorified by Israel's restoration.

Therefore I would paraphrase :

xi. 15. "For if the loss of them meant the world's reconciliation ; what shall their taking home be, but a very resurrection ?"

At this point, mentally, we must make a little insertion. It would run somehow like this, 'When all is said and done, it is they that are the ἀπαρχή, which consecrates all the φύραμα ; it is they who are the "root" from which the branches spring.'

Otherwise, we can only appreciate the new thought of the writer by a very forced translation.

> xi. 16. "It is, if the 'first fruit' (of the dough) be holy, that the whole baking is holy too; it is, if the root be holy, the branches are holy too."

And, even then, we should have to add; 'And, mind, you are but of the φύραμα; you are but among the branches.'

There follows the well-known image of the 'wild olive' graft upon the fruitful tree, a proceeding, as S. observes, in itself entirely non-natural. So strongly is the Apostle convinced of Israel's priority in the matter of God's favour.

Ἀγριέλαιος and καλλιέλαιος are Aristotelian terms. Ἐκκλάειν simply means to 'break,' or 'tear,' off.

> xi. 17—24. "If some of the branches were broken off, and you being but wild olive were engrafted among the branches, and became with them a sharer in the stock, the source of the olive's richness, then glory not

over the (rejected) branches. If you
do, remember this; it is not you who
bear the stock, but the stock that
bears you. You will say, The branches
were broken off that I might be grafted
in. True. They were broken off because they disbelieved; while you—
you stand by faith. My friend, be
not highminded, but fear. If God
did not spare the natural branches,
He will not spare you either. Mark,
then, in God both kindliness and severity. On them that fell is severity;
on you is kindliness—provided you
cling to that kindliness. Otherwise,
you too will be sacrificed. And they,
too, if they do not stay on in unbelief,
will be engrafted; for God is able to
engraft them once again. For if you
were cut off from the naturally wild
olive, and were set as a graft in the
fruitful, how much more shall these,
which are naturally part and parcel
of the olive, be engrafted in their own
tree?"

Apart from the curiousness of the
whole image, the verses explain themselves. Olives grow to a fabulous age,
and grafting, it would seem, is essential
to their fertility; though nobody grafts,
of course, a good tree from a wild one.
'Εκκλάειν is not technical. The ἐν αὐτοῖς
is curious : it means the branches left, not
the branches that are broken off. 'Ρίζα is
more than 'root.' Καλῶς recognises the
truth of what the Gentiles urge. Τῇ
ἀπιστίᾳ and τῇ πίστει are slightly varying
datives. The first is plainly of 'cause,'
the latter is nearer 'manner.' The πεσόν-
τας in *v.* 22 is odd, because it is the very
word deliberately discarded just above.
'Επιμείνῃς τῇ χρηστότητι is, as we see from
the phrase below, for all intents equivalent
to ἐπιμείνῃς τῇ πίστει. One 'stays on' in
God's kindness by persistent exercise of
faith. The ἐκκόπτειν's, of *v.* 22 and *v.* 24,
are different. For the former we should
have expected ἐκκλάειν to be used. In
the one case it is a process of 'unkind-
ness'; and in the other of 'kindness.' In

the παρὰ φύσιν of *v.* 24 is the kernel of
the whole figure.

Cf.
St Luke
xxi. 24.

 xi. 25—29. "For I would have
you know, my brothers, this solemn
truth, that you may not think yourselves wise. A partial hardening has
befallen Israel, till the full number of
the Gentiles shall have entered (into
the Kingdom). And, when that has
befallen, all Israel shall be saved. As
Holy Scripture says; *There shall
come from Sion the deliverer, and
shall turn away from Jacob impieties.
For this shall be with them my Covenant, in the day when I shall take
away their sins.*"

 "So far as the Gospel goes, they
are (God's) enemies for your sake:
but in regard to the election, they are
beloved for the fathers' sakes. For
the gifts and the calling of God are
irrevocable."

There can be no question that, for
Gentile believers, there is a prodigious
temptation to look on themselves as

φρόνιμοι (cf. St Matt. xxv. 2) in contrast
to Israel's foolishness. Only, consideration
forbids it. There is a μυστήριον involved;
and μυστήριον, in this place, comes very
near the sense with which we use 'mystery.' It is a truth a man could never
possibly know save by revelation. The
'πλήρωμα of the Gentiles' would seem to
imply that, in the writer's thought, there
is a definite number of Gentiles awaiting
salvation—a number only known to the
mind of the Most High. When that
number is achieved (οὕτω), there will be
'saving' for πᾶς Ἰσραήλ. The latter phrase
is rightly interpreted, "Israel, as a whole."
In the quotation, which is a free one, there
is an amazing variety of reading. St Paul
says ἐκ; the LXX ἕνεκεν; the Hebrew
'to.' All, obviously, make good sense,
but the divergence is very startling. The
LXX text of Isaiah (lix. 20) says,

And there shall come for Sion's sake the
    deliverer,
And shall turn away impieties from Jacob,
    and this is for them my Covenant....

The clause "When I shall take away..."
is borrowed from Isaiah xxvii. There it
reads "his sin." The fidelity of God to
His promises is a commonplace in O.T.
In *vv.* 30 and 31, though ἀπειθεῖν must be
rendered 'disobey,' yet the sense of 'dis-
belief,' 'unfaith' is not far in the background. The datives in *v.* 31 are a well-
known difficulty.

> xi. 30—32. " For as you once dis-
> obeyed God, and now have received
> mercy, thanks to their disobedience;
> so they too have now disobeyed, that,
> when you have received mercy, they
> also may meet with mercy. For God
> has made all disobedient alike, that
> on all He may have mercy."

Here indeed is a spacious hope. Good
out of evil is portended on the very largest
scale.

Coming to lesser matters, let me say
that the second νῦν, in *v.* 31, is greatly
better away. One gathers that the 'disobedience' of the Gentiles first befell
in point of time; then came Israel's

'disobedience,' distinguished as later by
νῦν. It belongs to the same period as the
'mercy' of the Gentiles. Both are νῦν.
But we do not want a third, for the final
'mercy' of all—which is not yet. After
ἠπείθησαν should be a comma (v. 31).
The τῇ τούτων ἀπειθείᾳ is a semi-causal
dative. Τῷ ὑμετέρῳ ἐλέει has nothing of
'cause-meaning' in it. I have rendered it
in the way which, I think, best expresses
the sense. It represents indeed a 'dative
of attendant circumstance' (equivalent to
'*with you visited in mercy*'). The συνέκλεισεν metaphor is better disregarded in
English. In Galatians iii. 22 we have
had it before. The whole statement must
be taken not too literally. God does not
'make' men sinners. Somehow, in unknown ways, 'sin' does subserve His purposes. In so far, God συνέκλεισεν.

The whole doctrinal section closes with
a very exultant paean, in which the Apostle
celebrates the glories of the knowledge of
the Christian revelation. In the course
of it he employs the same Scripture he

had used in the first letter to Corinth. In 1 Cor. ii. 16 we read "*For who hath known the mind of the Lord, that he should instruct Him?*" Combining the citation here and that there in one saying, we have the whole of the text of Isaiah xl. 13. Τίς ἔγνω νοῦν Κυρίου καὶ τίς αὐτοῦ σύμβουλος ἐγένετο, ὃς συμβιβᾷ αὐτόν; In 1 Corinthians there is appended the highly significant statement, "But we have the mind of Christ." That must be taken to throw some light on the passage here. For the question naturally rises, Is this wisdom and this knowledge the wisdom and the knowledge that are in the All-wise; or are they the wisdom and knowledge that form the Christian σοφία, communicated to men by the Holy Spirit of God? The latter seems to me to be infinitely more likely. A passage in 'Colossians' (ii. 2, 3) lends further confirmation. That says, "that their hearts may be comforted συμβιβασθέντες ἐν ἀγάπῃ καὶ εἰς πᾶν πλοῦτος τῆς πληροφορίας τῆς συνέσεως, εἰς ἐπίγνωσιν τοῦ μυστηρίου τοῦ Χριστοῦ, ἐν ᾧ εἰσὶν πάντες οἱ θησαυροὶ τῆς σοφίας καὶ γνώσεως ἀπόκρυφοι." In these words it seems to be suggested that he who has knowledge of Christ is admitted to the stores of wisdom which are hidden away in Christ. Furthermore, the passage shows that our 'riches' refers to 'wisdom,' and not to grace or mercy.

xi. 33—36. "O unfathomable wealth of the wisdom and knowledge of God! How unsearchable are His judgments and His ways beyond tracing out! Aye, *who hath known* Isaiah *the mind of the Lord, or who hath* xl. 13. *been His counsellor? Or who hath given* Him *first and shall be recom*- Job xli. 11. *pensed?*"
(Here the text of Job, in our English, runs, *Who hath first given to Me, that I should repay him?*)

"For from Him, and through Him, and unto Him are all things. To Him be Glory for ever and ever, Amen."

In the very last verse of all there have

been who have sought to trace some reference to the Trinity. And ἐκ, truly, does
suggest 'Fatherhood'; while διά is the
preposition appropriate to the Redeemer;
but the εἰς is absolutely decisive against
any such underlying meaning. To put it
in more modern forms, what we should say
would be this:

> 'He is the universal Origin,
> and He the moving Power, and He
> the End.'

The εἰς αὐτόν would seem to point to
that teaching which we find in 1 Corinthians
xv. 28. There the goal of the whole process
of creation and regeneration is declared
to be nothing but this, ἵνα ᾖ ὁ Θεὸς πάντα
ἐν πᾶσιν. There is a 'wealth' indeed in
a wisdom and a knowledge which can see
as far as that.

§ 16. A FEW LAST WORDS

When I was a schoolmaster (and they
were very happy days, as all schoolmasters
find them) there was no department of my

work which pleased me more than the teaching of the New Testament. The 'fly in the ointment' was the necessity of examination; for I was very well aware it was almost certain that that test would not be conducted on lines such as I myself approved. The difficulty was this; that it would have been wholly possible, in many cases, for a boy to make half marks *without knowing his text at all*; for a good half of the questions always dealt with 'introduction.' One had to know—that is, the boys had—not what the Apostle said himself, but what some one else said about him. This I could not believe to be right. For me, the one object was, so far as I could compass it, to make my pupils understand as of infinitely larger importance the Apostle's own pronouncements. The longer one reads St Paul, the harder one seems to find it to be absolutely sure of his meaning in any section. Still a student must be unfortunate beyond the common, who cannot carry away many definite ideas from careful perusal.

As one reads the familiar words of an Epistle like ' Romans ' again and again and again, it comes ever more home to one, that though he writes in Greek and cites the Greek Old Testament, he is really at bottom a ' Hebrew.' A great gulf separates his whole method from that with which we became familiarised in the days when our minds were given to the lucid writers of Hellas. It is when he is definitely arguing that he carries his readers least with him . Of their kind, no doubt, his arguments are very excellent : but it happens not to be the kind in which we ourselves have been trained.

Therefore we love him best when he leaves all logical processes far behind, and discarding ' reason,' as such, surrenders himself entirely to a species of intuition. It is in his dithyrambic vein when the tide of inspiration is flowing strong and free that he is for modern minds far most convincing.

When I first gave my mind to the task of investigating what he says about justification, I was led in that direction by a conviction that English readers are greatly led astray by terminology. My desire was to show any readers I might get that nothing could be done in the way of understanding the dogmatic ideas in St Paul till the reader had grasped two things, the Pauline outlook for one, the Pauline vocabulary for another.

It was for me of very deep interest to discover that somehow or other, starting merely from the Apostle's own statements, I had worked back to what appears to have been his natural mentality. 'Natural' I mean in the sense of what would have come to him from training and from environment. This was brought home to me by reading a little essay of Professor Kennett, entitled ' Hebrew Conceptions of Righteousness and Sin.' There I found that the interpretation, which had forced itself on my mind from the study of the Pauline text of 'Galatians' and of 'Romans' —say as to the meaning of 'righteousness'—corresponds almost completely with

Israelitish conceptions. It is decidedly comforting to a mere 'Hellenist' like myself to discover that his views on the meaning of δικαιοσύνη, as expressing a desirable *status*, are substantially in line with established Hebrew teaching. A perusal of the essay mentioned will demonstrate that it is so.

For the rest, quite apart from definite mistakes in interpretation, of this passage or of that, I feel sure my readers will say, Why did you not throw your ideas about the Pauline dogmatic on this head into Essay form? My answer is very simple, Because I could not. 'Paulinism' is not a system; it is rather an attitude. You cannot 'formulate' it—at least I hold so strongly—but you can 'feel' it. Only if you are to 'feel' it, you have first to master the structure of the shrine that houses the spirit; and that shrine is the text itself. If anyone should say, What in your opinion is the teaching of St Paul? I should answer 'Read and see.' This little and trivial book is an attempt to make such reading more easy and more profitable. One more question maybe will suggest itself, Why have you roamed so far? Why deal with all the chapters from i. to xi. ? Ah! that is just the difficulty. With St Paul, when you once begin, you simply cannot stop. His vivid personality, his own overpowering interest in that of which he discourses, carry you on from point to point. And so it comes about that you only cease to follow when he ceases to go before. It is for that reason I could not pause till the whole of the doctrinal section of ' Romans ' was, more or less, covered. Those on whom the spell has fallen, will not blame me for that. They will recognise the fact that the apostolic writings cannot be chopped up into lengths ; they must necessarily be taken, each letter, as a whole. With the end of the doctrinal section reached we may fairly say *claudite jam rivos pueri*—and alas! the meadows may have drunk too much already.

1983-84 TITLES

0104	MacDonald, Donald	Biblical Doctrine of Creation and the Fall: Genesis 1-3	18.95
1401	Bennett, William H.	An Exposition of the Books of Chronicles	17.50
1903	Cox, Samuel	The Pilgrim Psalms: An Exposition of the Songs of Degrees	9.50
2703	Wright, Charles H. H.	Studies in Daniel's Prophecy	13.95
3202	Kirk, Thomas	Jonah: His Life and Mission	12.95
4503	Olshausen, Hermann	Studies in the Epistle to the Romans	16.50
8803	Westcott, Frederick B.	The Biblical Doctrine of Justification	15.25
8804	Salmond, S. D. F.	The Biblical Doctrine of Immortality	26.95
9516	Harris, John	The Teaching Methods of Christ: Characteristics of Our Lord's Ministry	16.75
9517	Blaikie, William G.	The Public Ministry of Christ	13.25
9518	Laidlaw, John	Studies in the Miracles of Our Lord	14.75

TITLES CURRENTLY AVAILABLE

0101	Delitzsch, Franz	A New Commentary on Genesis (2 vol.)	30.50
0102	Blaikie, W. G.	Heroes of Israel	19.50
0103	Bush, George	Genesis (2 vol.)	29.95
0201	Murphy, James G.	Commentary on the Book of Exodus	12.75
0202	Bush, George	Exodus	22.50
0203	Dolman, D. & Rainsford, M.	The Tabernacle (2 vol. in 1)	19.75
0301	Kellogg, Samuel H.	The Book of Leviticus	21.00
0302	Bush, George	Leviticus	10.50
0401	Bush, George	Numbers	17.95
0501	Cumming, John	The Book of Deuteronomy	16.00
0601	Blaikie, William G.	The Book of Joshua	15.75
0602	Bush, George	Joshua & Judges (2 vol. in 1)	17.95
0603	Kirk, Thomas & Lang, John	Studies in the Book of Judges (2 vol. in 1)	17.75
0701	Cox, S. & Fuller, T.	The Book of Ruth (2 vol. in 1)	14.75
0901	Blaikie, William G.	First Book of Samuel	16.50
0902	Deane, W. J. & Kirk, T.	Studies in the First Book of Samuel (2 vol. in 1)	19.00
0903	Blaikie, William G.	Second Book of Samuel	15.00
1101	Farrar, F. W.	The First Book of Kings	19.00
1201	Farrar, F. W.	The Second Book of Kings	19.00
1301	Kirk, T. & Rawlinson, G.	Studies in the Books of Kings (2 vol. in 1)	20.75
1701	Raleigh, Alexander	The Book of Esther	9.75
1801	Gibson, Edgar Charles	The Book of Job (available December)	10.00
1802	Green, William H.	The Argument of the Book of Job Unfolded	13.50
1901	Dickson, David	A Commentary on the Psalms (2 vol.)	32.50
1902	MacLaren, Alexander	The Psalms (3 vol.)	45.00
2001	Wardlaw, Ralph	Book of Proverbs (3 vol.)	45.00
2101	MacDonald, James M.	The Book of Ecclesiastes	15.50
2102	Wardlaw, Ralph	Exposition of Ecclesiastes	16.25
2201	Durham, James	An Exposition on the Song of Solomon	17.25
2301	Kelly, William	An Exposition of the Book of Isaiah	15.25
2302	Alexander, Joseph	Isaiah (2 vol.)	29.95
2401	Orelli, Hans C. von	The Prophecies of Jeremiah	15.25
2601	Fairbairn, Patrick	An Exposition of Ezekiel	18.50
2701	Pusey, Edward B.	Daniel the Prophet	19.50
2702	Tatford, Frederick Albert	Daniel and His Prophecy	9.25
3001	Cripps, Richard S.	A Commentary on the Book of Amos	13.50
3201	Burns, Samuel C.	The Prophet Jonah	11.25
3801	Wright, Charles H. H.	Zechariah and His Prophecies	24.95
4001	Morison, James	The Gospel According to Matthew	24.95
4101	Alexander, Joseph	Commentary on the Gospel of Mark	16.75
4102	Morison, James	The Gospel According to Mark	21.00
4201	Kelly, William	The Gospel of Luke	18.50
4301	Brown, John	The Intercessory Prayer of Our Lord Jesus Christ	11.50
4302	Hengstenberg, E. W.	Commentary on the Gospel of John (2 vol.)	34.95
4401	Alexander, Joseph	Commentary on the Acts of the Apostles (2 vol. in 1)	27.50
4402	Gloag, Paton J.	A Critical and Exegetical Commentary on the Acts of the Apostles (2 vol.)	29.95
4403	Stier, Rudolf E.	Words of the Apostles	18.75
4502	Moule, H. C. G.	The Epistle to the Romans	16.25
4601	Brown, John	The Resurrection of Life	15.50
4602	Edwards, Thomas C.	A Commentary on the First Epistle to the Corinthians	18.00
4603	Jones, John Daniel	Exposition of First Corinthians 13	9.50
4801	Ramsey, William	Historical Commenary on the Epistle to the Galatians	17.75
4802	Brown, John	An Exposition of the Epistle of Paul to the Galatians	16.00
4901	Westcott, Brooke F.	St. Paul's Epistle to the Ephesians (available December)	10.50
4902	Pattison, R. & Moule, H.	Exposition of Ephesians: Lessons in Grace and Godliness (2 vol. in 1)	14.75
5001	Johnstone, Robert	Lectures on the Book of Philippians	18.25
5102	Westcott, F. B.	The Epistle to the Colossians	7.50
5103	Eadie, John	Colossians	10.50
5104	Daille, Jean	Exposition of Colossians	24.95
5401	Liddon, H. P.	The First Epistle to Timothy	6.00
5601	Taylor, Thomas	An Exposition of Titus	20.75
5801	Delitzsch, Franz	Commentary on the Epistle to the Hebrews (2 vol.)	31.50
5802	Bruce, A. B.	The Epistle to the Hebrews	17.25
5803	Edwards, Thomas C.	The Epistle to the Hebrews	13.00
5901	Johnstone, Robert	Lectures on the Epistle of James	16.50
5902	Mayor, Joseph B.	The Epistle of St. James	20.25
5903	Stier, Rudolf E.	Commentary on the Epistle of James	10.25
6201	Lias, John J.	The First Epistle of John	15.75
6202	Morgan, J. & Cox S.	The Epistles of John (2 vol. in 1)	22.95
6501	Manton, Thomas	An Exposition of the Epistle of Jude (available December)	14.00
6601	Trench, Richard C.	Commentary on the Epistles to the Seven Churches	8.50
7000	Tatford, Frederick Albert	The Minor Prophets (3 vol.)	44.95
7001	Orelli, Hans C. von	The Twelve Minor Prophets	15.50
7002	Alford, Dean Henry	The Book of Genesis and Part of the Book of Exodus	12.50
7003	Marbury, Edward	Obadiah and Habakkuk	23.95
7004	Adeney, Walter	The Books of Ezra and Nehemiah	13.00
7101	Mayor, Joseph B.	The Epistle of St. Jude & The Second Epistle of Peter	16.50
7102	Lillie, John	Lectures on the First and Second Epistles of Peter	19.75
7103	Hort, F. J. A. & Hort, A. F.	Expository and Exegetical Studies	29.50
7104	Milligan, George	St. Paul's Epistles to the Thessalonians	12.00
7105	Stanley, Arthur P.	Epistles of Paul to the Corinthians	20.95
7106	Moule, H. C. G.	Colossian and Philemon Studies	12.00
7107	Fairbairn, Patrick	The Pastoral Epistles	17.25
7108	Cox, S. & Drysdale, A. H.	The Epistle to Philemon (2 vol. in 1)	9.25

TITLES CURRENTLY AVAILABLE